NATIONAL FORESTS

NATIONAL
RESOURCES LAND

N

D1293629

PUBLIC GRAZING LANDS

William Voigt, Jr.

PUBLIC GRAZING LANDS

Use and Misuse by Industry and Government

RUTGERS UNIVERSITY PRESS

New Brunswick, New Jersey

HD
241
V64

Library of Congress Cataloging in Publication Data

Voigt, William.
    Public grazing lands.

    Includes bibliographical references.
    1. Grazing—United States—History.   2.   United
States—Public lands—History.   I.   Title.
HD241.V64   333.1'1   75–42250
ISBN 0–8135–0819–3

To Art, Billie and Sandy—not necessarily in that order

Contents

Preface

This began as a simple account of how an aggressive clique of public land-using stockmen in the West attempted a colossal grab of public domain and national forest grazing areas, only to be countered by a straggly but determined aggregation of conservationists who didn't admit they were outgunned and fought back to at least a temporary victory.

At the end of December 1971, William Sloane, director of Rutgers University Press, whose death in 1974 was a blow indeed, suggested that my approach should have historical perspective and cover more than a few short years of the 1940s and early 1950s. Now, three and a half years later, I hope I have come at least close to writing the kind of manuscript Bill Sloane visualized and wanted. It is chronological to the degree that appeared practical as the writing progressed, and has been divided into what seem to me to be logical parts. The first deals with the early-day West when grazing was unrestricted, before any major part of the public domain had been put under statutory control. Next comes the Forest Service phase, and the third deals with the lands under the Bureau of Land Management and its predecessor agencies. The final brief segment is a sort of summing up. What may be called a land-grab way of thinking, and variations on the theme, run through the entire book.

I've known for years that sooner or later my knowledge and impressions of land-grab times would have to be written. The unknown until Bill Sloane wrote the letter mentioned above was the direction in which the writing would lead and what the outcome would be. As research moved beyond the events of the late 1940s and the first half of the 1950s, when I was participant as well as observer, my conviction grew that the land grab attempt was but the visible trunk of the tree; that was underlain by a considerable and sprawly root system. More was at issue than whether a few western stockmen, who were privileged to graze their cattle and sheep on federal lands, might gain title to the pick of them for a pittance. No sooner was one question answered than another arose.

The coming land grab was warming to a boil when I joined the Izaak Walton League of America staff in Chicago in 1945 as assistant executive director under Kenneth A. Reid. Volunteer League workers in Wyoming and Colorado had been collecting evidence for some time, and they convinced Reid that the threat was a growing reality. He evolved the organization's basic public lands policy, to the effect that the federal lands were held in trust for a variety of public uses, and no privilege granted to private commerce or industry should ever be allowed to transcend the public's rights and interest.

Such a policy precluded any sale or giveaway, and reinforced the popular view in the conservation community that all the public lands contained multiple values and should be managed for multiple purposes. Open areas might grow forage that fed domestic animals; it also supported ruminant wildlife—and predatory species put there by nature, too—that had been there long before cattle, horses, sheep, or goats were brought in by newcomers from the Old World. Every upland acre had watershed values vital to irrigation farmers and lowland urban communities, and the streams themselves harbored fish important for food and sport. Timbered and other regions were underlain with minerals even as their scenic qualities delighted the eye of resident or casual passerby. The livestock industry was part of all this, not the whole of it. It could have its share of the products of the western public lands along with the rest of us but had no right to their exclusive use.

We learned there was excessive use being made of the ranges, at what looked to us like a mighty handsome subsidy in the form of very low grazing fees. Most of us who had lived in or traveled through the West, as well as the home folks out there, had seen or heard tales of the devastation that came to the ranges because of overuse in the World War I emergency, and learned that the government did not have the heart to reduce use as deeply as needed when harsh depression and drought came in the 1930s. We conservationists saw the stock industry's leaders and lobby using every argument they could lay tongue to in order to prevent even a smidgen of federal action that might hit their pocketbooks, no matter what the reason or justification. When the cadre of leaders then had the effrontery to try for the whole thing, that was just too much.

I had lived in Denver in the late 1930s and through most of 1942, and when the League decided to open a western office there, primarily to work on public land conservation problems, I was moved out from Chicago.

In his 1864 classic, *Man and Nature,* George Marsh wrote that "man has too long forgotten that the earth was given to him for usufruct alone, not for consumption, still less for profligate waste." We had become the richest nation on earth not alone through wise husbandry, which certainly has not been universal in this country, but largely because of the natural resources we discovered and could turn into money. The Ken Reids of the comparatively small conservation movement at land-grab time had come to see that our world had finite limits, a truth that still seems unpopular in much of America. They saw that instead of unlimited expansion and growth, the day was approaching when we would experience shortages instead of superabundance. Only a comparative few wrote and spoke about such things back then. William Vogt did so in his *Road to Survival* (and Bill Sloane was his publisher); Fairfield Osborn did so in *Our Plundered Planet.* Paul Sears put blunt truths into his *Deserts on the March.* Reid and I, and others who would write for us for little or nothing, said similar things in perhaps less eloquent ways in the pages of *Outdoor America,* the League's small magazine; and we did much speechmaking and pamphleteering.

What I am trying to say, I think, is that we who were a part of the conservation movement were in or moving toward a frame of mind that would cause us to rise in determined protest just as the livestock leadership was getting ready to draw and fire. And we shot right back at them. That phase of the story is not overlooked in this book, but it proved to be only part of the whole. My research turned up much that I had not known before about how pressure could be heaped upon public servants and cause some to bow to superior strength—political rather than physical or economic. It brought information on contributory causes of what has eventuated in the management of the public lands in the West, both the national forests and the lands that became privileged stockmen's domain under the too-friendly clauses of the Taylor Grazing Act of 1934. Memory was refreshed about purged officials of my acquaintance, and new information poured in concerning others whose chief fault appeared to be devotion to what they considered duty under what they believed to be official policy.

It sounds sort of crazy and mixed up, hard to believe or credit in this brief, oversimplified summary. I am convinced the narrative will make sense, though, as it unfolds. I hope I have captured the essence of a strange, complicated mixture of actions and motivations that encompass an original wealth of vegetative resources, a significant part of an industry that in the 1940s remembered wild and woolly earlier times and insisted on having its way in one guise or another, and federal officials whose concepts of how best to manage the public estate Out There could vary 180 degrees.

The book's dedication mentions three of many persons who have helped tremendously in this work, from long before it took form until now. Billie is my wife; she was my secretary in land-grab days and has stimulated me in this undertaking every step of the way. Art is Arthur Hawthorne Carhart, conservationist supreme, author, and former resident of Denver, now retired to Escondido, California, who was my close associate and friend then and now. His voluminous files supplemented my skimpy ones, and jogged memory on many aspects of the narrative. Sandy is Earl D. Sandvig of Portland, Oregon, who was assistant regional forester for range and wildlife management in Region 2, with offices in Denver, from August 1944 until he was humiliatingly removed seven years later. In Sandvig the Forest Service had one of its most perceptive and knowledgeable range specialists; from late 1949 forward it refused to utilize his talents and shortly shunted him into a career siding until retirement. I have not tried to count the folders of letters and documentation of many sorts, or the reels of taped conversations, exchanged between Sandy and me since this writing began. Let us just say that the manuscript would have been far less than it is without Sandy's contributions.

Kay Collins, staff chief of the Conservation Center of the Denver Public Library, and her coworkers in the Western History Department helped tremendously. They made available a rich store of source material. Included were tape recordings of recollections of many persons of whom I knew or with whom I was associated in land-grab times. Not the least of Kay's benefices was her providing the retirement address of her father, C. K. Collins of Albuquerque, who then sent me a taped account of his experiences as supervisor of Uncompahgre National Forest in western Colorado, one of the hottest of the hot spots in the era of the land grab attempt.

Ralph Hill and Herb Schwan, of Denver, provided a variety of information about national forest aspects of the manuscript. So did Forest Service officials at Region 2 headquarters there, especially Deputy Regional Forester Basil K. Crane. Frank J. Smith, director of range management at Forest Service headquarters, patiently answered innumerable questions, regardless of how pointed or seemingly unreasonable they might have appeared to be. Ed Cliff, retired chief forester whose policies I have felt were not in the best interests of either the national forest ranges or their owners, the general public, answered letter questions that filled in informational gaps. Walt L. Dutton, forty-two years a forester who ended his career in 1953 with nearly twenty years as director of range management, gave me a deeper insight into Forest Service phases of the story than most others—except Sandvig, of course. Charles F. Brannan, Secretary of Agriculture in a significant period, let a frank on-the-record interview be taped in his office in Denver in 1972.

On the Interior Department side, my warm thanks go to Dr. Glen D. Fulcher and his associates on the standards and technology staff he heads at the Denver regional center of the Bureau of Land Management; also certain Washington officials such as Jim Lee, information specialist who had squirreled away rare documents that he made available for note-taking; and Kay Wilkes, chief of the division of range, most especially Betty Cullimore of his staff who assembled tables of data, often on short notice.

For at least three years the staff of the Government Document Section of the Pennsylvania State Library—one of the country's best, in my opinion—must have wondered when I'd ever get through asking for House and Senate documents, old issues of the *Congressional Record*, obscure statute citations, and much more. They would seek out the volumes and stack them high for me, sometimes so much I needed two trips to get them out to my car—and I'd better not forget to thank the capitol officer who'd let me park in spaces right at the door reserved for cabinet officers who were temporarily away.

Many, many others have helped. Clarence Forsling, long retired as the last director of the former Grazing Service and an outstanding figure in the Interior phase of the book, was located in Albuquerque and has freely contributed files and facts from memory, including one long tape recording. Dr. Marion Clawson and Charles H. Stoddard, both former BLM directors, gave generously whenever asked. I cannot be casual in my thanks to these and others who provided material that made the manuscript possible. I appreciate what each one did, and hope the outcome can be considered a fragment of historical fact and opinion—for it must consist of both—that is meaningful in today's America. Yet the book is written under my name as author, and I take full responsibility for the contents.

Blackshear, Georgia   William Voigt, Jr.
October 1975

I

Foretaste and Foundation

1

A Stage Setting

The men wore no six-guns to be checked at the door on the way in, which might not have been the case some years earlier. In fact, the gathering that summer day in 1946 at a Salt Lake City hotel would have looked commonplace to a casual observer, for few aspects of American life are more ordinary than people coming together in a meeting room for business purposes. It happens often in nearly every community that boasts a hall for hire. Clothing and demeanor of the 150-odd men on this occasion were conventional for the locality. Faces differed little from others seen in western cities and towns.

The factors that set this occasion apart were its composition and its cause. Present were about an equal number of representatives of the American National Livestock Association (cattle), and the National Woolgrowers Association (sheep). It had been only a few decades since men from the two groups faced each other with open hatred. Antagonisms that then had bred mayhem, arson, murder, and senseless slaughter of innocent domestic animals had quieted considerably. Cowmen and sheepmen had learned that their differences were fewer than things they had in common. Now the two were joined in what, if successful, would become one of the most colossal peacetime land grabs in this or any other nation's history.

In their evolving plans the immediate objective would be title in fee to the best forage-producing portions of the 142 million acres of our public domain that had been incorporated in grazing districts, and of another fifteen million acres in isolated tracts not so organized. Soon the goal would be enlarged to encompass the lushest of about eighty million acres of range in western national forests, and sizable but untotaled segments of the National Park System.[1]

The acquisition would be cheap. Public domain would go at from nine cents to $2.80 an acre. The schemers didn't get around to setting prices publicly on national forest and national park land but there is little reason to believe they would be higher for acreage of comparable quality.

And the public's land would go to a very exclusive group. Only those ranchers then privileged to hold permits or leases for the grazing use of the federal lands would be allowed to participate. These favored ones would have fifteen years in which to make up their minds. Then, if they chose the title route, they would be allowed another thirty years to pay out, with interest on the mortgage at 1.5 percent. Timber and minerals, if present, were to go with the grass. This was heady stuff to dream on and seek to achieve, and became little less so later when minerals were dropped from the proposition.

Elected heads of the two livestock organizations presided jointly that day.[2] They were William B. Wright of Deeth, Nevada, of the cattlemen's association, and G. Norman Winder of Craig, Colorado, a sheepman. Out of the discussions came the organization of what was called the Joint National Livestock Committee on Public Lands, consisting of people from both organizations. The assembly chose Dan H. Hughes of Montrose, Colorado, head of a large family-owned livestock operation and former district judge, as chairman. J. Elmer Brock of Kaycee, Wyoming, former president of the ANLA, became vice-chairman.

Not to be overlooked was the presence at the meeting, as observer and counselor, of United States Senator Patrick A. McCarran of Nevada. Only a few weeks earlier Pat McCarran had wound up five years of intermittent investigation, mostly in western cow towns, of the chief land-managing federal agencies.[3] It began with emphasis on the Grazing Service of the Department of the Interior, which administered the livestock use of the district lands under the Taylor Grazing Act of 1934.[4] This law finally ended the totally unregulated livestock utilization of public domain that had been going on ever since we began our brutal shoving aside and subjugation of the Indians out there before and after the Civil War. The McCarran committee also had looked into the doings of the venerable General Land Office, which leased the isolated tracts under the Taylor Act and performed diverse other duties. And before McCarran closed down for lack of continuing authorization and appropriated money, he paid considerable attention to the administration of grazing by the U.S. Forest Service. Only a month before the Salt Lake City meeting and as one outgrowth of the hearings, the Grazing Service and the General Land Office were merged in a combined agency in Interior called the Bureau of Land Management.[5] It had been a shotgun sort of marriage in one sense, but likely an inevitable one. Both bureaus dealt with public domain, though in different ways. The Grazing Service had no responsibility other than grazing of livestock on district lands. In addition to leasing the isolated tracts, the GLO also disposed of public domain that had not been put in reserved status, administered mining law, sold timber where there was any, and carried out surveying duties.

At all his hearings McCarran had listened attentively to his public land-using constituency; he was indefatigable in its support. At times he would lead witnesses, and from the start he had solicited complaints. But his presence at that meeting had significance beyond mere solicitude. It was visible evidence that the livestock leaders had political support in high places. McCarran was nobody's fool, and in his counsel to the joint committee he undoubtedly advocated that they be sure their ducks were in a row before starting action. And to some extent, at least, they must have listened, for they were determined that their land grab should have legisled respectability. McCarran himself might not be the chief sponsor of the giveaway bill to be drafted and sent to what they hoped would be a docile Congress, but his advice might help them avert a misstep. Drafting the legislation was the primary task given the joint committee. It also was to enlist support from others.

The leadership did not believe getting a suitable bill enacted would be difficult. The two associations and their state affiliates already had the allegiance of nearly all members of Congress from the eleven western public land states. They also had other potent allies.[6] The politically strong American Farm Bureau Federation and its western state organizations were on their side. So were members of the staff and influential elected leaders of the Natural Resources Department of the Chamber of Commerce of the United States. The National Association of Manufacturers was coy but friendly. The political strength of this combination of agricultural and business interests was considerable.

Certainly it would not be difficult to get the desired legislation before the House and Senate for votes. By the 1940s the committees of Congress that passed on public land measures had little more than token representation from states east of the Mississippi.[7] Most easterners in Congress seemed to consider such stuff a western internal matter, an attitude members from the West welcomed when they did not cultivate it. As a result the West had almost complete charge of public land bills.

During the gestating period of the grab others who could stand to gain if the stockmen were successful were alertly watchful. Mining interests already had things pretty much their way under the archaic Mining Claims Law of 1872, and may even have been instrumental in having subsurface values dropped from the stockmen's goal. However, one could never tell surely where the next bonanza might be discovered, and this could be in the evolving bill. Timbermen took a similar attitude of restrained interest.

The decision to form the joint committee and press for action was not the result of a sudden thought. The land grab germinated over a good many years. Sentiment among the industry's elected and hired leaders rose and fell at various times but was present somewhere, at some degree of intensity, from the moment Gifford Pinchot proved in 1905 that he had authority to control livestock grazing under law that had existed since 1897.[8] Some evidence indicates that when the time was deemed right to pounce the industry was not of a single mind about the grab.[9] Its leaders were an aggressive, powerful, usually well-to-do minority of grazing permittees and paid executives of the national and state associations. Many individual ranchers, often smaller ones, and even a scattering of local livestock associations opposed it; some did so forthrightly, others more timidly.

The abolition of the Grazing Service and General Land Office and the creation of the Bureau of Land Management had been a victory for the associations and the livestock lobby of which they were a major part. The associations assembled complaining witnesses at the McCarran hearings. Their staff and elected leaders themselves gave persuasive testimony. The Grazing Service had been considered their creature. The hearings nailed down that belief as established fact. They were convinced now that they were on their way, unstoppable in whatever they wanted, and thought the Taylor Act itself blessed their ambitions through ambiguous introductory language which to them declared the district lands to be held in little more than custodial status "pending final disposal."[10] Everything seemed to be coming into focus for them. They had the world on a string with a downhill pull. So, why not go whole hog, as it were, and "dispose" of those many millions of acres at one giant gulp?

At the end the leaders of the grab movement were defeated in the attempt to secure title in fee. This occurred, though, only after they had broadened their objectives to include national forest and park system lands. It may be pointless to do so, but it is difficult to resist speculating what the outcome may have been if the grab had been limited to the Taylor lands. Vast areas of the public domain had a deceptively barren, worthless appearance. They did not excite the public imagination and inspire affection as did the national forests and parks. The original form of the land scheme just might have succeeded had its more aggressive spokesmen been restrained from reaching for more.[11]

The defeat of the grab was administered by a ragtag army of opponents that the livestock leaders scoffed at as starry-eyed dreamers, and belittled as "poolhall" conservationists.[12] True, these troops were about as disparate a band as the imagination could conjure. They had no central rallying point beyond conviction that somehow or other something had to be done to guard and preserve an increasingly precious public heritage that was situated in a region far more ecologically fragile than its grand sweeps of distance, massive contours, and impressive relief implied. And they did respond to cries of alarm that came from field forces in the West and zealous writers and others in the East and Middle West. The South was apathetic or dormant in the land-grab years.

The attempt to rip off the choicest areas in the Taylor districts, the even more desirable national forest ranges, and those parts of the National Park System where grazing was permitted, all at one feast of acquisition, probably was the last outright land grab attempt of any consequence affecting our West, certainly in this century.[13] We are not likely to see a repetition of the effort of the late 1940s for as far into the future as the human mind can project. The Taylor lands to a degree, the national forests by all means, and those national park lands have without question grown far too valuable in too many ways related to the realities of our era for this nation to allow them to slip out of public ownership. Some livestock hotheads will continue their clamor at every opportunity, as they have for nearly seventy years, but outright grab results will be nil.

If only the salient facts about actions in the 1940s required telling, this narrative could be relatively simple and brief. However, that was but one part of a complex tangle of events and attitudes that must be lined out if what has happened, and is still happening, in and to the western federal range is to be understood and its significance appreciated. The grab is long dead, but there is still much to be done if our western federal lands are to be fully safeguarded and allowed to achieve their potential.

Out there, except near proliferating metropolitan centers such as Denver, Salt Lake City, Albuquerque, Phoenix, and a few others, it seems one can stand in clear air and see all the way to tomorrow. Splendid vistas loom in every direction, but all that has affected or been affected by grazing federal lands is not as sharply limned as those peaks and peaklets rising against the blue. A great deal that has touched and still touches us all, east and west, north and south, is obscure. What is clear, though, is that over time no other of the multiple uses we make of our vast western estate has entailed more conflict, controversy, chicanery, wheeling and dealing, cussedness, hellraising in general, and political infighting than has the grazing of domestic livestock.

This began early and has seldom diminished in intensity or variety for long at a time.[14] It began before there were distinctions between this and that category of western public lands. It has been present through the birth, the growing-up era, and the years of maturity of the National Forest System. True, it has been somewhat muted in recent times in ways and for reasons to be explored later, but has never wholly died away. It has been part and parcel of the grazing use of the public domain since the drive westward gathered steam at the close of the Civil War. It has been less pervasive in the National Park System, chiefly because relatively few units of the system are grazed, but even there evidence points to incidents of sharp dealing and the application of pressure to that most sensitive of bureaucratic areas, the political.[15]

It would be nice to say that the victory against the land grab had lasting values, but it would not be true. That turned out to be little more than a holding action followed by a more subtle threat. Somewhere along the way the livestock leadership came to the conclusion that outright ownership was not necessary if other measures could assure the perpetuation of its privileged status on public land. Why own it if you could have all or nearly all the prerogatives of ownership without the cost and bother? This seems to sum up the change in attitude that occurred, and it points the direction of travel thereafter.

The attempted great land grab has been singled out for this early and special attention, first, because it was conceived and carried forward on so grand a scale and with such sublime confidence that it could and should succeed. That it was bungled does not diminish the dimensions of the concept. Second, it provides what appears a true reflection of a carried-over attitude toward public land that long flourished in the West. Some who were in on the deal believed in taking public resources, for free or for a pittance, as an inherent right that went with pioneering. And some appeared still to consider themselves pioneers, even as they tuned electronic appliances in well-furnished homes and looked after livestock on horses only where powered off-the-road vehicles could not go. Next, the grab attempt was accompanied and followed by an attitude or philosophy that, to me, has fully as unpleasant connotations for the American public that owns these western lands as the land scheme itself. I have called this the influence or authority grab,[16] and its central theme has already been mentioned—that it is silly to secure title and pay taxes and insurance and all the other things that go with ownership if you can get benefits without recording a deed at the courthouse. It is a smoother, more suave and sophisticated technique of arrogation, and its bad features and results generally are difficult to root out and expose to light. They show, however, in many places on the land itself, in large areas where condition is poor and productivity lowered. They show in internal differences among public servants over interpretations of their duties, and policies to pursue. They show in bland assumptions by leaders in a generally stable and respected western industry that whatever they craved they could get and whatever they opposed would not come to pass. They show in the dollar costs to taxpayers of trying to prop up and sustain a livestock clientele that is constantly dwindling.

By far the greater number of western ranchers were and are fine people—genial, frank, friendly, possessing an openhanded hospitality as famous as that of the Old South. The people wearing the black hats in the land grab were a mere handful of influential men holding important offices in the associations, and their staff leadership. It is toward these, not the unblemished majority, and at those in the federal agencies who bent to their wishes, that the accusing finger is pointed in this narrative.

It took more than a century for all this chapter has said and hinted at to come about, and the end is not yet in sight. In examining events and their portents, we will touch lightly on the early history of the public domain and the rise of the livestock industry that used and overused it. The narrative then examines occurrences affecting the Forest Service, and the Bureau of Land Management and its predecessor agencies, and looks into their significance, all in relation to the grazing of domestic animals and its consequences.

2

An Incredible Empire

How we, starting as a thin line of underpopulated country along the eastern seaboard, acquired a vast and incredibly rich hinterland that in less than three-fourths of a century reached three thousand miles from sea to sea, and embraced one and a half billion acres of land and water, is the material of which epics are made. Equally epic was the nation's eagerness to be rid of the empire, to turn the bulk of it over to private ownership as quickly as practical, for both military and economic reasons. The acquisition and dispersal programs began before the treaty of peace with Great Britain was signed at the close of the Revolutionary War. An understanding of both acquisition and disposal can help illuminate the tremendous material progress and the complexities inherent in any account that concerns the public land West.

Americans had been testing their frontier for generations before Independence; they thrust points of their brand of civilization into and across the Appalachians as explorers, hunters, fur gatherers, traders, and settlers. They pitted their strength and ingenuity against wilderness whose only other human occupant nearly everywhere was the Indian; and they usually considered the red man just one of many obstacles to be overcome—subdued or slaughtered—in order to make the hinterland productive according to their immediate needs and their definition of the term.

As the frontier moved westward, by fits and starts but relentlessly, the magnitude and scope of the resource wealth unfolding was but partly perceived. In fact, it was only after the industrial revolution struck America in full force that some of its natural resources were found to be of value by the measure that appeared to matter most—the dollar mark. Nevertheless, a country of seemingly endless extent was bared by each new penetration. Usually the settlers were after land that could be farmed easily, and until they reached more open areas near and across the Mississippi the almost solid timberlands encountered were considered as much hindrance as benefit.

In their wisdom, the nation's founders had pitched an early course toward settlement to westward in a fashion intended to lead quickly to a stable political organization that could contribute both to material development and national defense.[1] Seven of the original states, claimants in colonial times, were persuaded to cede parts of their holdings to the new United States. New York made the first cession in 1781, two years before the official end of the Revolutionary War; Georgia was last, in 1802. These, coupled to boundaries prescribed in the treaty, put our western borders generally along the line of the Mississippi. However, the lower end of the river was owned by France, which had acquired it from Spain as part of more than a half billion acres stretching north and northwest from the Gulf of Mexico to Canada. This became ours in 1803 through the brilliant Louisiana Purchase by Jefferson, whose emissaries to Napoleon went for a river's mouth and returned with an empire. An 1818 accord with Britain stabilized the northern border of the Purchase at the 49th parallel. To the south, the boundary was pushed to a long arc of the Gulf of Mexico when we bought Florida from Spain in 1819.

Shortly afterward Mexico gave Moses Austin permission to settle in what is now Texas. He did, and was followed by others. Soon there was discord with the host country, which ended in Texas declaring its independence and winning it at the battle of San Jacinto in 1836. Nine years later Texas voluntarily joined the United States. At the time it claimed some eighty million acres more than are inside its present extensive borders, and these—comprising parts of what are now Oklahoma, Kansas, Colorado, and New Mexico—were sold to the United States in 1850. Texas retained jurisdiction over its public lands when it joined the Union.

In 1846, partly because of the Texas matter, Mexico was provoked into starting war with the United States, and out of that followed cession by Mexico of all of California, Nevada, and Utah, and parts of New Mexico, Arizona, Colorado, and Wyoming. We paid Mexico $15 million for this huge region. It is one of the quirks of history that less than two weeks before the treaty of peace was signed in

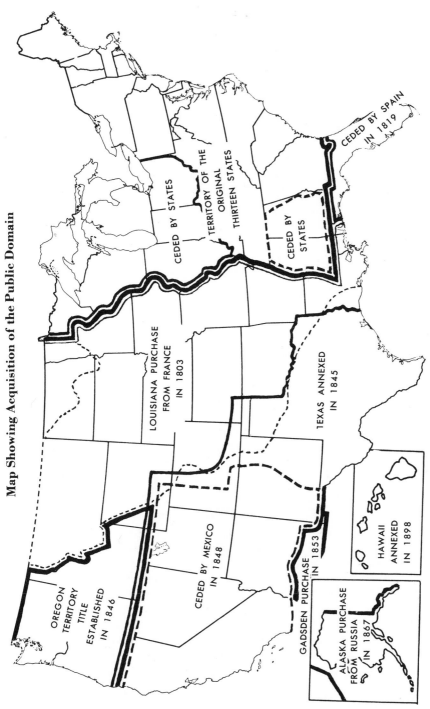

Map Showing Acquisition of the Public Domain

CEDED BY SPAIN IN 1819

TERRITORY OF THE ORIGINAL THIRTEEN STATES

CEDED BY STATES

CEDED BY STATES

LOUISIANA PURCHASE FROM FRANCE IN 1803

TEXAS ANNEXED IN 1845

HAWAII ANNEXED IN 1898

OREGON TERRITORY TITLE ESTABLISHED IN 1846

CEDED BY MEXICO IN 1848

GADSDEN PURCHASE IN 1853

ALASKA PURCHASE FROM RUSSIA IN 1867

U.S. Bureau of Land Management

1848, but without knowledge of the fact in either Washington or Mexico City, gold was found in California, first in the stream that powered Captain John A. Sutter's sawmill. Further, gold from California mines worth nearly a half billion undepreciated dollars would be recovered in the next seven years.

Conflict simmered in the Pacific Northwest for years over the fur trade, and in 1827 the British and Americans began to administer the region jointly. An 1846 settlement of claims resulted in all lands below the 49th parallel coming to the United States; this consisted of some 183 million acres comprising today's Oregon, Washington, and Idaho, and large portions of Montana and Wyoming.

A few miscellaneous acquisitions rounded out what became our first forty-eight states. A Southern coalition wanted to build a railroad to the West Coast, and part of the projected route crossed what then was Mexican territory. The Gadsden Purchase of 1853 cleared that, adding parts of what are now New Mexico and Arizona. Interior real estate in north central Colorado had not been claimed as part of the original Texas, nor was it in the Louisiana Purchase; Colorado got it when admitted as a state in 1876, though it was American territory *de facto* prior to that year. In southwestern Louisiana another detached tract was relinquished to us in the 1819 treaty with Spain. Other land not in the 1803 Purchase and lying far to the north, east of the Red River Basin, was recognized as ours by Britain in the 1818 accord. Finally, on a date that is in dispute, Britain turned over to the United States all of the Red River Basin south of the 49th parallel, comprising parts of the Dakotas and Minnesota. This and the other agreements with Great Britain made the 49th our border with Canada from the Great Lakes drainage to the Pacific.

In just seventy-two years—1781–1853—almost one and one-half billion acres had been acquired in one way or another and added to the public domain (Alaska, bought from Russia in 1867, is not included in this total.). This was 7.5 times as much acreage as there was in the thirteen original states plus Maine and Vermont. It staggered even the most imaginative minds, and contained natural wealth in undreamed of quantities and kinds. By standards of the times it was limitless, containing far more than the existing population and its technology could possibly use. It would take decades of swift industrial advancement, a population gathering latent forces for an explosion yet to come, and exploitative development beyond the visions of the most avaricious or ambitious, to bring the United States to the point where one might question the popular myth of inexhaustibility and be heeded.

Even before the young nation began to flex its muscles and look westward with acquisitive eye, it set out to dispose of public land; later this parceling out, which began as a trickle, grew into a torrent. Hundreds of millions of the acquired acres went in many ways and to all kinds of people. Grants of land went to veterans of the Revolution and later conflicts. Land was sold in large blocks to speculators, and in smaller acreages to settlers. Squatters got the land they had moved in on before it was surveyed, even before there were courthouses in which to register deeds. Grants went to states for education and other purposes. Great tracts were given to railroad companies in return for their promise to lay tracks to meet the two-way transportation needs of the growing nation. Hewing and hacking, driving the Indian tribes deeper into the unknown or segregating them in reservations, and ruthlessly breaking or ignoring treaties of eternal friendship and respect as they did so, Americans worked and fought and bought and connived their way westward down the slopes of the Appalachians, across the rest of the Ohio-Great Lakes Basins, through the shoulder-high prairie grasses and wooded flood plains of the Mississippi valley, and on to the Missouri where the river reaches the state that bears its name. The dates when states involved in this great pioneering march entered the Union indicate the accelerating pace of travel to them and to jumping off points for the Great Plains and beyond: Kentucky, 1792; Ohio, 1803; Indiana, 1816; Missouri, 1821.

In retrospect it seems inevitable that the not very latent greed inherent in humanity should manifest itself in the methods by which federal lands went into private ownership and control. A book I have not found in my research might be devoted exclusively to the almost innumerable ways so much public acreage got into private and corporate hands. It would include methods that were legally and morally right, and also many kinds of fraud, misrepresentation, thievery, lying, cheating, malfeasance, misfeasance, bribery, graft, chicanery, and unlawful appropriation.

Here we are not particularly interested in when or the manner in which public land became private, especially those areas east of a line roughly corresponding to the 100th meridian, which is commonly accepted as approximating the precipitation line that separates the long-grass prairie from the short-grass plains. It is enough to say that methods east and west differed mainly in respect to the kinds of use to be made of the land and the products thereof, and to climatic conditions that exercised almost dictatorial control over the actions and activities of man. It was where the plains began that ranching took first place and farming second. The westerning hordes who sought a farming destination discovered that beyond the 100th they were in an intermediate kind of country that could not or would not respond consistently to the raising of row crops as did the more humid easterly areas whence they came. The sodbuster plodded as far toward the sunset as the terrain and dwindling annual precipitation let him go. Thereafter, homesteading was most successful in the region Bernard DeVoto called the "interior West" [2] when fingers of settlement were thrust up stream valleys until elevations were reached beyond which irrigable crop and pasture lands could not be found. It is anticipating the story a bit but it is as well to say it now as later: In the doing, the farming settler slowly, inexorably pushed the public land or open range-using rancher toward the higher, drier plains, toward mountain meadows and perennial stream valleys, and toward elevations where there was at least as much forage for domestic animals and wildlife as there was standing timber. When the stock grower got to these kinds of lands the nester could push him no farther, for climate and slope exercised a restraining control superior to the strength of the yoked oxen and the endurance of the man behind the walking plow.

Shortly after Jefferson purchased the Louisiana Territory in 1803 he sent the Lewis and Clark expedition to answer the puzzling question of what the $15 million purchase price actually had bought. Though it dashed lingering hopes of finding a northwest passage for watercraft, the party did travel to sources of the Missouri, crossed the Continental Divide, and descended through still alien Oregon country to the impressive lower valley of the Columbia before returning in 1805. Captain Zebulon Pike struck out across the plains and in 1806–07 explored the valley of the Arkansas River to the vicinity of the peak in Colorado given his name. Soon after, Major Stephen Long led an expedition along a more northerly route, generally following the Platte and South Platte Rivers, where he, too, found a peak in the Rampart Range of the Rockies to be named in his honor.

Books were written about all three expeditions—by Nicholas Biddle on the basis of the Lewis and Clark reports, by Pike himself, and by a Dr. Edwin James who went with Long. A fourth was written by a man identified by DeVoto only as "a literary person" who traveled with John Jacob Astor's fur hunters. [3] These and other accounts served both to excite and deter readers of the day, for they told not only of the marvels seen but also of the perils to be encountered. Not the least of the latter were the risks to life that were natural to the plains, which for decades were looked upon as the Great American Desert. The Rockies farther on towered above perennial snow lines, and might or might not be readily passable or life supporting for those enticed by their grandeur and beauty. The combination of arid or semiarid plains and forbidding mountain ranges tells in large part why the interior West was relatively ignored in earlier pioneering times. Travel into the region for more than a generation after the explorations of Lewis and Clark, Pike, and Long was mainly for trapping, trading, and adventure. When the first few settlers and missionaries started out, the plains and mountains were primarily obstacles to overcome en route to California and Oregon, as much so as the immense herds of bison in their paths and raids by nomadic Indians. The Pacific Coast was far better known than the interior West by reason of several expeditions by sea, penetrations as far as northern California by the Spanish moving out of Mexico, and travel into the Columbia Basin by the British who, like Astor and other Americans, wanted furs.

A major turning point in the history of the American West came when fur traders broke wagon trail across the South Pass of the Continental Divide in Wyoming about 1832.[4] Later, along this trail, there would be deep ruts to be followed by each new westering family or group of families and help guide them to coastal destinations. Proof that common vehicles of the day could traverse the Rockies made possible what DeVoto considered the most significant single event in the West's evolving history. This was the coming of white women to share pioneering wealth and woe with their men and to bear their children. In due time this would mean villages instead of isolated camps, and towns, schools, churches, stores, factories, government, and all the rest of the symbols and trappings of our civilization. The first group containing women went westward in 1836.[5] True, there were but two in the party—Eliza Spalding and Narcissa Whitman, wives of missionaries—but it was a momentous beginning. They were bound for Oregon and made it before the end of the year. Thousands more would come along in the thirty-odd years that would pass before the railroad made wagon trains obsolescent.

It was in this period that livestock ranching had its start in the interior West, but it was far from new elsewhere out there. It had been practiced for upward of two centuries in the Southwest, where each Spanish mission had its flock of sheep and other cattle, and

where favored men grew wealthy on extensive crown grants of rangeland. Even before the missionaries came, military explorers had
driven flocks and herds as they marched; this was a way of assuring
a meat supply if wild game proved hard to come by. Raising domestic
livestock was a thriving business in what are now Texas, New Mexico,
Arizona, California, and parts of Colorado, Utah, and Nevada long
before the first ox, cow, bull, or calf began the long walk from the
line of the Missouri toward the West. Osgood's *Day of the Cattleman*
tells well the origins of cattle ranching in the Rockies and adjacent
regions.[6] Towne and Wentworth have traced in detail the trails followed by sheep in *Shepherd's Empire* [7] and other writings; they show
that the raising of mutton and wool had been established progressively in nearly all parts of the Southwest long before the close of the
eighteenth century. Cows grazed along with sheep in much of the
Southwest in those early times, a practice now frowned upon because it practically guarantees overuse and damage.

Though ranching today seems an almost inevitable pastoral industry in the westerly plains and mountain country, it could be said
to have started there almost by happenstance. DeVoto records that
in 1838 when Captain Sutter and a group of missionaries traveling
toward California reached Fort Laramie they exchanged worn, footsore horses for fresh stock.[8] Laramie had been built as a shelter and
supply base for one of the early fur companies, and trading rested
and fattened horses for lean and weary beasts of travelers became a
sideline of the main business transacted.

Soon afterward its practitioners began to change ranching from
sideline to chief occupation. Fur traders saw a chance to make
money off the growing numbers of pioneers by supplying them with
essentials they had not stocked in sufficient quantity when starting
out, that had spoiled, or had been lost as a result of carelessness,
ignorance, accident, storm, or Indian attack. Some stock strayed from
the wagons, some was driven off by Indians, some looked too worn to
last the journey and was left to die, but instead fattened on grass that
dried to nutritious hay on the stem. Those who ran small trading posts
set up at river crossings where trails merged or divided, and at other
strategic places, often picked up a few stray head here, more there,
and almost naturally grew into the livestock business. Some families
simply tired of the long trail and halted along the way to hole up in a
dugout in the side of a hill or in a primitive sod hut to try to make a
go of it where they chose to stop. If they survived the havoc wrought
by the elements—on frequent occasions violent tornadoes and bone-

chilling blizzards strike the open plains—or if they were not killed by Indians resentful of the white man's intrusions and double-dealings, they usually ended up running early-day livestock operations.

The population and ranching build-up was a relatively slow process in ox team and Conestoga wagon times. The largest single band of settlers in the 1840s was that which founded Mormon Utah. The gold discovery and other events that were shaping up, however, would bring swift, earthshaking change to the vast plains and mountains country over a very few years. Aided by generous political favors, railroad lines were being laid down by the hundreds of miles and being pushed ever closer to the advancing frontier. The Gadsden Purchase in the Southwest, to benefit a proposed transcontinental railroad, was mentioned earlier. This was enmeshed in controversial affairs that helped lead to the outbreak of the Civil War in 1861, and the war delayed that line's construction. By 1862 more northerly transcontinental rail routes were nearing certainty, as a result of congressional action no longer hindered by members from the South. Eighteen-sixty-two also saw passage of the 160-acre Homestead Act, which had been blocked in earlier times by Southern fear of what it would mean to the institution of slavery. The war, too, could claim at least partial responsibility for another event, a phenomenon actually, whose effects would be felt in cow country for years. This was the huge rise in numbers of cattle in Texas, brought about by natural increase and lack of markets after Grant in 1863 cut the line of the Mississippi for the Union and split the Confederacy in two.

The end of the war would bring explosive elemental forces to bear on the interior West, and in part shape its future condition even to this day.

3

Those Were the Days

In *The Americans: The National Experience,*[1] Daniel J. Boorstin wrote of the tremendous 1,800-mile leap made by covered-wagon pioneers across difficult terrain, often in the face of great danger, from the Missouri River at Independence to the Pacific Coast. To question whether it was a leap or a crawl would be nitpicking. The travelers trudged or rode slowly ahead, with their thoughts more on rainbow ends on the western shores than on what lay to either side of the long trail. There was the lure of gold to be found in California and of various kinds of riches in fabulous Oregon Territory. The barren appearance of so much of the high plains and the forbidding peaks of the Rockies and other mountain ranges of the interior West at first seemed to repel more than to attract.

This altered radically after the Civil War, though the ferment of change had been building before that fratricidal conflict. When the war ended, the region extending roughly from the 100th meridian to the Sierra Nevada in one direction and from Canada to the southward bend of the Rio Grande in Colorado in the other then became the last physical frontier in what are now the contiguous states. Filling that interior frontier was the final chapter in the settlement of those states.

We are reminded by more than one historian that a series of momentous events—the passage of the 160-acre Homestead Act, the close of the war, the first drives of Texas longhorn cattle to Kansas and beyond, and the linking of the east and west coasts by rail—all took place in less than ten years. One of the results would be the filling of that last frontier with livestock and the establishment of the open range livestock industry. Another twenty years brought old-style open range ranching to an end in an epic period of boom and bust.

At the time of the Civil War the interior West had already changed considerably from what it was in the wild and woolly years when mountain men tended trap lines with an eye peeled and an ear cocked for sight or sound of Indians. Frontiersmen of earlier years had already discovered the nutritive qualities of plains grasses at all seasons and the possibilities the range held forth as pastureland. The incidents and undertakings that disclosed it were isolated but cumulatively built a fund of knowledge and experience that, coupled to events of more massive import, would turn the region into a ferment of human activity.

Freighters' oxen would be deliberately wintered in numbers on the open ranges of the western plains before 1860. In the spring they would be rounded up over a broad span of countryside, sleek and strong, ready to be yoked once more to pull wagonloads of freight westward, much of it human. These roundups were a foretaste of a similar spring roundup rite to be practiced by hundreds of participants upon tens of thousands of cattle in the boom years just ahead.

Before the 1850s the interior frontier saw only a few domestic animals around a nester's home or trading post. Osgood [2] hinted at what was in the offing when he wrote of the existence of a herd of six hundred cattle there as early as 1856, but that was a rarity. Hard facts tended to hold back a widespread or lusty livestock industry until a bit later. There were few nearby markets of consequence, transportation was primitive, and the Indian still was an adversary to be feared.

The close of the Civil War released forces that had been pent up, tied down, or gathering strength for four years. Before the war slavery-serving Southern forces had prevented passage of the 160-acre Homestead Act, which easily was enacted after Secession and for decades influenced the pattern and nature of settlement in those portions of the frontier suited to walking-plow agriculture, and in some that were not.

Railroading had north–south aspects, but the main thrust was east–west. The war spurred approval of a midcontinent crossing through cooperative efforts of the Union Pacific and Western Pacific, and this had an impact on the growth of the new range livestock industry almost impossible to overemphasize. Then, the checkerboard land ownership pattern that resulted from railroad and other land grants was to have widespread and significant effects likely not foreseen when they were so freely dispensed by Congress. Granting every other section laterally from the rights of way for as many as twenty miles on each side caused them to be interspersed with public domain, other public land, and private ownerships into an intricate design bound to bring administrative headaches later.

Lee's surrender freed hundreds of thousands of men from uniform and tight discipline. Hordes of them, Union and Confederate alike, were eager to forget the past and seek new lives in the rapidly opening lands Out West. As the military forces consisted of all kinds, so also would the travelers and their settlements. A considerable number worked at building railroad lines and it would take only until 1869 for crews moving westward from Omaha and those coming east from California to meet at Promontory Point, Utah. Lines had penetrated deep into Kansas and Nebraska by the mid-1860s; the Union Pacific had reached Wyoming in 1867.

The rail coupling in Utah was fully as significant to the future of the interior as was the earlier proof by Bonneville and Sublette that wagons could cross the Continental Divide and go on through mountain country to California and Oregon. Horses or oxen and wagons were adequate to handle relatively small volumes at a comparatively slow pace. The railroad could move men and materials at far faster speeds and at lower cost.

The end of the war also released the great herds of Texas longhorn cattle that had come about by natural increase during the conflict. Texas cattle had been a long way from substantial markets even before the 1860s. The Confederacy consumed much of the surplus in the earlier war years. Then General Grant and the Union Navy cut the line of the Mississippi, divided the South, and deprived it of its Texas meat supply. By 1865 Texas was almost bulging with longhorns. Meantime, the war had depleted cattle supplies in the Union states and there was a ready market if only the Texans could get their beef to it. Trail herding to railhead was the immediate answer, with lengthening tracks providing ever more sidings where chutes could be built to load cars. Trail herding began in 1866, and by the 1890s millions of cattle had made the long walk north. While the destinations of many were sidings from which steers could be rolled to feedlots and butchers, open range ranchers needed first a few, then increasing numbers of bulls, cows, and their young. Not all the cattle that soon filled the interior came from Texas. Others were driven, later hauled by rail, from the West Coast and from numerous easterly sources.

The filling took a remarkably short time, considering the vastness of the region. John Clay [3] notes there was almost no livestock business, as a business, there as the 1860s came to an end. A. W. Sampson [4] reports there were 4.6 million cattle in the seventeen western states in 1870, mostly in Texas, and a total of 26.65 million only twenty years later. A table in the Nimmo report [5] shows 600,000 Texas cattle on the trails in 1871 and that 5.2 million had been trailed northward from 1866 to 1885 inclusive.

It would be difficult to overemphasize the importance to the swift development of the region of qualities peculiar to the native grasses. It has been noted earlier that livestock had been wintered on them without supplemental feed. J. W. Powell [6] remarked that these grasses cured like hay on the stem instead of deteriorating into life-lessness as did those in more humid areas. Footsore stock freed by Forty-niners and others and left presumably to starve, were found by following wagoners the next spring sound of wind and limb, in re-markably good condition.[7] This quality of the forage, combined with the abundant free public range over which livestock could roam unhindered gave great impetus to the open type of ranching that pre-vailed until the disaster of the later 1880s led to its close. Nor were there restraints in the earlier years such as the barbed wire that was to be invented in 1874 [8] and would itself contribute to the unseen coming disaster.

It appears futile to dwell at length on the plight of the Indian in this era. It is enough here to note that the increasingly rapid en-croachment by whites on land that was Indian by right of prior occu-pancy, then by treaty, and the killing off of the wild game that com-prised so much of the natives' food supply, made the tribes desperate. One of the most publicized of the resulting conflicts was the Sioux War, 1875–77. The death of flamboyant General George A. Custer in south central Montana brought immediate military vengeance, and the red man's fate was quickly sealed. By the end of the 1880s the worst the livestock industry could expect from Indian neighbors was an occasional sporadic raid to kill a steer or two to feed hungry fami-lies on the reservations.

The 1870s brought the great cattle buildup and the decade that followed brought unparalleled greed and recklessness. Its natural disasters toppled some of the mightiest cattle empires created in the boom. Free range on the public domain continued until the mid-1930s, but the old technique of letting stock run loose, nearly always without provision for feeding and care in bitter winter weather, had to

Clear stream, heavily grassed plain, when being surveyed in 1870, Uinta County, southwestern Wyoming. *USFS photo*

Same stream, 67 years later. In 1937 lush grasses had been replaced by big sage and rabbit brush; only traces of grass left after overgrazing. *USFS photo*

give way to better ranching methods. Open range ranching was common in Spain and we inherited it from Mexico via our Spanish-speaking Southwest. There the climate encouraged the practice. The mistake then made lay in the belief that it could be followed all year in the far more rigorous weather conditions encountered from Colorado to Canada and at higher, colder elevations. Ambition and avarice were accessories, but even the aggregate of miscalculations and speculative actions that hit so hard when the bubble was bursting would not have caused so much livestock suffering and loss if the barbed wire fence had not been invented.

As the open range industry in the interior frontier originated alongside the trails, it naturally gravitated to lands near the railroads as the lines were laid down, then spread out on either side in irregular patterns dictated largely by the presence or absence of water. Often the chief asset of a stock owner, other than the stock itself, was possession or control—which are different things—of one or more strategically situated watering places such as a perennial stream, spring, pond, or lake. To these should be added a few cowhands, a branding iron, and a corral or two. Little more was needed then, for the grazing land itself was free, mostly federal public land. Even the checkerboard railroad land was not as securely held against trespassing livestock as the titles granted by the federal government would indicate, for those alternate sections could not be fenced economically, nor could they be adequately policed. Ranchers bought railroad sections containing water mainly because by doing so they could control grazing on surrounding dry acreage. There the cattle ran loose until rounded up for branding or for sale.

The belief that bigger is better—which prevails so broadly even today—led the ambitious to acquisition of ever increasing numbers of waterholes and livestock. The former would be acquired legitimately, by purchase or by homesteading, or illegitimately by any of a dozen or so types of fraud or loose dealing, reported often and fruitlessly by commissioners of the General Land Office and others writing on the doings of the times. Gifford Pinchot [9] put it succinctly: The highest grade citizen was the one who'd gotten the most, which made material riches synonymous with virtue. All whose writings have come to my attention have told of the many kinds of fraud, the ruthlessness of those who perpetrated fraud or hired it done in their race for strategic water, and of the harsh manner with which they clung to what they had gained. E. S. Osgood quotes from the preliminary report of the Public Land Commission of 1879, wherein a Colorado cowman told that he had two miles of running water on his 320 acres of patented land, and that the next water in one direction was twenty-three miles away. He had control of reachable forage between the two as though he held title to it.[10] All the variations of the Homestead Act [11] were used in their time to build new livestock empires or to increase existing ones.

Broadly speaking, the higher the elevations of land the better the water situation and more lush the forage, but the shorter the growing and grazing seasons. This factor has no paramount bearing on the subject matter of the present chapter but did dictate how the higher country might be used to extend the empires of the larger operators as or when the filling or pre-empting of regions at lower levels crowded out ranchers of less power and prevented newcomers from getting a start.

The actual open range boom began in a big way about 1880.[12] A few years later the incessant drive for growth had crowded more stock numbers on the ranges than they could possibly stand. And it was accompanied by an era of wild speculation that lasted a mere six years before bad weather and human errors brought a sudden disaster and its lasting influence.

The lure, of course, was the spectacular gain to be had from an interest in a flourishing livestock business. Doubtless nonexistent operations were fraudulently peddled here and there, but the incredible fact is that it usually was not necessary to be overtly crooked to turn a fast buck in cattle. Many of the speculators bamboozled were eastern Americans; other investors lived overseas, and few ever saw the countryside or the livestock on which they spent their money and from which they expected large dividends. Sportsmen out to hunt big game took back tall tales of how the invested dollar could be doubled in a year or so and at small operating cost. Cheyenne and other population centers became scenes of wild buying and selling that was aided and abetted by press and government reports.[13] Legislatures voted money to promote the boom in pamphlets and in other ways. English and Scottish newspapers picked up the story of the bonanza from cow-town papers mailed home by visitors and journalists on assignment. Bill Nye, the humorist, wrote wry tales quoted by historians of the era, one of the favorites being of the mythical tenderfoot who ended with a big herd of cattle allegedly started by the natural increase from a single steer.

Government reports often were notable for their optimism, a tendency that seems to have persisted and to which we will refer in later chapters. The Nimmo report,[14] issued only months before disaster struck, quoted "intelligent observers" as saying the range as a whole could stand two to four times as many head of stock as then were on it. A few observant livestock operators contradicted Nimmo by their actions. Clay [15] wrote that by 1884–85 the range was showing signs of being overstocked. Osgood [16] said that by the first half of the decade it had become unwise to depend entirely on free grass and that some of the more thoughtful bought or otherwise obtained as much patented land as possible to hedge their bets. Others were lucky or foresighted enough to move stock to less crowded Canadian ranges or to sell 'and ship at peak prices just before the balloon burst. A few more prescient editors also warned of dangers of overstocking and speculating. However, given the lack of hard knowledge of range productivity and management in that day, it is plausible to believe it would have been difficult for anyone to say surely just what harm was being wrought.

The tendency of the strong to take what they wanted, and their desire to hold what they had was one factor in the evolution of the boom period, and of the customs and practices it brought. They only partly deterred the smaller operators seeking desperately to grow, and the newcomers who tried to crowd their way onto the bonanza train, regardless of whether they were welcome or there was enough territory and grass for their stock. Clashes were inevitable, as were impromptu or more reasoned methods of dealing with problems that arose. Vigilante thinking and processes were among the solutions attempted by the haves against the have-nots.

Long before there was overcrowding and a swelling boom, leaders among the ranchers found it desirable to join together in associations to protect their interests.[17] The first of these of consequence was formed in Wyoming in 1871, though smaller groups had come together in Colorado as early as 1868; larger ones were formed there by 1872. The stock growers of Montana organized in 1874. The Wyoming Stock Growers Association, which was to assume great power in a short while, grew out of the Laramie County Stock Growers Association set up in 1873 at Cheyenne.

Such associations came into being initially as a result of questions of ownership of stock running at large, and of the "right" of a rancher to graze his stock, exclusively or otherwise, on this or that tract of land. The operators didn't want government interference with their free use of the open range. By banding together they hoped to settle internal differences between members of the club and keep outsiders from horning in on their good thing. Bunched as they were in their associations, the operators constituted a formidable force; they still do in Wyoming and elsewhere, though their application of power is no longer physical but through political processes. In the boom-and-bust era the Wyoming association was the boss of the territory in livestock and public land matters. The legislature of 1884 put the association in charge of all maverick (unbranded) cattle found on the ranges, as trustee for the territory, and gave it widespread control over roundups and brands.

These were important prerogatives. By setting roundup rules the members could prevent participation by nonmembers, which was hardship enough to put a man out of business. And if a brand was ruled against, all stock bearing it could be treated as maverick and impounded for disposal as property of the territory, disposal that often meant turning it over to influential association members. The Wyoming organization lost some of its legal powers in the late 1880s, but stayed strong otherwise.

Sheep came to be a complicating factor to the cowmen of the interior West rather early in the day. Southern Colorado, especially the Rio Grande River valley, was genetically New Mexican, so to speak. Spanish-speaking settlers had pushed up the valley from the south long years earlier, bringing their customs and livestock, mostly sheep. By the late 1860s Colorado had a sheep population of more than two million.[18] The Mormons had taken sheep as well as cattle with them to Utah in 1847, and sheep spread into Wyoming and Montana in the early 1870s. They predominated in southwestern Wyoming by 1884, and by that time embattled cowmen had come to the conclusion that the only effective way to deal with the problem was to build fences or use force. Often both were employed in the brutal sheep–cow warfare that continued from that era until well into the twentieth century. Sheep, however, figured only peripherally in the great boom-bust experience. That was primarily a cattle phenomenon.

The noted "Green Book" [19] of the Forest Service, to be referred to at some length later in other relationships, at one place had this to say of the rousing boom years and the practices of those times: "The newness of it all plus the size of the outfits left Americans without guide or standard . . . to gauge either security of cattle . . . or ability of forages to stand up. . . . Cattle instead of grass came to be regarded as the raw resource."

In the wild speculations one fatal lack was accurate information as to actual numbers and kinds of livestock bought and sold. Buyers took "book" counts—the numbers in the ranch house or corporation office records—as actual numbers on the range, whereas they may have been far out of line, either due to the making of rough estimates in rougher country or failure to note losses from disease and other causes, or both. Book counts in some instances likely were outright frauds perpetrated to jack up prices. In the era of unrestrained speculation prices paid for the same livestock or ranch holding multiplied within days or weeks on the Cheyenne and other markets. Investors in this country and abroad were interested only in dividends, and for a time these were spectacular.

In the end weather collaborated with barbed wire and a collapsing market to close out a phenomenal era in the history of grazing the public land West. The ranges were crowded to the limits of their capacity and beyond when combinations of severe winters and dry summers struck hard. Results might not have been quite so bad if there had been no fences.

The coming of barbed wire had been seen as a godsend by the stock industry. It was a comparatively cheap way to keep one's own cattle in a given area, and to keep the other fellow's out. A rancher with plenty of barbed wire fence up didn't need as many horses to feed or cowboys to ride them. Soon after its invention, large acreages were put under barbed wire, nearly all of it on public domain. Much of the rapidly increasing tonnages annually produced went to the interior frontier. According to the General Land Office report for 1888, two Colorado corporations had fenced a million acres each, three million acres were fenced in two New Mexico counties, and numerous operators elsewhere each had as many as a quarter million acres of public land under wire. The GLO wrote that some 7.25 million acres were fenced in fourteen western states and territories, turning them, in effect, into private pastures.

Without fences the range stock could have drifted ahead of the blizzards. Many might have been saved by finding shelter in some stream bottom or a dry coulee. As it was, they wandered downwind until they could go no farther, then died huddled against the barbs by the tens of thousands. Such stock as survived the terrible storms failed to gain protective weight in dry, poor-forage summers that followed, and thus were hit that much harder in succeeding winters. Clay wrote of the "appalling . . . murder" of livestock in those harsh times, adding that the truth often didn't dawn upon snowbound ranchers and corporation managers until spring roundup time. He wrote that the 1886–1887 winter struck the industry from southern Colorado to Canada and from the 100th meridian to the western slope of the Rockies.[20]

The combination of forces involved—ruinous speculation, greed, poor management, weather, barbed wire, and a failing market—killed an era and "changed the range-cattle industry from an adventure to a business." [21] After the panicky period, the Green Book says, "the history of the range is largely the story of the struggle between the big owner and the little owner, with the 'rustler' an unrecognized but inevitable ally of the small owner." It evolved into an era of summary executions of suspects in "cottonwood justice."

The further intrusion of sheep into what had been cattle country aggravated the situation for all concerned. Years later an elderly Nevada cowman told a Senate investigating subcommittee [22] that in those days "you'd get up in the night and head for the spring" with the cattle, and on arrival "find nothing but dust" because "somebody else had beat you there." While that witness may have been talking of intruding sheep or cattle, it was the moving in of the former that brought on the bloodiest, rawest, bitterest conflicts. In some ways and regions the increase in sheep numbers was a sort of vacuum-filling process following the sharp cuts in cattle during that series of bad winters and dry summers. Often the flocks were owned by nomads, without a home base, who wandered wherever public land promised grass. The range itself got little relief from heavy use, and there may not even today be a truly widespread recognition of the lasting impact of the damage to forage and soil started during the boom era.

4

Small Voices

We are prone to consider American conservation problems and steps to counteract environmental adversity as recent, the product of an overnight awakening, which isn't so. What has been true is a tendency toward slowness to recognize problems and reluctance to act decisively upon them in timely fashion.

We were deep into the nineteenth century before resource conditions reached a stage that would concern the federal government, and the problems that brought this about involved the public lands of the West. Timber was the first resource to rouse the nation to action, with water second. That either could stimulate substantial concern was due to a slowly spreading awareness that inexhaustibility of resources might in fact be a myth. This came coincidentally with the boom-and-bust cattle era in post-Civil War decades.

It was a time of surging growth in the industrialization of our nation. The agony of the war was behind us. Everywhere we were expanding and enlarging and pressing outward and upward. It was a time of careless, wasteful exploitation, an age with a seemingly insatiable appetite for lumber and other wood products. Timber barons, with a reckless disregard for posterity, would pursue careers of cut-out-and-get-out in the nation's virgin forests, leaving devastation as they went. New England's native stands of timber had been logged off long before the time of which we speak. The soft pines of New York and Pennsylvania went next. The mixed hardwoods of Ohio, Indiana, and southern Illinois were being cut right and left, and those tremendous stands of white pine in the Lake States were being penetrated deeply by sawyers and axmen. The pine lands of the South survived in virgin stands a little longer, as did the live oaks and cypress of that region's wetlands. It was the rape of the tall timber of the Lake States, and the sight of barren or slashed hillsides to the east that brought realization to a few that the course being pursued could have but one ultimate consequence: woodland disaster. Not even the unparalleled forests of pine, redwood, fir, cedar, hemlock, and spruce of the West and Northwest could be guaranteed a future unless protective steps were taken soon.

Though he was not the first to mark a need for caution in the treatment of our natural resources, George Marsh in his *Man and Nature*, published in 1864, is often given credit for the initial stimulus toward creation of something approaching a conservation movement later in the nineteenth century. His message came at a bad time for resources conservation, as the Civil War was in its late throes and the nation was preoccupied with its demands. But the book survived, and its provoking precepts found fertile ground later, when there was time for other things.

Marsh wrote with concern of man's capacity to derange the harmonies of nature and, like many who followed him, was far more disturbed by the stripping of trees from the earth than he was with what might happen to the lowly grasses underfoot. In truth, it must be said that at the time he wrote the grasses had not suffered greatly over widespread regions of the United States. It is equally true that even at the end of the century whatever benefits came to forage through conservation did so largely as a by-product of action intended to prevent destruction of timber resources. Little conscious thought was given to the preservation of a forage base on the land. Trees, on the other hand, not only provided fuel but were needed to build the dwellings and shops and factories whose expansion in all fields and directions was the wonder of the western world. A supply must be assured.

Deterioration of forage is not always easy to detect. It can be a slow, insidious process. The contrast between grassland abuse and forest abuse is as that between drought and flood. Drought creeps slowly, stealthily, causing a gradual, almost imperceptible withering and death of annual and some perennial things. It shows itself in trees, as a rule, chiefly in growth rings narrower than in wetter times. Flood, on the other hand, often rises swiftly, with obvious power to crush, overwhelm, and destroy. Trees stand tall; magnificent specimens may have required centuries to reach maximum proportions. Then, suddenly, the ax and saw take them down. They may go overnight. The change is highly visible, dramatic as a flood is dramatic. Thus it was that timber, not grass, with water supply close behind— for it was even then believed that trees steadied and conserved stream flows—first brought the need for conservation to national attention.

The names and connections of those who initially lifted almost unheard voices in protest against wanton timber destruction have been well documented in numerous books and reports; no need to duplicate here at tedious length. Hibbard, Cameron, Dana, Pinchot, Clepper, Stegner, and others bring the times vividly to life and may be consulted for names and activities of outstanding individuals and for other details. The active earlier organizations most often named in the literature are the American Association for the Advancement of Science and the American Forestry Association. The former memorialized Congress as early as 1873 to do something to prevent unrestrained destruction of timberlands, and is credited with influencing the lawmakers to provide for the hiring of our first federal forester, Franklin B. Hough.[1] He was assigned to the Department of Agriculture—an incident that takes on increased significance as we proceed —with duties limited to collecting and disseminating facts and figures on the timber industry. It was a small step, but larger ones were to follow.

Those who have written of the era tell us that numerous forces were working slowly toward stimulating an awareness of the need for what Aldo Leopold later termed [2] a "land ethic," but achieving widespread acceptance of the concept was something else entirely. The West itself had little organization devoted to resource conservation. What was there concerned itself largely with water and consisted mostly of John Wesley Powell's followers. Their good intentions were confounded by others who might have profited if Powell's concepts [3] of land and water utilization had been accepted and put into practice; they, however, were interested only in material benefit to be secured through other means.

The strongest organizations in livestock country were the associations of ranchers, and these seldom concerned themselves with resource conservation. They were organizations of, by, and for the industry they both led and served, and such organizations seldom have proved good at self-regulation and self-restraint in resource utilization and exploitation. They usually are preoccupied with protecting the "rights" of their members and warding off regulation or other impingement on custom or privilege. The undertakings, previously noted, of the Wyoming Stock Growers Association during and after the boom-and-bust era should be considered the rule rather than the exception. In more recent years the national organizations of cow and sheep ranchers, along with state and some local affiliates, demonstrated time and again that they were in finest fettle when openly or covertly opposing ecological verities. Some specifics will be indicated in later chapters. No record I have found shows any western livestock organization supporting Powell's fundamental premises of land use, or the stands taken in the 1870s and 1880s by AAAS and the AFA.

In addition to the activities of self-interest groups, part of the long delay in bringing at least partial order out of chaotic resource use was simply due to lack of widespread understanding and effective communication. Powell may have come closest to recognition of the essential oneness of nature, and his writings and speeches certainly should have aroused favorable interest and action, yet there were limits to even his pursuit of the concept of natural unities, and much of his career, after publication of *The Arid Lands,* was spent in frustrating political infighting instead of constructive work on the land.

Marsh was preoccupied with what destruction of timberlands did to water flow; he wrote at length of findings by French and other observers abroad. This seems to have been his chief contribution to conservation thinking. Powell devoted little direct attention to timber. He seemed to take it for granted that the western highlands would remain wooded on into the future. He concentrated instead on seeking methods by which each landowner might have access to water with which to irrigate hay meadows whose product would supplement the livestock forage produced naturally on benchlands.

There is a strange similarity between Powell's proposals for laying out livestock farms in the semiarid and arid west and the pattern of landownerships that actually has prevailed since long before his time in upstate New York, where he was born. There farms often reach out laterally from valley streams to ridgetops. The stream waters serve many uses, including stock water and supplemental irrigation. Row crops are raised in the flood plain; livestock pasturage is found on the rising benchland; and a perennial supply of timber for fuel and other purposes grows on the higher slopes and ridges. The whole constitutes a self-contained subsistence unit. Though Powell was born near Jamestown, New York, his family moved westward when he was small. It is possible that he may have heard his parents and their friends talk of the land-use pattern back in the Genesee or Susquehanna basins. He may have visited upstate New York when adult and noted the custom in parceling out land. If so, he failed to provide linkage in his writings. Wallace Stegner, Powell's biographer, has no material to substantiate the hypothesis.[4] Nevertheless, it is a possibility that, to me, seems worth noting.

Doubtless one reason the livestock industry saw little to acclaim in Powell's proposals was that he wrote chiefly in terms of the homesteaders, the small family farmers as it were, rather than broad spreads of huge operators who would control hundreds of thousands of acres and tens of thousands of head of cattle or comparable numbers of sheep. Ranches of this magnitude were just over the horizon when Powell's report was published in 1878; it was no time for thinking small.

Powell apparently had a greater awareness than his contemporaries that the grasses of the high plains and mountain meadows were vulnerable to overuse. In Mormon Utah, where he carried out much of his field work, Powell found [5] that in a relatively short span of thirty years cattle and sheep had "destroyed native grasses" over large areas and had "everywhere reduced them." Where ground-covering vegetation had once slowed erosion when rare rains came, often in brief cloudbursts, "there is now only an open growth of bushes that offer no obstruction" to flooding, water dissipation, and soil loss. He wrote of trampling by stock and that soil around springs and elsewhere was impacted to the point that water could not percolate into the ground to nourish root systems; it ran off swiftly so stream beds were low or dry later in the spring or summer.

Here Powell was writing of things people of the West did not want to be told or that were beyond their comprehension. Too, his comments on the overuse of forage were comparatively brief, not highlighted nor emphasized, and generally overshadowed by the social engineering aspects of the main thrust of his report, which now seems a pity. Except for Powell's almost casual reference to overgrazing in Utah, I've found little in the early literature, official or otherwise, on that subject, and nothing to indicate that forage had an appreciable influence on the course of conservation events in the last half of the nineteenth century. Even Powell gave overgrazing and its effects less than a printed page. The AAAS focused on timber in its 1873 memorial to Congress. The name of the American Forestry Association almost guaranteed it would do likewise.

These two organizations, in particular, continued to agitate for an effective restraint upon the then unbridled exploitation of forest lands, and a number of bills were introduced in Congress, without, however, getting very far until a measure stimulated by the AAAS eventually was enacted in 1891. It became law as a rider attached to a bill whose chief intent was a general revision of land laws, including changes in provisions for homesteading.[6] The section provided that such lands as might be set aside as forest reserves were not to be open to homesteading, and that the reserved lands need not necessarily bear commercial stands of timber. Under it President Benjamin Harrison created more than thirteen million acres of forest reserves from public domain.

The enactment brought almost immediate problems, since it made no provision for the administration and use of the reserves. They were effectively locked away from any utilization under the strict, conservative interpretation given the language of the act by the Department of the Interior. There is a certain irony in the fact that desire for commercial and industrial exploitation of western timber was a chief reason why the law was changed in 1897 into an enforceable instrument for natural resource conservation. Corporate giants such as Anaconda Copper of Montana, and Homestake Mining of South Dakota's Black Hills, which used considerable timber in their mining and related operations, were in the forefront of the attack on the original forest reserves law, and they had plenty of allies. Richard G. Lillard identified some of them as cattle interests, the railroads, and lumbermen.[7]

Because it was so restrictive, allowing no use whatever of all those millions of reserved acres, conservationists feared the 1891 law would be lost through repeal. Their strategy was to try to correct the law's weakness, and they moved in that direction. The National Academy of Science named a forestry commission to study alternatives, and both President Grover Cleveland and Interior Secretary Hoke Smith were consulted. Cleveland's deep personal interest shows strongly in Pinchot's account of what occurred.[8] Pinchot was one of a three-man NAS committee appointed to express preliminary thoughts. He quotes Cleveland as advocating that the forestry commission give first attention to the organization of a forest service, with the setting aside of additional reserves to come later. He wanted a plan that would look small, and not cost much at first, but would lend itself to growth over time. These were admirable political precepts! In them we may see root and bud of every bureaucratic empire in government today.

The commission followed Cleveland's counsel in every respect. It urged an administrative structure with adequate personnel and funds. Cleveland might have been satisfied with that, and let favorable action on the NAS proposals be taken by Congress and his successor, for his term was ending. Instead, despite the warning in the temper of the times that it might be well to make haste slowly, Cleveland set up thirteen additional reserves at once, totaling twenty-one million acres, by proclamation. They included areas in Montana and the Black Hills of South Dakota.

This was too much for the opponents of the 1891 law to take, and they promptly mounted additional attack. The first step was to try to void the new reserves by law, and the Senate voted to do so the day a bill for that purpose was introduced. Things were different in the House. Congressman John F. Lacey of Iowa, who drove home the truth of what was in the wind with the words, "There is nothing so sacred as an abuse," [9] led the counterattack. He drafted modifying language that would let timber be cut and used for mining and domestic purposes, and would allow the Secretary of the Interior to "make all needful rules and regulations to further the purposes of said reserves, and for the management and protection of the same." There was some modification when the bill was in House–Senate conference. These angered Cleveland, and he pocket-vetoed the bill on his last day in office in 1896. Pinchot said it was a brave act that focused attention on the forest situation on front pages of the nation's newspapers.

Senator Richard F. Pettigrew of South Dakota had no reputation as a conservationist, but his name, nevertheless, is intimately tied to the bill that gave federal forestry substance and practicality. He introduced his bill in the early days of President William McKinley's administration. It had been drafted at Pettigrew's request by Charles D. Walcott, director of the U.S. Geological Survey. The provision that made the difference between passage and defeat suspended for nine months the date when Cleveland's thirteen reserves might enter the system. This gave mining interests, speculators, and others time to set up claims in them under the mining and homestead laws.

Though the motives behind the bill were far from pure, it nevertheless became the foundation for today's national forest system. Like so many other laws on the nation's books, it began with a curiously negative tone. It said that "*No* public forest reservation shall be established *except* to improve and protect the forest . . . , or for the purpose of securing favorable conditions of water flow, and to furnish a continuous supply of timber . . ." (italics added). Further, there was no intention in the act, it said, to include in forest reserves land that would be more valuable for mineral or agricultural purposes. However—and here was the real crux of the matter for times yet to come—the Secretary could "make such rules and regulations and establish such service as will insure the objects of such reservations, namely, *to regulate their occupancy and use* and to preserve the forests therein from destruction" (italics added). Pinchot called that clause the "milk in the coconut." [10]

The clause truly was more flexible than westerners had anticipated, and there would be many second thoughts about its inclusion after a few years had passed and the more imaginative and aggressive hands of Gifford Pinchot held the administrative reins. This was not to come about for another nine years, years in which Interior did little more than leave the reserves untended. This was partly because of the anomalous situation that found the reserves in Interior, which had no foresters in its employ, while Agriculture employed a number of foresters but had no forests to administer. In addition, Interior was reluctant to strike out boldly; it did not assume that action was permitted if not prohibited, but took the position that without explicit authorization, nothing could be undertaken.

In the interim, forest trees continued to put on new wood annually—except where they were cut by means legitimate or otherwise. Forage within the boundaries of the reserves continued to grow—except where overuse by livestock or use at wrong seasons of the year put or kept it on downgrade. The watersheds continued to produce life-giving flows to nourish irrigated farms and growing communities downstream—except where stripping off timber and skinning off grass and browse accelerated flows in the runoffs from spring rains and snowmelt and left channels dry or merely damp in the heat of summer.

This was an intolerable situation to Pinchot and, though he was an employee of the Department of Agriculture, he managed in one way or another to insinuate himself ever deeper into matters affecting the federal forests. While the reserves were under that suspension order for the rest of 1897 and part of 1898, Pinchot himself wrote an assignment he would undertake for Agriculture as a confidential special agent, to examine the lands in their various aspects and, in the end, draw up what he considered a workable plan to establish a Forest Service.[11] Following the inspection tour Pinchot, in mid-1898, became head of the USDA's Forestry Division with the title of Forester, which was itself new. He took the job with full intention of bringing the foresters in government and the forest reserves together,

Vigorous vegetation inside protected area, compared with overused range outside fence, Malheur National Forest, Oregon, 1939. *USFS photo*

with himself in charge. From that time forward, until the deed was accomplished early in 1905, it is hard to judge whether Pinchot worked harder at being Forester than he did at bringing about the transfer of the forest reserves to Agriculture.

It is not my purpose to follow every devious or straightforward step Pinchot took in the intervening years, but a look at one or two footprints may not be amiss. Through Hiram Jones, an important figure in the Interior Department setup whom he had cultivated, Agriculture in the summer of 1899 was asked by Interior to make an investigative inspection of western forest reserves, and the task of course went to Pinchot. The request made special reference to problems involving grazing, and this brought Pinchot into communion with Albert F. Potter, an Arizona Woolgrowers' Association official who was later to become the first Chief of Grazing for the Forest Service. The assassination of President McKinley put Theodore Roosevelt in the White House in 1901, and soon Pinchot had the satisfaction of seeing presidential messages advocating a unified Bureau of Forestry flow from the Oval Office to Capitol Hill. Pinchot and his associates in the department and elsewhere early on took the position that forestry was rightfully an agricultural undertaking. One of them, Overton L. Price, declared in an appropriations committee hearing that "every source of wealth grown from the soil" was a function of agriculture; therefore forest work should be in USDA, not Interior. Price testified, in fact, that the Department of Interior "is overloaded and has officially asked to be relieved of its forest reserve work," a task, he added, that the Department of Agriculture was "thoroughly prepared to handle." [12] This sort of ground preparation has not often come about by chance in Washington's official circles, nor is it common to have one of the departments of the executive branch volunteer to give up one of its bureaus. Theodore Roosevelt and Pinchot had by then become close associates, officially and otherwise, and it is difficult to believe that Interior had been persuaded without White House intervention stimulated by Gifford Pinchot. At any rate, and whatever had gone on in the interim, Congress enacted the law in February 1905 that provided for transfer of the reserves to Agriculture, changed their names to national forests, had created a Forest Service for their administration.[13]

This act was far-reaching in many respects. It put the forest reserves in hands that would administer them with unprecedented vigor, and in ways that broke new administrative ground right and left. More than that: National forest administration under the new regime spelled the inevitable doom of the free range that ranchers had for so many decades enjoyed on the public domain in the West. Putting public domain ranges under federal control was almost three decades in the future, but once the national forests were no longer free the rest of the federal West simply had to follow; the two were but separate organs of the same animal. As this was written they had not yet been joined in a single federal department, but in my view this, too, will eventually come to pass.

II

From Hope and Vigor to . . . What?

5

Growing Pains

Managing the timberlands of the new National Forest System began from scratch, so to speak, since there was no comparable undertaking upon which the fledgling administration could draw for knowledge and experience. The history of how the forestry part of it was accomplished has been recorded by others in detail, not least by Pinchot himself, and it has no extensive place in this account, where grazing is the central interest. It should be noted, though, that a few schooled, trained, and experienced foresters were available whom Pinchot could recruit. Administering the grazing lands was different, in that the science of range management had yet to be born. A searcher would have found it hard to locate range management literature in any library. Yet a start had to be made, and quickly. Pinchot, ever bold in such circumstances, was eager to get going.

His instincts, bolstered by his towering intellect—or vice versa—led him to actions that seem almost prescient. Transfer of the forest reserves from Interior to Agriculture was still nearly five years in the future and not at all a certainty when Pinchot met Albert Potter, a rancher and a leader of ranchers in the Southwest. Yet without livestock ranges to manage and no surety that he would get them, Pinchot in 1901 persuaded Potter to leave the staff of the Arizona Woolgrowers Association and join him in the USDA forestry office.[1] Soon he sent Potter on surveying assignments which gave him opportunity to observe ranges and range use throughout the West. Thus, when in 1905 the federal forests were transferred from Interior to Agriculture, Pinchot had in Potter perhaps as well qualified a man as he could have found anywhere to put in charge of range use aspects of national forest management.

Though Pinchot was first of all a forester, and forestry was ever to be his primary love, the practical side of his nature told him that grazing domestic livestock would claim a large share of his attention. No doubt it all would have been much simpler if he could have started with virgin range, previously used only by creatures of the wild, so he could let in varying numbers of domestic stock as experience showed what differing areas could accommodate without deteriorating. But he took charge of range stocked for decades and in places badly depleted. Cattle and sheep were already there, and their owners would have to be dealt with. It seems obvious now that the situation and its problems were on Pinchot's mind frequently in the years from 1898, when he went to the forestry bureau in Agriculture, until opportunity laid them in his hands in February 1905.

Pinchot and his close associates in and out of government had talked and thought a great deal about how the national Forest System should be administered. When the transfer was accomplished, Pinchot was ready with at least the framework of an administrative pattern that in basic respects remains to this day. The instructions that went into a letter, written by and addressed to him but signed by Agriculture Secretary James Wilson the very day of the change-over, may be said to contain the essence of the conclusions on policies Pinchot had reached in the years just before and after the turn of the century. Few other administrative directives have been more frequently quoted than this one, and selected passages must have a place here, too.

In administering the forests, the letter read, the "most productive use for the permanent good of the whole people" should guide rather than the "temporary benefit of individuals or companies." And *use—* italicized as quoted by Pinchot in his autobiographical *Breaking New Ground* [2]—would be the administrative keynote, "under restrictions only as will insure the permanence of those resources"; at the same time it must be an emphasized *"conservative use"* which, he believed, would not conflict with the "permanent value" of the forests. The use would be carried out "under businesslike regulations, enforced with promptness, effectiveness, and common sense." He wanted "local questions . . . decided upon local grounds." Next was a stricture that came to bother conservation forces in the late 1960s and early 1970s, in the era of the Public Land Law Review Commission; [3] he wrote that the "dominant" industry should receive first consideration in determining

use. Near the end was the sentence quoted most often, ". . . where conflicting interests must be reconciled the question will always be decided from the standpoint of the greatest good to the greatest number
in the long run."

Here were idealistic objectives Pinchot must have felt attainable.
Some were achieved, a goodly portion in those exhilarating younger
years when hitting all targets dead center was the aim of a growing
army of mostly young men Pinchot sent forth to right wrongs of the
past and to hold the forests against selfish utilization or plunder. A
disturbing question raised in this narrative is whether, over the long
run, the Service has remained fully dedicated to the hallowed proposition of the greatest good to the greatest number, most particularly
with respect to grazing.

When Pinchot acquired the federal forest system few restrictions
on use were spelled out in statutes. With respect to livestock grazing,
a rancher had acquired or retained the use of public range within an
area that went into the system in one or more of several ways—by
force, subtle persuasion, or custom involving accommodation with
neighbors. Under the 1891 law grazing ostensibly had been prohibited
along with other uses, which proved no greater deterrent to ranchers
than to loggers, miners, or others who took whatever they found of
value there.[4] Livestock ranged as freely as in earlier years, since there
was no specific provision for regulating or policing. This had changed
little even after the 1897 organic act was passed because Interior
failed to see or was too timid to grasp the opportunity in the law.

The 1905 situation was complex, with few ready-made solutions
to problems that must be tackled. The new Service was faced with accomplished facts and grazing was a major one. Several thousand
ranchers lived on land adjacent to the national forests or on privately owned interior holdings surrounded by government property.
Some of the land produced lush forage to which the users held almost
the equivalent of title by reason of proximity. Under Service control
there should be a fair rationing of available forage, for there was not
then and still is not enough to satisfy the desires of all who would like
a share. And, human nature being what it is, each rancher believed
his situation was special if not unique. So an early task had to be a
choosing of ranchers who would be privileged to continue to run their
stock on forest range.

In addition to ownership or control of base property within or
near the forests, the choosing involved a factor called "dependency."
To what degree was the rancher accustomed to using a particular

segment of range dependent upon it to maintain a year around operation? What was the base property's capability in terms of stock numbers and seasons of use? Did the rancher also adjoin public domain and, if so, when and to what extent did he use that to graze his herd or flock?

The base property factor was critical in that it virtually eliminated the nomad as a grazing user of national forest ranges. This was to have far-reaching effect, bring unhappiness and ugly incidents that were not totally eliminated until the enactment nearly thirty years later of the Taylor Grazing Act.[5] An immediate result was to crowd the nomad's livestock, often sheep, off the forests and onto the already overstocked public domain. Those thirty intervening years were painful in many ways.

The field staff to handle this and many other matters was at first larded with Interior Department holdovers, for many of whom Pinchot had little liking. Those he considered political hacks or incompetents were weeded out quickly, and replaced [6] with a Pinchot staff as fast as talent and payroll money became available. For the most part the men out on point—supervisors of individual forests, of course, but most of all the district rangers—were young and relatively untried. Some of the first came straight from ranch to Service and had little formal schooling. Soon new employees, however, were graduates of forestry and agronomy colleges or universities that usually were located in the East. Forty and more years afterward there still were heard nagging complaints [7] in the West and in Washington about those damned easterners who didn't know one end of a cow from the other yet were in national forest country to tell experienced ranchers how to run their business. Pinchot took the best he could find and most of the field staff seemed as determined as he to get on with the work. Ranchers would simply have to become accustomed to an official presence and to the imposition, the enforcement, of new, strange, often unwanted and frequently resented rules and regulations.

Social engineering was a part of forest administration. Hardy, sometimes foolhardy, settlers were still moving westward looking for almost free government land, taking up homesteads wherever they thought they could make a go of it. My paternal grandfather was one of those who picked poor dry farming land—that is, without a source of irrigation water—in the Arkansas River Valley near LaJunta, Colorado. He lost it and moved on. When a homesteader staked a claim near a national forest he usually wanted to join the brotherhood of the privileged and put some livestock on federal range, even if it meant taking away from settlers who had been there for years. We still considered ourselves fundamentally agrarian, and the homesteader was loved by all humanitarians and every aspiring politician. Unfortunately, those elected to Congress did not seem to know how to handle problems of settling the western hinterland other than by amending the homesteading laws to tack on a few more acres to what a man could try to bring to patent. By then it was the exceptional settler who was able to find homesteadable land that would support a family without other resources.

So the Service set out to devise a way to help new settlers and others who were operating at subsistence level or below, such as poorer natives of Spanish-Indian derivation. Redistribution of the grazing privilege was decided upon, taking from those with much to give to those with little. This brought with it a system of grazing floors and ceilings. Ranchers with a set minimum would not have their grazing reduced below that level. Ranchers running more cattle or sheep might not graze numbers above a predetermined ceiling for the area. The system of floors and ceilings remains in effect today, but redistribution dwindled away and finally died in 1953.[8] It had caused much permittee unhappiness through the years and led to many heated but unpublicized arguments within the Service. We will encounter the subject again later.

The numbers game involved judging more than how many head of livestock a rancher might graze. Determinations had to be made on where they would graze; when they might go on the forest range in the spring and when they must come off in the fall, with dates varying from year to year and place to place. Altitude was a factor. Also, how heavy had the snow pack been the previous winter? How completely had it melted? Was spring early or late and had the growth of tender young shoots reached a stage proper for grazing? The soil should not be soggy wet and soft so hooves would chop or trample. Fall considerations included the seeding traits of various kinds of forage, how much should be left standing for erosion control, and what the fire hazard would be if too much remained. There were others; these are enough for illustration.

Central to management factors was the explosive question of grazing fees. Pinchot called them "highly controversial,"[9] which to me seems understatement. Pinchot expected to sell timber, and considered the government was also in the business of selling forage. Loggers could not get trees for the asking. Neither should stockmen get grass without pay. The upshot was that in May 1905, with Pinchot in office only three months, Secretary Wilson sent a carefully worded inquiry [10] to the office of the Attorney General. He asked three questions: Did he, the Secretary, have authority under existing law to grant permits or leases for the use and occupancy of national forest areas? If so, could such permits or leases be for terms longer than a year? Finally, could "reasonable compensation" to the government be a permit condition?

Affirmative replies to all three came within two days, which may be a bureaucratic record for speed in a matter of such importance. It hints that someone in a high place greased the travel ways or, at least, that there had been preliminary consultation between principals. S. T. Dana writes [11] that the greasing and consulting was done by both Pinchot and President Theodore Roosevelt. The reply to the third question was worded as carefully as the inquiry had been: A charge could be made "whenever, in your judgment, such a course seems consistent with insuring the objects of the reservation and protection of the forests therein from destruction." In short, "yes," with perhaps some emphasis on national forest protection, which could mean against any number of adverse actions or effects.

In retrospect it seems incredible that the livestock industry's leaders could have overlooked or ignored the implications of the exchange of correspondence. The swiftness of the action may have taken them by surprise, or the stockmen may have been temporarily lulled by the fact that the questions seemed to apply to a matter remote from western range. It dealt with an application to install and operate a fish-salting plant in far-off Alaska.

Immediately after receiving the answers he wanted, Pinchot and his associates began setting up a fee system, and it was put into effect at the start of the 1906 grazing season. Surely the initial fees were modest enough. Charges for a cow and her calf ranged from twenty to twenty-five cents a year; those for a ewe and her lamb were from five to eight cents a year. Quality of range and length of season accounted for the differentials. A year meant from three to twelve months, depending on location and local conditions. Table 1 shows the fees charged through the years.

Pinchot's *coup* is the one instance I have found where the Forest Service—or the grazing agencies of Interior after the public domain was brought under federal administration—got the jump on the livestock industry in any matter involving fees without engaging in a tremendous struggle in advance. This time the struggle came afterward, for the stockmen reacted strongly when they did learn the im-

Growing Pains   49

Table 1 *

Average Grazing Fees, National Forest
in Western United States, 1906–1975

Year	Cattle Sheep ($ Per Animal Month)		Year	Cattle Sheep ($ Per Animal Month)	
1906	0.05	.0100	1940	0.15	.0370
1907	.05	.0100	1941	.16	.0385
1908	.05	.0100	1942	.19	.0460
1909	.05	.0100	1943	.23	.0550
1910	.04	.0140	1944	.26	.0625
1911	.03	.0130	1945	.25	.0610
1912	.04	.0150	1946	.27	.0625
1913	.09	.0450	1947	.31	.0750
1914	.09	.0450	1948	.40	.1000
1915	.10	.0450	1949	.49	.1100
1916	.10	.0450	1950	.42	.1075
1917	.10	.0350	1951	.51	.1225
1918	.11	.0350	1952	.64	.1525
1919	.13	.0350	1953	.54	.1175
1920	.13	.0350	1954	.35	.0900
1921	.13	.0350	1955	.37	.0900
1922	.13	.0350	1956	.35	.0875
1923	.13	.0350	1957	.34	.0900
1924	.13	.0350	1958	.39	.0975
1925	.13	.0450	1959	.50	.1025
1926	.13	.0450	1960	.51	.0925
1927	.14	.0450	1961	.46	.0875
1928	.12	.0375	1962	.46	.0775
1929	.12	.0400	1963	.49	.0900
1930	.14	.0425	1964	.46	.0900
1931	.14	.0450	1965	.46	.1025
1932	.07	.0225	1966	.51	.1175
1933	.09	.0200	1967	.56	.1225
1934	.08	.0240	1968	.56	.1150
1935	.08	.0270	1969	.60	.1325
1936	.13	.0340	1970	.60	.1325
1937	.13	.0370	1971	.78	.1700
1938	.15	.0425	1972	.80	.1750
1939	.13	.0330	1973	.91	.1925
			1974	1.11	.2300
			1975	1.11	.2300

* Source, U.S. Forest Service, Washington

plications of the letter exchange. Having enjoyed nearly ten years of free forage under the same law that now would be used to make them pay for it, they were in no mood to give in without a fight.

Something was being taken away from them; and something they considered sly and underhanded had been put over on them by that smart aleck forester, Pinchot. They wouldn't put up with it.

They had long since learned that western members of Congress were sensitive to their wants and ready to rush to the rescue when their property interests were affected or they felt some privilege was being curtailed. Congressmen and industry leaders descended upon Pinchot and Roosevelt in swarms. Neither would budge. Very well; there were other ways and means. The West added an amendment to the 1907 farm bill that removed from the President and vested exclusively in Congress the power to set aside new national forests in the six western states—Colorado, Idaho, Montana, Oregon, Washington, and Wyoming—that had most of the remaining timbered regions outside the National Forest System. And Roosevelt had only so many days in which to approve or veto the bill. In that short time, Pinchot's people prepared needed papers and Roosevelt executed orders proclaiming new national forests totaling sixteen million acres in those six states. Then he signed the bill.[12]

Naturally, this infuriated the westerners. Other interests—timber, mining—took part, but the livestock industry was in the forefront. The upshot was a rebellious Public Lands Convention, held in Denver.[13] It was an explosive assault on the Forest Service, but it survived the violent oratory and hot resolutions adopted.

Shortly afterward, elements in the industry tried legal action as a way to break the Service. Cameron tells [14] that rangers in New Mexico were indicted for larceny after seizing livestock found in trespass. In the same region another ranger was charged with murder when he killed a trespasser in self-defense. These cases challenged the authority of the Service to control livestock grazing, and the power was affirmed when the accused were acquitted in both. In two others, then, livestock were deliberately put on national forest ranges without payment of fees to challenge the Attorney General's letter–opinion. Both went to the U.S. Supreme Court before being decided in favor of the Service.[15]

In addition, a rash of complaints and contentions of other sorts came after the Denver convention. Whether they were stimulated by it may be moot, but numbers increased to the point that paper work began to overwhelm the field forces. By the end of 1908 the rangers were bucking so much to supervisors which they, in turn, sent on to headquarters in Washington, that it was felt another echelon of organization must be created. Therefore, in December of that year,

Pinchot established district offices at strategic locations, to which the forest supervisors reported. The new system spread the burdens of administration and, with two exceptions, completed the decentralization Pinchot had envisioned from the start. "Local grounds" upon which "local questions" might be solved, as outlined in the celebrated 1905 Wilson letter, then took on three dimensions—the local ranger district, the individual national forest, and the intermediate district office. To eliminate confusion, these were later renamed regional offices. Now, presumably, there would be no reason to lean on the office of the Chief Forester unless a problem was of massive proportions or critical importance or concerned matters extending beyond regional boundaries. Later chapters will tell of times when it did not work out quite as contemplated. However, Pinchot's system of decentralization exists today much as he conceived it.

One of the exceptions noted above was the establishment of the national Forest Products Laboratory at Madison, Wisconsin, in 1910. The other was the evolution of a system of forest and range experiment stations; the first that carried on range studies was located in Arizona in 1911.

Findings of scientists and their helpers at the range stations were to contribute greatly to the Service's knowledge. Indeed, they have added much to the sum of human knowledge of forage lands and have advanced the still comparatively young science of range management. By the nature of such things, facts developed through on-the-ground experimentation become accepted only after the passage of time. Lack of sound scientific knowledge in the earlier years undoubtedly accounts in part for the excessive grazing use that occurred and perhaps for undue optimism of the foresters over range grazing capacity, all of which had its part in the depletion of so much public land.

In June 1902, a Pinchot team in Agriculture produced the first edition of what came to be known as the "Use Book." [16] The pamphlet-size booklet was ready when the Service was created in 1905. It still is called the Use Book but there is a world of difference between the original version, a slim volume a ranger could slip into a hip pocket before setting out for a meeting with a permittee or other user of forest products, and the formidable shelf set of today. By the 1950s it had swollen to seven thick volumes, and an annual report declared a serious effort would be made to reduce its bulk and complexity. Somehow the slenderizing and simplifying never came about. Frank J. Smith, director of range management of the Service, wrote [17] me on October 30, 1972, that the manual still consisted of seven volumes, but several separate handbooks of instruction had been added. And it still is the chief guide to the actions of the staff of the Forest Service, from Chief Forester down to district ranger's assistant.

Generally speaking, the official with whom a national forest user deals most of the time is the district ranger. From the beginning the ranger has lived on his district or in an adjacent community. Such a community usually would be small and accustomed to depend considerably on forest resources for its livelihood—the timber, forage, minerals, fish and game, scenic or other recreation-related attributes, or some or all of them in combination. If single, the ranger likely courted the daughter of a forest user or of a town businessman dependent for part of his profit on the trade of forest users. If married, the ranger and his wife and children were part of the user-community's social, cultural, and economic life. All these factors inevitably injected personal elements [18] into his work and crept into decisions he was required to make. Subtle pressures could be and were exerted, and at times they were not so subtle. If a ranger arrived at a decision a permittee considered adverse, his kids could suffer at school or at playtime. His wife could endure snubs or worse. And what bore on the ranger's family weighed on him as well. He was in the same position as the leader of an infantry patrol in hostile territory; he would take the first fire. He was the highly visible local symbol of that far-off authority in Washington whence came the guidelines and strictures that irked or chiseled away at next year's cattle or sheep profits.

In any administration the personal element determines ultimate success or failure. Policies and guidelines are important, but people carry them out. Through the years the personal element has always been important, but it was especially critical in the formative era of the Forest Service. In the front office sat a leader who knew no fear, was sure of himself and of the cause he served. He had confidence in the course he would follow to further that cause. He showed skill in choosing the kind of talent he believed his operation needed. He envisioned an elite corps as dedicated as he was; he obviously hoped to instill a spirit that would linger long after he himself might be gone from the scene. By the time Pinchot departed—fired in 1910 by President William Howard Taft after a profoundly disturbing dispute between Pinchot and a high Interior official over the leasing of coal deposits under national forest lands in Alaska [19]—the elitist spirit was deeply ingrained.

Table 2 *

Animal Unit Months of Grazing Use
of National Forests in
six Western Regions

Year	AUMs (000)	Year	AUMS (000)
1908	14,000	1955	8,849
1913	15,600	1956	8,712
1918	20,400	1957	8,372
1923	17,200	1958	8,376
1928	12,600	1959	7,938
1933	12,200	1960	7,961
1938	11,100	1961	7,758
1943	9,800	1962	7,426
1945 **	9,100	1963	7,596
1946	8,664	1964	7,590
1947	8,050	1965	7,174
1948	7,982	1966	7,638
1949	7,646	1967	7,618
1950	7,434	1968	7,617
1951	7,338	1969	7,477
1952	7,322	1970	7,408
1953	7,337	1971	7,300
1954 ***	8,836	1972	7,300

* Source, U.S. Forest Service, Washington
** No figures were published for 1944
*** Reflects increase from taking over LU lands from Soil Conservation Service (LU lands now called National Grasslands)

I have seen little discussion of one aspect of range administration in the Pinchot and a few post-Pinchot years that I consider had a good bit of influence on actions and attitudes. We are prone to believe that even as the Forest Service came into existence it was faced with overused rangelands. That undoubtedly is true as to large areas but was it a servicewide condition? Statistics on grazing show that, through excessive optimism or through new discoveries, Service officials considered that forest areas contained forage that was then underused. Whatever the facts may be, it is true that even before the emergencies of World War I came upon us, a steady annual increase in grazing was allowed on national forest ranges. The figures are in Table 2. I won't go deeply now into whether this was right or wrong, other than to mention that two former officials [20] with whom I have consulted are of the opinion that the service has from the start been consistently high in its estimations of carrying capacity.

Service statistics disclose that between 1908, when calculations of use in animal unit months [21] (AUMs) began, and 1920, grazing rose gradually from about 14 million AUMs to an all time peak of more than 20 million. Between 1908 and 1913 AUMs were allowed to creep up from 14 million to 15.6 million. They continued to rise slowly until the war was at its height, then rocketed upward as the government itself pressured stockmen to crowd on every head of cattle and sheep they could lay hands on.

The early-year increases, though, are unexplained in documents I have seen. They certainly were not as a result of appreciable enlargement of the National Forest System. When President Theodore Roosevelt left office in 1908 national forests totaled somewhat more than 150 million acres. Clawson writes [22] that this figure stood for thirty years. Since then the increase in acreages administered by the Forest Service has been for the most part cutover land east of the Rockies, purchased for watershed conservation purposes under authority of the Weeks [23] Act, and Bankhead–Jones Act land,[24] purchased from distressed farmers and ranchers in the Great Depression and transferred from the Soil Conservation Service to the Forest Service in 1954.

Whatever the case, it seems clear that a combination of rising AUMs of grazing before World War I, long seasons of use, and the huge increases allowed by the Service during the war, just about skinned the ranges bare. Before his ten-year regime ended, Henry S. Graves, Pinchot's successor, ordered a gradual reduction. Since then the numbers have grown irregularly smaller, until today they are not much more than a third of the 1920 total (Table 2). The pattern has been highly irregular, and this irregularity in the curve reflects conflict between the Service and the stock industry as well as conflict within the Service, to which we will come in due course.

Questions of tenure, so important to the stockmen in assuring a stable ranching operation in which public range was employed, rose early. Initial permits had been for only one year. Soon they were lengthened to five years, and increased to the present standard ten-year term in the 1920s. With term permits came what amounted to a cementing of the permit preference; thereafter it was rare for a permittee to be forcibly deprived of his grazing privilege. Even when a permit was taken away it was, as a rule, only for gross, willful, and often repeated violations of the law or the rules and regulations laid down in the Use Book. In time, renewal of basic permits became almost automatic.

The Service encouraged stockmen to organize associations and advisory committees from the beginning. I suspect this reflected the influence and thinking of Albert Potter, Pinchot's range chief, because of his own background as chief staff officer of the Arizona Wool-growers Association. Potter and Pinchot recognized that through consultations with local and statewide associations, or with advisory groups that might or might not be set up by an association, they could achieve better communication on range conditions, problems, and needs.

These groups were especially active in discussions and actions concerning range improvements. Users of national forest range had long been accustomed to installing improvements or conveniences on public lands. They drilled wells and put up windmills to pump water for their stock to drink. They built corrals for holding and count-ing the animals. They built fences. And so on. In its early years the Service had little funds for range developments such as these and since they assisted or were useful in permittee operations the practice was allowed to continue. To the extent appropriated dollars became available, they were used to supplement permittee money and labor and equipment and materials for range developments of many kinds. Table 3 contains range improvement statistics.

The developmental work by the permittees had, however, a self-contained problem that was to surface often as time passed. The Service held the position that anything built on federal land was federal property.[25] And the permittees sometimes made substantial investments on Service range, in money and in kind. Complications rose when a permittee sold the ranch, or died and the heirs disposed of part or all of the estate.

The subject of money inevitably brings us back to fees. I doubt if Pinchot at any point wanted to gouge the ranchers grazing national forest ranges. Surely the rates he began charging in 1906 were modest enough. Fees started lower and they have remained considerably under what ranchers have had to pay to rent private pasturage. It was not long before permittees discovered that the low fees they paid gave their stock and their home bases a value considerably higher than that of a neighbor in comparable territory who did not have a grazing preference. Permittees began to take advantage of this, add-ing a specific amount to a sale price for each head of livestock or AUM of use specified in their permits. Officially, the Service frowned on the practice, disowned it—more so in earlier years than later times —but other than tut-tutting in speeches and writings it did nothing

Table 3 *

From 1905 through 1917 the Forest Service received no funds specifically for range improvement or revegetation work, though it did get small appropriations "for experiments and investigations of range conditions within national forests," which were used to begin the range experiment station program and helped shape range betterment activities in later years. It then received additional funds expressly for what now would be called range improvement at a rate of $50,000 a year for 12 years, through 1929. From 1930 through 1934 it was granted $528,820 for range improvements. There were no appropriations directly for range improvement from 1935 through 1945 (all but the last three of which were years when the CCC received separate funding); however, the service was appropriated substantial sums for investigations that embraced grazing management, reseeding, and range economics. Range reseeding funds rose from $110,000 to $553,996 between 1946 and 1947. Thereafter statistics were standardized in a form that separated "revegetation" from "range improvement," though part of each was accomplished with appropriated funds, part with assistance furnished by permittees in the form of cash, use of equipment, labor, or supplies, singly or in combination. Separated also were "management" appropriations, which indicate the year by year cost of supervising both revegetation and range improvement. Following are the annual statistics starting with 1948:

Fiscal Year	Management (000)	Revegetation (000)	Improvement (000)	Total (000)
1948	2,172	720	784	3,676
1949	2,313	1,009	764	4,088
1950	2,442	884	769	4,096
1951	2,468	908	1,586	4,964
1952	2,470	925	1,563	4,959
1953	2,412	903	1,100	4,416
1954	2,404	750	1,375	4,529
1955	2,304	661	1,158	4,125
1956	2,415	878	1,592	4,885
1957	2,765	1,128	1,655	5,548
1958	3,204	1,368	1,815	6,387
1959	3,355	1,667	2,131	7,153
1960	3,365	1,671	2,136	7,172
1961	3,859	1,911	2,388	8,158
1962	4,610	2,540	3,180	10,330
1963	4,832	2,674	3,203	10,709
1964	5,008	2,714	3,252	10,974
1965	5,254	2,780	3,383	11,417
1966	5,362	2,810	3,379	11,551
1967	5,527	2,854	3,442	11,823
1968	5,831	2,895	3,996	12,722
1969	5,831	2,905	3,506	12,242
1970	6,571	3,252	3,728	13,551
1971	6,571	3,252	4,378	14,201
1972	7,290	3,419	4,641	15,350
1973	7,000	3,600	4,700	15,300

* Adapted from U.S. Forest Service Budget Branch figures

about it. The practice continues to this day. The low fees and the permit values they spawned tended to convert the permittee's grazing privilege into a property right, perhaps even more so than his constructing range improvements with his own money or labor. This, too, was destined to bring forth much controversy with the passage of time and the coming of change to the range.

The Service has had and still has thousands of grazing permittees with whom it gets along very well, solid citizens who are true husbandmen and consider themselves following a stewardship course in their use of and consideration for the land. Those with whom Pinchot and his men dealt in the first five years, or in the next ten under Henry Graves, approved most if not all the successive policies initiated in this newest of governmental land management undertakings. Not all, of course, did so. A minority, but a vocal and ingenious minority, often well-to-do if not wealthy, and often holding elected or appointed positions of influence, tended to be critical. This was especially true if there seemed even a remote chance that they would be adversely affected in the pocketbook. As we go along we will find the same questions rising in more recent times that wrinkled brows when Pinchot was spreading his philosophy across the land.

If finger pointing is justified in fixing blame or setting reasons for anything, we must center upon World War I as a root cause of the major troubles that beset the Service soon after the conflict ended.

Elements of Conflict

Over its first twenty years of existence the Forest Service had been assailed in various ways, notably at the Public Lands Convention in Denver in 1907 and in court actions, but it had not yet been subjected to a full-scale congressional investigation led by hostile westerners. The first came in 1925 [1] and, like so many events in the saga of grazing public lands, had several causes. What appears to have triggered it, however, was a proposal that the Service should charge fees comparable to those being paid for rental of private pasturage of similar quality. This likely was not as important as problems connected with unregulated grazing of the public domain, which were being looked into in the same investigation, but it sparked a great deal of oral fireworks. Moreover, the hearings provided exhibition halls in which to display all the small and large grievances that can accumulate over time.

It has been noted that the earliest fees charged by the Service were very low, a few pennies a year for a cow and her calf, less for a ewe and her offspring. Over the years the Service gradually increased fees, but less on established formula than *ad hoc* judgment. Attempts were made to assure that charges were about the same wherever forage production was comparable. Fees were raised a few cents in 1910, and again in 1915. The next year the Service made a study to compare its charges with those made for privately owned forage. This was followed by a late 1917 order increasing rates annually for three years, through 1919, with $1.50 per year as top limit.[2] Upon our entrance into World War I in 1917, congressional voices began to be heard expressing the view that the fees were too low, that they should be raised in keeping with the general rise in all costs during the critical era.

These voices became insistent as the war ended, especially so from members of the Congressional Appropriations Committees, who demanded that stockmen pay higher rates to help reduce the heavy war debt. The Department fought off one congressional proposal to put a 300 percent increase in the statutes, and in late 1920 agreed to make the study. A reason given why fees should not be manipulated by statute was that the Service had in 1919 issued new five-year permits, and increasing fees immediately afterward would throw that segment of the industry out of economic kilter and result in justifiable protests.

The study was assigned to C. E. Rachford, chief range inspector, who assembled a team and worked out the techniques to be employed. Among the fee formulas considered was one tied to the market price of beef and lamb on the hoof. Another was fair market value. A third was open competitive bidding. Fair market value won out. Rachford and his helpers spent two years on the study, in which time the team visited and judged values on more than 1,500 privately owned ranges totaling more than 16 million acres. These were compared with nearby national forest ranges. After facts had been gathered they were evaluated and conclusions reached. In the 1923 season permittees paid an average of 10.4 cents per animal unit month (AUM) for cattle and 2.9 cents for sheep. Rachford's report [3] recommended averages of 18.1 cents for cattle and 6.2 cents for sheep. This entailed increases nearly everywhere in the public land West except the dry ranges of the Southwest.

Thereafter, some four hundred meetings were held, attended by about nine thousand forest range users and others. All were adamantly against the new scale except those from the Southwest who would enjoy a reduction in cost. The meetings and discussions took considerable time, and the longer they ran the more intransigent the livestock leadership became, the more insistent its protests to friendly western members of Congress. The study ended in late 1923; debate continued long afterward.

Meantime the seemingly endless argument over the future of the public domain went on, and related issues became involved. There was the question of whether stock-raising Indians should have additional range or if still more should be taken from them. Expansion of the National Park System, which usually meant denying use of range to domestic animals, raised tempers of stockmen and their allies in

Congress. Soon all these issues became intertwined, but none caused as much argument as did complaints against the Forest Service and the question of how or whether to bring the public domain under control. It was in such an atmosphere that the Senate Committee on Public Lands and Surveys ordered the investigations of 1925.

With Oregon's Senator Robert N. Stanfield presiding, the hearings began almost sedately in Washington in April 1925. Stanfield himself was a rancher and a forest range permittee. His people back home had run afoul of Service regulations,[4] which may or may not have caused the hearings he chaired to be more subdued than those conducted by certain others from cow and sheep country. He began by putting the entire Rachford report in the record, saying it had "seriously disturbed" the permittees.

The philosophy that ran through the Rachford narrative was to the effect that national forest forage was as much a commodity as anything else sold or traded in by permittees. It noted that "all other national forest resources are sold at their commercial value," and there was "no clear reason" why a fair price should not be charged the "favored few who have grazing privileges." He commented that the ranchers considered the "commercial value principle" to be "unjust, fallacious, and pernicious," in that the Federal Government would be capitalizing on the "pioneer efforts of a sturdy American citizenship." Rachford, however, could not see that the permittees had come from any sturdier pioneering stock than had their neighbors who did not enjoy use of national forest range; they had "contributed just as much to the development of the West as the favored few." The few, then, obviously should not be subsidized with low fees, but should pay the going rate for private pasture the same as any stockraiser who had no permit; which seems basic, unassailable logic.

Chief Forester William B. Greeley was the first witness called.[5] He held that the principal factors affecting fees were the proper use of the available forage in the public interest, the value of the forage to the livestock industry, and the effect of the fees on the ranchers. He reminded of the attempt made five years earlier to write a 300 percent fee increase into law, and this exchange followed:

Stanfield: You mean United States range lands should yield as much as private lands?

Greeley: Other factors being equal, Government land is worth just as much as private land.

After a further exchange, in which Stanfield implied that subsidizing permittees was justified, Greeley remarked that since the permittee had protection from competition and had a preference by reason of the location of his home base, it was only rational to ask him to "meet us on a fair business compensation basis."

Greeley said the Service had asked the industry to criticize its data; instead, it had "criticized our principles." Nevertheless, since there had been such an outcry from the industry the Department would hold off imposing increases until at least 1927, when definite instructions from the Secretary of Agriculture were expected. Meantime, there would be an "appraisal" of Rachford's study by a "competent man" outside Government.

Whether Greeley foresaw that the "competent man" would undercut Rachford and the Service is not known, but his making the announcement when and where he did took some of the fee increase wind out of senatorial sails for the duration of the investigation. Stanfield put the more significant field hearings, held in the Southwest, in the hands of Senators Ralph Cameron and Henry Ashurst, both of Arizona, neither of whom had a high regard for the Service; both seemed intent on having it shown to western audiences in as unfavorable a light as possible. They let fly with every oral weapon they could lay tongue to, castigating the Service right and left, and leading witnesses broadly so as to elicit derogatory statements. Questions of fees gave way to tirades and complaints.

At Prescott, Arizona, on June 12, 1925, Ashurst tried unsuccessfully to draw complaints from John Stephens, a cowman for forty years. From the record: [6]

Ashurst: You've never had a dispute with them?
Stephens: No.
Ashurst: They never practiced any tyrannies upon you?
Stephens: No.
Ashurst: You are to be congratulated. . . . I want the stenographers to put this in capitals, that here is a man who has escaped their tyrannies.

Under leading by John K. Bowden, subcommittee counsel, John Stanley of Chino Valley agreed that a permittee was under the thumb of "some official" who "could make or break you." [7] Greeley asked Stanley if he himself had had such an experience, whereupon Cameron broke in to say "you needn't answer that unless you want to"; then, addressing the audience, he declared, "We are here to get information from the stockmen. We'll do the questioning. The Forest Service people are here only to answer questions from us if we want to ask them. You don't have to answer any Forest Service questions at all."

The committee had sent out advance men to visit association leaders, soliciting information detrimental to the Service. They got some of what they wanted. C. H. Hinderer, a former employee of the Service who had become a Prescott banker, testified [8] that the officials wrote, applied, and interpreted the regulations, and that this gave them the notion that they were immune from anything they did not choose to do. John Lee, an old timer from Cornfield, Arizona, was unhappy because he had been ordered to take a cut and had been slow to comply.[9]

Then:

Bowden: You were told the Forest Service would take action?
Lee: Oh, yes, they threatened to do several little things.
Bowden: Such as?
Lee: Cut my permit for disobeying.
Bowden: They threatened to take away your permit?
Lee: Oh, no; just reduce me down to nothing.

At Flagstaff on June 15 Greeley was given an opportunity to make a statement despite the earlier brusqueness, or perhaps Greeley had asked for it in the interest of fairness. He outlined a three-point policy to which he was committed: [10] (1) to hold grazing to the safe carrying capacity of the ranges; (2) to issue clearly worded ten-year permits; and (3) to graze cattle and sheep in separate areas. (It is worth noting here that of the three, by 1975, a half century later, only the second had been fully achieved.) Greeley said he was willing to put a limit on the extent of cuts to be made for range protection, which he announced had never been brought up before (but which would be much like a policy enunciated by one of his sucessors in a Great Depression permit year).

After continuing in a general vein for a few minutes, Greeley went into the rationale for the proposed new schedule of fees. He was careful to stress two factors important to the Southwest where the hearing was being held: first, most permittees there would obtain a reduction instead of being raised; and, second, the Service already had been lenient because the region had been hit a double blow—the postwar depression and a simultaneous drought. Fees had been reduced or forgiven entirely in some areas. He ended with an appeal to a sense of business fairness; the Service, he said, should receive just "compensation for a commodity that is commercial in character and utilized for a commercial purpose."

Throughout the hearings information dropped here and there hinted at the deplorably depleted condition to which the ranges had been reduced. On June 19, 1925, at St. Johns, Arizona, Art Saunders [11] described what happened as a result of his cattle eating locoweed. He told how the seasonal drying process seemed to concentrate the active ingredients of that hallucinatory plant. When his locoed cattle went to water they'd put their heads down but not touch the water, go through the motions of drinking, and walk away as if filled. Within a month they would be dead. Saunders said his stock did not start eating locoweed until 1911 or 1912, because until then they had forage that was more palatable and without ill effect.

At the close of the hearings the senators reported [12] little or nothing about fees, concentrating instead on legislation intended to bring the public domain under control. There is little question but that they were holding back, waiting to see what would come of the independent appraisal of the Rachford report. They also appeared to be relying on the Service to continue to go easy on permittees in droughty parts of the country. The Service went further. While the Stanfield investigation was going on, Rachford's facts and figures were rechecked in-house and—whether from cause or under senatorial or other pressure is not clear from what I have seen— slashed them close to 10 percent. Proposed cattle fee increases were to be dropped from an average of 18.1 cents to 16.6 cents, and sheep price rises would only go up to an average of 5.9 cents instead of 6.2 cents.[13] If the Service felt this would quiet objections to an increase, it was wrong.

In January 1926, the Department chose Dan D. Casement, Kansas livestock dealer and one-time permittee, to appraise the Rachford report; he submitted his findings in June. Even the reduced Rachford formula was too much for Casement to approve. First, Rachford's proposed fees for Oregon and Washington, which were somewhat higher than those for most of the rest of the national forest West, must be brought down.[14] Then he would approve only 25 percent of the schedule of increases.

Why? He recognized that forage was a commodity, and that it should go at market value was fair "in the abstract," but he doubted its "wisdom and justice."

"This doubt," he wrote, "is induced solely by social and economic considerations and by the belief that the inauguration of a purely commercial policy now would be . . . inconsistent with the practice originally approved and hitherto followed . . . in stressing the social and economic motive in [the Service's] relations with its permittees."

Here Casement had reference to the many favors and privileges granted to settlers throughout the period of filling the West; the laxity in turning public lands to private ownership or control and general generosity in conveying public lands and the fruits thereof to almost any who chose to go there and exploit them; the general sympathy that marked the treatment of the grazing users of public lands, including the national forests. A broad statement of fact would be that, generally speaking, only one aspect of Forest Service social engineering met with stockman disfavor. This was the policy of redistribution of grazing privileges. Under it larger permittees were reduced, a little at a time, so new settlers adjacent to national forest range might have a go at its grasses. Probably no other policy, except one to be described in coming pages, caused more internal upheaval in the range management practices of the Service than did the policy of distribution. The policy dwindled away in practice in a short time as homesteadable lands dwindled, but it did not die [15] until 1953.

Amazingly (or not), the Service and the Department capitulated on fees without much fight. The Casement report was accepted [16] for application early in 1927. Not only would the increases be but a fourth of the already reduced Rachford formula, but they would be spread over the next four years—1927 through 1931—so that presumably they would hardly be felt by any permittee. Here it must be remembered that the nation had now come out of the postwar economic doldrums and was deep into the "Roaring Twenties," racing toward the October 1929 stock market crash and the Great Depression—but neither the industry nor the Service was clairvoyant. By the time the fourth increment was due, the nation was in financial straits and in mental anguish. Times were hard for all, and out West the weather was getting droughty again.

In 1928, first year of application of the Casement formula, the Service began setting fees on the basis of an animal unit month rather than an annual flat rate. The AUM had been used earlier, to calculate range use, but not in fixing fees. The ratio of five to one, to equalize costs as between cowmen and sheepmen, was stabilized at this time.

By 1931 the fees averaged 14.5 cents per head per month for cattle, and around 4.5 cents for sheep.[17] Then, with hard times at hand, the industry leaders remembered the earlier proposal by the Rachford team, which had been echoed by Casement, that fees be tied to the livestock market; from their viewpoint they had good reason to do so. The market for beef and mutton had plummeted just as had that for about everything else that went into economic indexes. It was a propitious time to push for a cut in fees, and once more the industry found the Service amenable. The formula chosen would go into effect for the grazing season of 1933, with fees pegged to 1932 prices, when the market average for beef cattle had been $4.13 per hundredweight and for lambs had been $4.18. This served to reduce the average fee for cattle from 14.5 cents to 9.05 cents per AUM, or less than 32 cents for a three and one-half months' grazing season. The average for sheep fell from 4.5 cents to 2.05 cents, or less than a nickel for two months on nutritious high altitude range.

An objective observer likely would not question the justice of a reduction in grazing fees at that time and under existing circumstances. Rather, he would concentrate on whether the formula was equitable to all concerned. The livestock market price system succeeded one that was based on little more than a judgment value, a guessing game that had gone on for twenty-six years. The new method would linger nearly twice as long before being supplanted by a formula nominally related to the fair market value of national forest forage, akin to the technique that Chris Rachford had recommended in 1924. That vindication of his judgment came long after his death, and virtually had to be forced upon the Service by the Bureau of the Budget, as described in a later chapter.

It should not be assumed that in the decade and a half from the end of World War I forward range administration was dedicated exclusively to the topics so far discussed. Problems outlined in the previous chapter continued or recurred. If, for example, trespass was brought under control in one area it could be expected to be a bother in others at any time. Trespass by the nomad or tramp operator was an ever present hindrance to smooth forest operations, prior to his elimination in the mid-1930s through passage of the Taylor Act [18] for administration of grazing on the public domain.

The stockmen's persistent agitation for what they considered a less painful method of bringing use down to something approaching range carrying capacity resulted in what came to be known as the transfer cut. This had been recommended early on by industry leaders in Idaho and was accepted widely until after World War II, when it was assailed as were distribution and all other kinds of downward adjustments. If a permittee sold his ranch or his stock, or the home base changed hands through inheritance, the Service would apply a reduction upon the successor. If the ranch changed hands, the reduction would be 10 percent; if only the stock was sold, a 20 percent cut would be imposed. The theory was that this would not hurt the rancher moving out, and the one coming in knew in advance what the grazing privilege would amount to in AUMs.

For a time and in some areas the transfer cut appears to have been almost the only kind applied. The combination of the Great Depression and the widely prevailing droughts—for this was the disastrous Dust Bowl Era of the first half of the 1930s—appears to have subdued desire for more drastic action by the Service to reduce grazing to true carrying capacity. Drought meant poor feed production; depression meant fewer ranchers could raise and fatten livestock on anything approaching the levels of wetter years. Even so, there was overproduction in various parts of the country, leading to slaughter of livestock under government orders in an effort to bolster prices to the producer. The Service actually allowed a small increase in total AUMs on forest ranges in part of this adverse era, to favor hard-hit permittees.

President Franklin D. Roosevelt's array of New Deal programs brought considerable help to national forest ranges. The Civilian Conservation Corps was created in the early 1930s to provide public work outdoors for the jobless young, and thousands were housed in camps on or near national forests until World War II caused the program to be terminated in 1942. Under technical leadership by Service personnel the CCC youngsters plugged gullies, cut roads and trails, built drift fences and corrals, developed water holes, and worked at other range improvement practices. They also were used in Service experiments in reseeding and even total rehabilitation of depleted ranges, which was to give rise to a development a few years later that in my opinion constituted perhaps the most important revision of basic policy in the history of national forest range administration since the Pinchot era. This policy put primary reliance for range betterment on improvement practices, and is treated in more detail later.

The middle 1930s were marked by bitter fighting between the Departments of Agriculture and Interior over the control of public domain grazing. Interior outsmarted Agriculture when the Taylor Act was going through Congress, offering to administer the Taylor lands at a ridiculously low cost, while the Service put forward more realistic figures. This made Agriculture very unhappy. I have not found conclusively that the action was inspired by the Department of Agriculture, but the record shows that not long after the Taylor Act became operative the Forest Service had a team of specialists busy writing a lengthy report for the Senate Agriculture and Forestry Committee. It was published in 1936 under the title of *The Western Range*, as Senate Document 199 of the Seventy-fourth Congress, Second Session. The committee resolution requesting the report simply said the USDA had a "large amount of information on the original and present condition, and the social and economic importance of the range and its conservation," and would the department be so kind as to report [19] on those things and recommend "constructive measures"? The department would be happy to oblige.

The central message of the report was simple: Nowhere in the Federal Government was land being administered nearly as well as it was by the Forest Service and, since range utilization was agricultural in nature, Interior's western range should be wrested from it and placed in its rightful home in Agriculture. Without grazing regulation the public domain's forage values had gone to pot. The Grazing Service setup in Interior was too young and inexperienced to be entrusted with all those millions of acres being put in grazing districts. The Taylor Act was no prize package, except to the ranchers to whom it was granting monopolistic rights to federal ranges. Under the beneficent guiding hand of the Service the national forest ranges had recovered marvelously from the ravages of overuse in World War I and earlier times. The Taylor lands could do so, too, but only if administered by and under the policies of the Forest Service.

The Green Book, as *Western Range* came to be known, was overkill pure and simple. It got nowhere with Congress, and one of its principal effects was to intensify animosity between the services, feeling that has died away somewhat in recent years, surfacing mainly when the subject of agency transfer is revived in Congress or by the Office of the President.

Records fail to pinpoint a date when interagency rivalry and dislike commenced. It doubtless predates the turn of the century, and Pinchot's habit of speaking plainly surely aggravated it. He chafed when the forest reserves were under Interior while he was in Agriculture. It seems entirely likely that an eagerness to be rid of the reserves, cited by Overton Price before an appropriations committee in 1904, may have been forced upon Interior by Teddy Roosevelt and did not truly represent Interior sentiment. Pinchot resented having to hire General Land Office employes in 1905, and those who did not fit his scheme of things quickly departed.

Pinchot also resented having to bow to Interior on mining claims filed under the 1872 mining claims act. Anyone could file on any piece of land that looked enticing, if it had been public domain before coming into the forest system and if it had not been thereafter put in a specific reserved status. Pinchot had questioned some coal mining claims on national forests in Alaska when R. A. Ballinger was Commissioner of the Land Office, later Secretary of Interior. This became a celebrated controversy in its time and was a principal cause for Pinchot's forced resignation in 1910. The Pinchot–Ballinger case certainly did not engender tender feelings between Interior and those service people who thought the sun rose and set at Pinchot's command. Then, too, national forests and public domain had common borders for thousands of miles in the West; this caused brush fires of friction to flare. And there always were partisans in associations and elsewhere to take sides and feed flames. The Green Book notes that "no less than a dozen bills to transfer forests to Interior had been introduced since 1911." [20] It says nothing of bills that would have put public domain in Agriculture.

Agriculture's reaction to the Ickes *coup* whereby he underbid the Service to assure his control of the Taylor lands was amply reflected in the Green Book. Some of the language verged on the resentful. Elsewhere, in addition to overly biased comparisons, there were contradictions. In one place it spoke of hundreds of millions of acres so badly depleted it would take a century to bring them back to original productivity; [21] later it told of the "remarkable ability" of western range country to recover, provided it was given to Agriculture to manage. There were slurring references to Interior's handling of public domain; in effect the Service was criticizing Congress in a report to Congress, for it was the legislative branch that had enacted the poor, inapplicable, indifferent laws under which the General Land Office puttered and fumbled its way toward oblivion. The Taylor Act, with all the faults so carefully pointed out in the book, was the will of Congress.

In retrospect, it is amazing that the Green Book was written as it was. What it said about the deterioration of public domain was unquestionably true; what it boasted the Service could do with it is not so surely veracious. It left itself open to indignant accusations that it was overplaying its capabilities, misrepresenting its accomplishments, and deliberately denigrating a sister agency. As one example of boasting the record simply does not support, the report said only 5 percent of national forest range was deteriorating while 77 percent was on the upgrade.[22] Later a chart showed overstocking on only about 8 percent of national forest range.[23] Records show the Service allowed some 11 million AUMs of grazing in 1933, cut it by about 26 percent to 8.1 million by 1947, and was then saying[24] that heavy further reductions were needed to bring grazing within carrying capacity. The Green Book was either falsifying right and left or the boast was just another example of inexcusable optimism.

This has not been a belated critical review of the Green Book so much as an attempt to indicate that its writing and publication probably hurt rather than helped the Service, causing resentment and disharmony. It lashed out at private landowners and their management practices, saying that 85 percent of their ranges were on the downgrade—which may have been close enough to pass as truth but immediately added that group to the list of Service enemies. It claimed that states and counties were doing even worse, with 88 percent of their lands deteriorating. Indian lands, also administered by Interior through its Bureau of Indian Affairs, were performing slightly better; only 75 percent were trending downward. By comparison, the Forest Service was managing its ranges in such exemplary fashion that only 5 percent were deteriorating. All national forest grazing permittees had dependent private property, and many also ran their stock on public domain, Indian reservation range, or state land part of each year, so the Service, through the Green Book, was criticizing nearly every rancher with whom it had dealings.

Many passages in the report were incontrovertible truth. In various ways and places it constituted a basic manual of range management; numerous passages could be used as text for elementary classes in the science. At other places it brought out clearly how dependent many small communities were on good range conditions.[25] These are basic enough that they might have been the central theme of the book. Range condition and trend then were and still are vital. Whether permittees should be cut in numbers or seasons or both depends on these two factors. Reductions are result, not cause. In the heyday of petroleum production in Oklahoma and the rest of the midcontinent oil region in the 1920s and 1930s, the news media were full of admonitions to landowners not to treat oil and gas royalty payments as income but as capital to be invested. Those who paid attention prospered; those who did not found that the initial gushing flow soon dwindled and, in time, petered out altogether. In a comparable way, as the book pointed out, the land beneath the forage, and the stubble and roots of that forage, had to be conserved so they could continue to produce grasses and forbs to nourish and fatten the livestock that meant dollar income. The forage and its land base constitute capital, not income. In oil country depletion is a mathematical certainty. In range country the mathematics may be a bit less precise but depletion is eventually inevitable if the land is overused.

Some of the troubles of the following decade might have been avoided if both the stock industry and the Service had followed more closely the textbook aspects of the Green Book.

The decade and a half of happenings recounted in this chapter constitute a curious mixture, but in separate ways they all hang together and have been reflected in later events affecting the grazing of western public lands.

The Forest Service's compliance with a demand for more realistic fees, from one Congressional committee charged with raising revenues to meet national needs, put the agency in conflict not only with its permittees but their firm friends in Congress on the Public Lands and Surveys Committee of the Senate. And the Service's willingness to cut back and in the Depression reduce rather than raise fees also can be related to events we shall reach in due course. The bickering between agencies has continued to surface from time to time, though it has been more subdued in recent years.

Toward Climactic Times

The Forest Service entered the ten-year permit term starting in 1936 under circumstances that would haunt it throughout the decade and play a part in subjecting it to perhaps the most severe tests of courage and fidelity of its career to that time.

Actions preparatory to the permit term had of necessity to be started a good many months ahead of the actual event. Judgment had to be passed on range conditions and trends, and conditions nearly everywhere had been worsened by the lingering effects of the Great Depression plus years of severe drought. Ferninand Silcox had been brought in to succeed Chief Forester Robert Y. Stuart in 1933, with orders to tighten internal controls and get things a bit more shipshape; they had been allowed to go somewhat slack.[1] He did reorganize, but was prevented by weather and economics from exerting a similar salutary effect on national forest ranges. They still were being overused, and pleas came in from all sides to be lenient, at least until the industry had recovered somewhat from the double-barreled disaster it had gone through.

Silcox agreed, and instructed that during the 1936 term there would be no more than a 15 percent reduction for range protection in a single year, and full term cuts were not to exceed 20 percent in the aggregate. Moreover, none were to be imposed before talking things over thoroughly with an affected permittee.[2]

The Silcox policy brought on imbalances galore. It hamstrung field forces across most of the national forest West. Any who recognized range damage and acted to bring it to a quick halt would be flying in the face of Washington Office policy. A few field men

Contoured cattle trails carried water that broke out and caused gullying in Sequoia National Forest, 1944. *USFS photo*

did, mostly in Region 1, as will be told later. No doubt Silcox recognized he was merely postponing the inevitable, but the West didn't take it that way. The '36 policy appeared to lull the industry into a belief that relaxed rules would last indefinitely. It then erupted into wild indignation when, as the next term year approached, it was told that perhaps heavier cuts than had ever been imposed before were needed to save deteriorated ranges from depletion and destruction. In the interim another world war would bring its full complement of complexities to range situations, and a rash of complications of other kinds would break out.

Even in the depressed years outdoor recreation in national forest areas tended to increase. Every new "dude" seen fishing, hunting, or camping in or near a permittee's allotment could be looked upon as a potential threat to his tenure, and as forest recreation seekers increased association spokesmen began complaining about their numbers and habits. As far back as 1927 the annual report [3] of Chief Greeley had noted that the industry was "inclined to question . . . recreation and game conservation."

The big game question was bound to be raised as improved state laws, regulations, and management practices tended to better

These cattle have good bloodlines but are in poor condition because of poor 'forage conditions. Cochise County, Arizona, 1943. *USFS photo*

conditions for wildlife as well as for hunters. The hard times of the 1930s had an effect on hunting, reducing opportunity to get to national forest hinterlands for those most disadvantaged by the Great Depression. It had a reverse effect on the game herds. They were under no compulsions except those imposed by nature, and multiplied rapidly under lessened hunter pressures. This situation was to grow much more noticeable long before the end of World War II, and would bring on agitation and acrimony between organized ranchers and organized outdoorsmen. This would also affect relations between the Forest Service and the western states; it would even bring threat of a federal law to give statutory authority to the Service to send men out on the forests to slaughter big game animals where they were considered too numerous.[4]

Hard confrontations still were ahead as the 1936 term began. Most of the public paid little attention to grazing on the national forests, unless it was a personal matter to them. Attention was focused abroad, where Hitler was nibbling ever more persistently at other people's property and prerogatives. Would this or would it not bring war? A few noted with rising concern that Japan was buying up all the scrap steel the western democracies would sell, and feeding the stuff into its armament furnaces. Far-sighted ranchers stocked up with more cattle and sheep in anticipation of a bonanza as the nation struggled out of the bad times. Rising war threats meant orders for nearly all of the things Americans produced from the soil or in their factories, including beef and hides or hide products, and mutton and wool or wool products.

In 1936, too, the considerable segment of the industry with a grazing interest in the public domain—more numerically than those who used the national forests—was maneuvering for all possible benefits available under the brand new Taylor Grazing Act. The grazing districts were being organized, and there was politicking among ranchers for election to the advisory boards that would have so much to say about who was allowed to graze how many head of what kind of livestock, and where and when. Since many whose stock grazed the national forests also used public domain, their interests were divided, not concentrated exclusively on the forests as they might have been at other times.

When war did come, the Forest Service refused to be stampeded as it had in World War I. Silcox by then had been succeeded by Earle H. Clapp, who retained the title of acting chief until he retired in 1943 and who may in some respects be considered one of the most underrated heads the Service has had. It was Clapp who geared the Service for extraordinary wartime production of forest products, and watched many of his best men get into uniform and leave, some never to return. But it was also Clapp who, in April, 1942, five months after Pearl Harbor, when patriotic fever was high and still rising, sent a two-page directive [5] to the field in which he gave strict orders that the overgrazing mistakes of World War I were not to be repeated. In doing so he ran a calculated risk. It might have been relatively easy for the profit-minded to mount a propaganda campaign that could have made holding down livestock numbers and seasons appear downright treasonable. It is to the credit of the stock industry that this did not occur.

Before he retired in 1943, Clapp had seen the beginnings of the long-drawn-out investigations of grazing begun by Senator Pat McCarran of Nevada in 1941.[6] McCarran centered much of his attention upon the Grazing Service, but did not overlook any opportunity to hear complaints against national forest grazing policies; those concerning the lusty and growing big game herds gave McCarran his major initial opportunity to look deeply into Forest Service matters. Before it was closed in 1945 for want of continuing authority and funds, the McCarran investigation would be fully immersed in the hassling of the Service that accompanied the harder policy against overgrazing that was to be inaugurated with the 1946 permit term.

When Lyle F. Watts became chief in 1943, the major range problems before the Service were the combination of excess livestock numbers and unduly long grazing seasons, exploding big game populations here and there, and the only partly pent-up yearning of the masses for the kinds of outdoor recreation to be found on the national forests. On taking office, Watts did not abandon or soften Clapp's range policies; he seemed to feel they were right and should continue to apply, though, like Clapp, he did try to leave unchanged the language of the 1936 ten-year term permits issued by Silcox. The annual reports are imperfect in a number of respects, and not wholly reliable guides to historical fact. If they are read carefully they do, however, provide hints of situations considered bothersome, even when most in the Service were preoccupied with wartime problems, and of directions of thinking that would loom large in future years. This was true in Watts's regime.

With the limited funds available the research arm of the Service continued to experiment with innovations in range management and improvement, including some initially tried in CCC days. Watts forecast in the 1943 report [7] that "careful seeding of selected sites" might increase from "six to well over ten times the grazing capacity of millions of acres of depleted range land." It was a heady prospect. The 1944 report [8] was more concerned with the approaching end of the permit term in 1945 than with range rehabilitation. Plans for the new term to start in 1946 were discussed with industry leaders who "generally welcomed" them—but the report did not go into plan details. A few sentences further on the report indirectly noted that parts of the total range were in sad condition by saying there was much to do before they could regain their "full potential productivity." That assertion could be construed as a prelude to the presentation of an ambitious six-year postwar program proposal in 1945, or as a hint of the drastic curtailment of grazing that would be ordered soon.

Most permanent federal agencies mulled over programs they would like to carry out when the war was behind us, and were encouraged if not ordered to prepare plans to execute them. They were dictated in part by the widely prevalent fear that the war would be followed at once by economic depression, as had happened after World War I. The Service dutifully drew up the six-year action pro-

posal and described it in the 1945 report,[9] issued about two months
after V-J Day. Of significance here is that it proposed to spend more
than $2.2 billion "to restore depleted forests and rundown range
lands. . . ." The report did not differentiate between timber and range
lands considered depleted and needing restoration. Would a half-
and-half division be fair? Even a formula under which three parts
went to forests to one part to range would provide a half billion
dollars for the latter, far above previous sums available for such
purposes, even in CCC times.

Surely the idea of expending huge amounts of appropriated
funds for range betterment churned in the minds of Forest Service
personnel in crucial years of the decade when livestock industry
criticism was rising toward crescendo. And surely such thinking
would have a significant bearing on critical decisions yet to be made.
No matter that the six-year program might be considered by the
pragmatists as little more than another study report to gather dust
on a library shelf. Let the program itself be no more than the stuff
of dreams to them; they could perhaps transform at least part of
the dream into practicalities. Maybe all that was needed was to
refine the proposal in the crucible of time; the process could be heated
by the friction and political pressures already becoming evident.

Range resources and livestock production were given top billing
in the 1945 report, ahead of timber, watershed protection, and other
national forest uses, which appears to give credence to the proposition that range was intended to get more than passing attention
under the six-year proposal.[10] "Our ranges . . . in the West, are generally heavily stocked and some are seriously overgrazed," it said.
The ranges simply were "not in condition to sustain the present numbers of stock." Public and private pastures were carrying a large
number of domestic animals. Rains following the dry mid-1930s had
helped tremendously to support high numbers during the war, but
the situation was "fraught with danger." The Service should reduce
AUMs "to forestall . . . losses . . . another drought would entail, and
safeguard the range itself."

In order to help the ranges recoup from World War I damage,
reductions of about 45 percent had been made since 1918. Still, because of "recurrent droughts and other adverse factors," there still
was much erosion and there were other undesirable conditions. So,
"in many places, further *drastic adjustments, sometimes involving
complete exclusion of livestock,* will be necessary" [11] (italics added).
Such stern language disclosed recognition of widespread adverse

Stock trample and overuse waterhole rims when there is no provision for their more scattered distribution. Beaverhead National Forest, Montana, 1960. *USFS photo*

situations, a determination to bring about correction, and decision not to rely entirely on a perhaps nebulous hope for future approval of a costly range rehabilitation program to accomplish it.

Postwar America would never be the same as it had been before, and Watts saw the national forests as the "people's playgrounds." With gasoline and tire production high, and new automobiles starting to move off the assembly lines at a fast pace despite one costly strike, there had to be a huge increase in recreational use of public lands of all kinds—and the forests were among the choicest of these. He could not escape the fact that wildlife had burst the bounds of reason in population and in demands upon the ranges for forage all year long. There was increasing competition by the larger vegetarians of the wild with livestock for available forage. Rising game numbers plus reductions in livestock AUMs were "bound to bring dissatisfaction" to permittees. The report complained that some states would not "liberalize restrictions on killing" big game. This was a reference to what is commonly known to wildlife managers as the "Bambi" complex, named for a Walt Disney cartoon film in which Bambi, an appealing fawn, repeatedly confronted danger from gunners. It was a carryover also of the oversell conservationists had given to the idea that the mothers of the herd were sacred and should not be hunted and killed. This may have been legitimate in the early years of the century when game herds reached their nadir in the West, but it could not be defended in the 1940s, when reducing the female population was essential to a slowing down of the population explosion. Deer and elk are polygamous, and killing a few, or even a great many, bucks and bulls only meant giving the remaining males larger harems. The Service had reason to deplore backward game management by the states, and it expended much effort over several years in consultations and argument intended to help overcome laggard public and official attitudes. It was not enough, and throughout the decade it had to face repeated complaint over damage done to stock forage by game.

It would be convenient if events came along in neat chronological order, for it would make this account much easier to write and the events of the era easier to comprehend, with each significant happening dropped into its own little niche in time. As has been said, Senator McCarran began his long series of hearings in Washington and the West in 1941, and he cocked an ear and listened attentively whenever the Forest Service was mentioned. This came frequently in 1943, when he offered his bill, S. 1152, to let the service slaughter excess numbers of game animals. About the same time he also was hearing testimony on a bill that would give legal status to forest grazing advisory boards, S. 1030 by Senator Edwin Johnson of Colorado. S. 1152 was quietly pigeonholed when McCarran came to the conclusion that the Service and the states would really come to grips with the big game surplus [12] problem. S. 1030 was not to die so easily. When it failed to pass, McCarran put in an almost identical bill under his own sponsorship. It was given the number S. 33 in 1944 and retained it when it was reintroduced in two successive Congresses. McCarran found the Izaak Walton League of America and a few other groups strongly opposed to S. 33 and the whole concept of giving advisory boards legal status. They believed the boards should remain advisory and not be riveted in law as district boards were under the Taylor Act. Spokesmen for the livestock industry, on the other hand, considered it a step toward converting their grazing privileges into rights; they enjoyed their Taylor Act prerogatives and would like to have them extended.

As is usually the case, when S. 1030 was on the agenda at a

hearing in Denver in mid-November 1943, the testimony was not con-
fined narrowly to the specific point at issue. Walter B. Sheppard of
Denver, not otherwise identified, was unhappy with the Service, the
industry, and Congress. He believed a service chief could exercise
little more authority than a Senate page.[13] The associations already
were powerful and shouldn't be made more so. The chain of influence went from the permittee to his local association, to the state
group, to the national association, to its Washington lobbyists, who
then went to members of Congress who, in turn, went into action
with dire results to the Service and the range lands in its charge.
When a Senator spoke, said Sheppard, "every place holder in Washington ducks." The typical bureaucrat, he went on, "almost literally
crawls on his belly to Senators and Congressmen who are not im-
pervious to influences incompatible with the public interest." Cabinet
officers come and go, he continued, whereas "the livestock lobbies
stay on forever." Such testimony before McCarran was rather rare;
most witnesses represented one or another segment of the stock industry.

The Service seems to have been a bit coy regarding the extent
of the reductions it would impose on use of run-down range at the
start of the 1946 permit term. It was not widely publicized in advance that some of the reductions would be severe. The facts would
come to light in a McCarran hearing at Salt Lake City in May
1945,[14] and be discussed with considerable heat at another, chaired
by Senator Joseph C. O'Mahoney of Wyoming, at Casper the following September.[15] The hearing at Salt Lake City came after V-E
Day, that at Casper after V-J Day, in an atmosphere of general
rejoicing over the ending of hostilities but of trepidation as to what
the postwar economic situation would be. Stockmen were, if anything, more wary and suspicious than at other times.

At Salt Lake City Walt Dutton, range management chief, took
the brunt of complaint from industry spokesmen. His opening words
were mild, conciliatory—which was characteristic of Dutton—almost
evasive, but he was pinned down by L. C. Montgomery of Heber
City, head of the state cattlemen's group. He brought from Dutton
admission that while the servicewide average reductions would indeed be fairly low, some would range from 30 to 50 percent. In fact,
in some instances stock would be removed entirely from the forests.
The record does not indicate whether the listening stockmen were
stunned by the figures and thus slow to react, but it is true that

Outmoded close herding of sheep; front ranks eat most palatable forage, later ones what's left, to bare ground. Inyo National Forest, California, 1931. *USFS photo*

Better scattered band of sheep grazing Medicine Bow National Forest, Wyoming, 1942. *USFS photo*

other Service personnel quickly stepped in with supplemental, sometimes diversionary information, and exclusion testimony was not then followed up.

Between Salt Lake City and Casper the stockmen's leaders had time to become better prepared to deal with what they considered heinous prospective cuts. Congressman Frank A. Barrett of Wyoming sat with O'Mahoney there; so did Senator E. V. Robertson of Wyoming. The first witness in the stockmen's well-organized presentation was Lester C. Hunt, Governor of Wyoming. Word of impending deep cuts, he said, had brought apprehension, worry, indecision, and discouragement to the stockmen, whose positions were insecure and whose operations were unstable. So, he proposed that the stockmen's local associations be given full power to rule on anything that had to do with administration of grazing. This, of course, was just what the conservationists at Denver in 1943 had forecast would happen if S. 1030 or S. 33 should be enacted and advisory boards be given legal status. Further, said Hunt, permit numbers should be prescribed by law, so they could be changed only by statutory amendment. Or, he said, *dispose of all federal lands*. In the meantime, please intercede with the Secretary of Agriculture and persuade him to forbid the Forest Service to cut stock numbers or time. In all, his was an amazing aggregation of pleas and declarations to come from so high an elected state official, one who presumably was thoroughly familiar with the complexities of administering public properties, including state-owned grazing land.

A parade of influential stockmen followed Hunt. Their testimony disclosed a large and widening gap between the industry's leaders and the Service. Nearly all mentioned prospective reductions, but the range of castigation spread across the whole broad front of differences that can arise when an agency deals with something that affects the livelihoods of a large number of people. Samples follow: [16]

E. V. Magagna of Rock Springs: With regulations subject to change at the whim of the Service, permits were unstable, binding only upon the permittee; the Service apparently intended to outlaw all grazing, since each new regulation cut AUMs, and areas were constantly being withdrawn to benefit wildlife, recreationists, and others.

J. Elmer Brock of Kaycee: It was high time Congress stepped in to stabilize an industry that had been maltreated under unsound, uneconomic, socialistic policies for forty years.

Oda Mason of Laramie, head of the state woolgrowers group: There should be no cuts, for the next good break in the weather would fix everything.

F. E. Mollin of Denver, staff head of the American National Livestock Association: The Service sent incompetents out to examine ranges.

In general, the Service was given a rough going-over. From time to time Dutton or some other official would respond to specifics, and toward the end Dutton disclosed that a meeting of the Service with the associations would be held within two weeks. The inference was that perhaps all these complaints could then be talked over more or less informally and agreement reached as to what was genuine and required corrective treatment and what was mere bombast. The 1946 report did not mention the meeting, and the rising tempo of actions and activities were sure portents that the industry had decided on a major uprising against any effort by the Service to bring grazing use within carrying capacity through reductions in AUMs.

Nowadays cattle use national forest ranges an average of about three to three and a half months a year, sheep around two months. Compare this with 1946, when, according to the annual report,[17] cattle averaged 5.6 months and sheep 3.1 months. This comparatively long grazing season, cutting into the early spring when forage and soil conditions usually were not yet ready to support grazing, and lasting into the fall when stock were eating seeds, cropping stubble too closely, and even uprooting plants, doubtless gave rise in good part to the assertion in the report that "much remains to be done" toward restoring 26 million acres that were in bad shape. Those millions represented a sizable percentage of the entire national forest range in the West. Then the report spoke of "mistakes of the past" in not correcting overgrazing because of consideration for the economic plight of permittees; adjusting seasons and reducing numbers of livestock had been delayed repeatedly so as not to hurt their pocketbooks. Decisive cuts "should have been made long ago." To have done so and achieved "complete" recovery would have doubled "forage production, overcome serious erosion," and stabilized the industry generally, as well as those dependent cowtowns out in the hinterlands.[18]

At the beginning of 1946, Watts wrote, permits had been renewed, good through 1955, with every prospect for "undiminished use" for "every permittee whose range is *properly* stocked" (italic added). I won't say the report was evasive at that point, but it contained nothing about permit conditions for ranchers using a substantial part of the western range whose allotments were *not* "properly" stocked. The cuts Dutton had forecast at Salt Lake City had been ordered. And it was at Salt Lake City, a year almost to the day after the hearing where Dutton disclosed the extent of the planned reductions, that the leaders of the two national associations assembled to organize the Joint National Livestock Committee on Public Lands and initiate the attempted Great Land Grab.

8

Script For a
Wild West Show

Before the end of World War II the congressional hectoring of the Forest Service had all been done by western senators. Now it was time for western members of the House to move in. The initiative was taken by Representative Frank A. Barrett of Wyoming, a lawyer and a stock grower, and before he got off stage center his performances and those of certain colleagues in field hearings would cause them to be labeled a "Wild West Show." [1] This was a reference to shoot-'em-up spectacles staged under the circus tents of Col. William F. (Buffalo Bill) Cody many years ago.

The events of the Barrett era didn't proceed in orderly chronological fashion. They varied considerably in nature and location, but all were related in one way or another to the determination of the livestock industry's leadership ,to have charge of western ranges, or else.

By the time his appropriations and renewal resolutions ran out, Senator Pat McCarran had made a shambles of the Interior Department's Grazing Service and General Land Office, and a subdued Bureau of Land Management had been created out of their merger.[2] Various reasons were given at the time as to why those two services were in disrepute, but I see these as significant: (1) R. H. Rutledge and C. L. Forsling, the Grazing Service's last two administrators, were convinced the Taylor Act really intended that grazing district lands should be operated under soundly conceived range management plans instead of being given minimal supervision on a custodial basis; (2) those administrators believed, as did the House Appropriations Committee, that fees charged should more nearly reflect the true value of public land forage being consumed; and (3) the venerable General Land Office indeed creaked as it slowly, ponderously went about administering grazing on isolated tracts not in districts, handling mining claims, disposing of timber where there was any, surveying, taking care of sharply declining homestead claims, and doing other miscellaneous chores.

These few highlights illustrate why the industry's leaders were in a heady mood. They had shown that their members of Congress and allies in other organizations would come at their call to trample the Interior Department agency that had dared try, even in a hesitant way, to manage the Taylor lands in the public interest rather than purely the stockmen's interest.

Now officials of the Forest Service were getting uppity here and there, as the stock associations saw it. So the thing to do was to pour on the same kind of heat that had brought Interior to heel. If direct pressure failed to result in submissiveness, go the congressional route. Members of Congress from the West controlled powerful committees, had proved they were in position to swing heavy clubs against public land administrators, and would do so willingly when asked.

Congressman Barrett became a livestock industry hero in the Jackson Hole National Monument incident. President Franklin D. Roosevelt had had the effrontery in 1943 to proclaim that broad Wyoming valley at the eastern feet of the towering Grand Teton mountains a national monument[3] without prior consultation with the state delegation in Congress. That was a snub as well as an action that a few sizable ranch operators did not want. So Barrett introduced a bill in the Seventy-eighth Congress to abolish the monument. It passed both houses, more on the issue of failure to consult than on the merits of the legislation, and Roosevelt pocket vetoed it. Barrett came back in the Seventy-ninth with H. R. 1330, another bill to abolish.

The stockmen's great interest in Jackson Hole has significant aspects. Much of the flattish valley was in federal ownership—public domain (Taylor land) or national forest. It lay just south of Yellowstone and east of the Tetons. It was split north and south much of its distance by the upper waters of the Snake River, in whose valley most of the privately held ranch land was situated, and a federal highway ran northward through the City of Jackson to become the southern entrance to Yellowstone. Horace Albright, when superintendent at Yellowstone in the 1920s, saw the beginnings of what he considered honkytonk development of those private lands near the highway and river. At Albright's urging, John D. Rockefeller, Jr., in 1927 began buying them and in all acquired about 33,000 strategic valley acres. He intended to operate the properties as ranches only until an appropriate time to donate them to the government as an addition to Grand Teton or Yellowstone National Park. Meantime undesirable development there would be forestalled.[4]

When Roosevelt proclaimed the monument, the boundaries were so poorly drawn they were not fully defensible. Some irrigated cropland had been included. The remaining ranch owners, some of them operators of large spreads, feared being thrown off the public range under National Park Service rules. All manner of propaganda was put out.[5] The county's tax base would be destroyed, it was said. It was rumored that a huge oil pool lay under the valley floor and in NPS hands that could not then be privately exploited. There was a legitimate big game problem. Thousands of elk summered in Yellowstone. The so-called southern herd poured each fall into Jackson Hole and overloaded the range. There was fear that if hunters were kept out under the Park Service's traditional rules, it would result in a greater overpopulation than already existed. Nobody relished the idea of wholesale slaughter by park personnel to keep herd numbers within winter range carrying capacity. Stockmen drew word pictures of their private lands being overrun by elk, their meadows and haystacks destroyed, their domestic animals deprived of winter feed.

In the middle 1920s the Izaak Walton League had become concerned about the plight of the southern herd. It sent Cliff Hallowell of Waterloo, Iowa, to the area. With donated funds, Hallowell bought two thousand acres of Jackson Hole land that was deeded by the League to the federal government to become the nucleus of the present elk refuge and wintering ground operated by the U.S. Fish and Wildlife Service.

Later, in the 1940s, as the McCarran hearings disclosed, stockmen and others would become perturbed over the rapid increase in deer and elk numbers in several western states. Critical areas developed in Colorado, Utah, the Modoc country of northern California, and a few other areas. These species had gone far down in numbers by the turn of the century, due to overshooting and habitat preemption. They began a slow but accelerating comeback after the national forests were created and were, of course, protected in the national parks. We have seen how game populations irrupted in the Great Depression, when fewer hunters had the price of a rifle, and how this accelerated in World War II, when younger hunters were away and ammunition was scarce. The big game story was part of the Jackson Hole controversy and the general unhappiness of stockmen over what they called the failure of the federal agencies to solve problems of deer and elk competition with their domestic animals for forage, mostly in winter.

In time the big game situation was brought under reasonable control, and so was the Jackson Hole matter. After dragging on for several years, it ended in a compromise in 1950. Certain unneeded lands south of the Gros Ventre River, which should not have been included in the boundaries as initially drawn, reverted to private status and the rest—the principal part of the valley east of the spectacular Tetons—was added to that national park, where it should have been all along.

Stockmen appearing before the McCarran committee in the war years complained bitterly over restrictions and shortages—as who did not? Help was not to be had. Materials and supplies were rationed, with high priority given the industrial sectors of the economy. Yet somehow the major elements of the stock industry not only managed to get along but to build up herds and flocks to unprecedented numbers. Both public and private ranges were fully stocked.[6] Prevented from excessive use of national forest ranges during the war, the public-land-using segment of the industry had nevertheless managed to increase its herds and flocks by bringing in feed from outside and by more intensive production of forage crops on available private land.

Acquisitive natures are not exclusively ranch-born or western. These traits are found all over and they are nothing new. So it should be considered natural that those doing well in the livestock business should want things to continue that way. They, just as their predecessors of whom Pinchot and others have written so vividly, were ardent believers that bigger is better and they wanted what they could get while the getting was good. They resented more than anything else reductions in either numbers allowed or time on and off the range. The industry was proving it could crack down on the Grazing Service for taking small, tentative steps toward putting users of Taylor lands under tighter management, and if the Forest Service failed to heed that implied warning, more specific steps would be taken. It might not be a bad idea to bloody a few Forest Service heads, figuratively of course, to make sure the message got across. That just might teach certain foresters that the industry leadership was not to be trifled with. Initial steps were taken before the Grazing Service was abolished.

The first widely publicized target to be hit had been Lee Kirby, supervisor of the Tonto National Forest with headquarters in Phoenix, Arizona. About the same time permittees turned against Supervisor Russell Beeson of the Modoc National Forest. (See Chapter 13 for details.) Both were shipped out, forced to accept unwanted and unwarranted transfers to other jobs. You may or may not be surprised how fast the grapevine gets that kind of word around the circuit. These, as it happened, were only forerunners of similar actions to come. And the obvious must not be overlooked: The associations did not sign the orders moving Kirby and Beeson; that was done by nervous officials of the Service. I have not been able to pinpoint just who was responsible for the Kirby and Beeson removal orders; and they may possibly have been isolated incidents, not wholly relevant to what occurred later. That is moot.

The associations found they could not dictate to a new team working in Region 2 from the Denver office of the Forest Service.[7] An easy-going regional forester had been replaced by a feisty new man, John W. Spencer. Earl D. Sandvig had come to Denver from Missoula, Montana, Region 1 headquarters, to be chief of the Division of Range and Wildlife Management. His division specialists— Art Cramer, Herb Schwan, Ralph Hill, Clarke Anderson—found "Sandy" a man who believed range condition was the prime criterion in judging allowed grazing use of the forests. That word went out quickly to the supervisors and rangers. Spencer backed Sandvig to the hilt. The goal in Region 2 was to get stock numbers down and the grazing seasons right wherever range was damaged. Then, when and as funds and manpower for range improvement practices should become available, they would be applied to speed up natural recovery processes. Spencer and Sandvig believed they had unqualified support from the Washington headquarters of the Service. They worried over what had happened to Kirby and Beeson, but those might have been aberrant incidents and their principal immediate effect was to cause Spencer and Sandvig to try to be doubly sure their readings of range conditions were right before going ahead with the planned program of grazing reduction and land rehabilitation.

Region 2 was home to some of the industry's most vocal firebrands. They included G. Norman Winder of Craig, Colorado, president of the National Woolgrowers Association and a permittee on the Routt National Forest, and J. Elmer Brock of Kaycee, Wyoming, a permittee on the Big Horn and a former head of the American National (cattle). Sensitive grazing situations had prevailed for years on both those national forests. And there were others: leaders of the Uncompahgre Cattle and Horse Growers Association on the Uncompahgre National Forest (see Chapter 14); Dan Hughes of Montrose, chairman of the Joint National Committee of 1946, a permittee on the Grand Mesa National Forest; and Farrington (Ferry) R. Carpenter of Hayden, first administrator of the Taylor Act, also a permittee on the Routt. A dozen or so other names might be added, but if only those of Winder and Brock had been listed, people who lived in Region 2 in the 1940s could nod their heads knowingly and anticipate much of the rest of this and later chapters.

In meeting after meeting, at all seasons, leaders such as these used every available stratagem to try to prevent reductions and to frustrate the efforts of the range managers to bring loadings within grazing capacity. Differences between user and Service, however, went far beyond these relatively simple and clear-cut issues. Violations of permit terms were widespread and of many kinds. It looked at times as though permittees were being persuaded to break the rules to test the mettle of the rangers, the supervisors, and the regional office staff, and as Sandvig wrote me, "many of us in range management walked lightly for fear of getting our heads chopped off." [8] Sandy undoubtedly had in mind the fates of Kirby and Beeson. Now it must not be assumed that all in Region 2 had strong backbones; Sandvig and his associates had to do some testing of their own, to learn where rangers and supervisors would stand firmly with them on principle. He wrote me he found men sprinkled across the region "who cared more for the resource and its condition than their ratings in personnel files," [9] and would try to stand fast against the pressures exerted by the livestock leaders.

When sweet talk failed to sway Sandvig and his people from the course they believed right, meetings often went sour and discussions turned rough, ugly. Things got worse as the calendar edged toward the coming 1946 permit term and the more the stockmen learned about the reductions planned. Now belligerent talk by the associations crystalized into the action described in Chapter 1, when the joint committee was formed with orders to advance to the legislative front. True, at the outset the bill to be written would speak only of Taylor Act lands, but the newspapers printing the story were but a few days old before Winder, Brock, and others were moving toward a significant broadening of objectives—objectives which may have lain in the backs of their minds all along. If the Forest Service refused to be persuaded by techniques previously used, they would threaten to have the whole eighty-odd million acres of national forest rangeland in the eleven western states ripped off and turned over to the grazing users. And while grabbing forest ranges as well as the better land in the districts, they would just include those thousands of acres that had been proclaimed a national monument out in Jackson Hole, plus whatever else could be taken from the National Park Service.

If Sandvig and his field people "walked lightly," officials in the Washington office of the Service appeared to tread even more softly. Dutton knew the right thing to do; he had been on nearly every rung on the Service ladder in the field and could read range as well as the best of the specialists, but he was essentially a man of peace who would seek ways to avoid conflict if they could be found. His superior, Assistant Chief Christopher M. Granger, leaned more toward administrative matters than range management, though he was not unschooled in that field. Granger, too, looked for acceptable compromises in preference to confrontations.

At the top, Lyle Watts was an unhappy figure. I am convinced he was sincere, earnest, and essentially honest, that he believed deeply in the doctrine of the greatest good for the greatest number, and wanted it carried out. I think he was convinced that the course followed by Spencer and Sandvig in Region 2 was proper, and at the time things were coming to a head he felt he was backed by real public opinion power through the leaders of the conservation movement. He relied much on Kenneth A. Reid, my predecessor as executive director of the Izaak Walton League of America. Another conservation counselor was Dr. Ira N. Gabrielson, recently retired director of the U.S. Fish & Wildlife Service who was beginning a new career as president of the Wildlife Management Institute. Then there were announced supporters in such other organizations as the National Wildlife Federation, National Audubon Society, American Nature Association, Society of American Foresters, The Wilderness Society, and the Sierra Club, then more sedate than it would become a generation later. Conservation leaders were in the early stages of perfecting the organization of the Natural Resources Council of America,[10] a network for the exchange of information about resource situations upon which the groups that held membership could then act independently—or not act—as they saw fit. The technique instituted by the NRCA came in handy to our side soon afterward.

The soundness of reasoning on the part of the technical people in the Service, the logic of such field leaders as have been named, and the belief that the conservation movement—newly burgeoning after years of wartime preoccupations and restrictions—would stand by and help prevent industrial or Congressional reprisals, all seem to have convinced Watts that he should follow the dictates of range realities rather than succumb to expediency. For the 1946 permit term of ten years he preliminarily approved heavy cuts where heavy cuts se,emed called for, and at the same time pushed for a broader, expanded program of range improvements to speed sick land recuperation.

The initial objective of the Joint National Livestock Committee on Public Lands was essentially simple, and twofold. The preparation of land-grab legislation and efforts to have it rushed through Congress was one. The other was to forestall and frustrate the Forest Service in its AUMs reduction program. The Joint Committee began working on the draft of a land-grab bill in the fall of 1946. Meetings were held in October and December. The December meeting, held in Denver, was revealing.[11] Chairman Hughes invited a number of organizations, including the Colorado and Wyoming Izaak Walton League Divisions, to attend. The Forest Service was there, represented by Sandvig. In Hughes's opening statement he said he thought the stockmen's wants were reasonable enough so all could support them. He seemed to believe most of the invited groups would approve. Then he asked outsiders to comment.

Dr. John W. Scott, professor of zoology at the University of Wyoming at Laramie, speaking for Wyoming Waltonians, told Hughes that since he had not seen a draft of the bill he did not feel he could speak to it. H. C. Kelly of Denver, secretary of the Colorado Division of the League, also took the position that comment would be premature. A representative of the National Education Association reminded the committee that the 25 percent of all receipts distributed by the Service to forest counties each year helped pay for the education of many children in livestock country; in other words, the stockmen should look out for possible side effects of any action they took. The Colorado Game and Fish Commission representative declined to approve the goals of the committee. By this time Hughes was getting uncomfortable; he said plainly that he was unhappy with the trend of the remarks from the invited guests.

At that point Frederick P. Champ, Logan, Utah, banker and chairman of the Public Lands Committee of the Chamber of Commerce of the United States, entered and Hughes called on him immediately. Champ obviously believed he was among friends, with no strangers around, and warmly endorsed the work of the Joint Livestock Committee. Earlier in 1946 his committee had circulated the U.S. Chamber's Referendum 88 on public land disposal, accompanied by a set of guidelines that inclined toward the land grab, to chambers of commerce all over the country. Many state and local chambers, not all of which knew precisely what they were voting on but trusted their national leadership, obediently endorsed Referendum 88. Significantly, Champ's home-town chamber in Logan voted "no." Its members remembered floods from watersheds denuded under private ownership, and campaigns that had been conducted all along the Wasatch Front in Utah to raise funds to buy such lands and turn them over to the Forest Service for rehabilitation.[12]

But Champ told the Denver meeting that the time had come when the trend of federal acquisition of lands should be reversed. It was essential to start moving all that federal land into private ownership. Much of it could serve its highest purposes only if in private hands. When Sandvig then spoke briefly Champ discovered there were other than stockmen present and he got the floor immediately to backpedal as fast as he could. This time up he said the issue was bound in the wise use of all resources and the Joint Committee must reconcile its interests with those of the rest of the country. The session ended without adding any recruits to the livestock leadership's existing roster.

Next day, when no outsiders were looking on, the committee agreed on certain "principles" to be incorporated in the land-grab legislation. It was determined at this meeting that subsurface mineral rights should not be demanded; they would be reserved for disposition by the government but the new private owners, if the plan succeeded, would have to be reimbursed if the surface should be disturbed by any mining or oil drilling. This information comes from the January, 1947, issue of *The American Cattle Producer*, publication of the American National Livestock Association. The same issue, in an article on page 8, then said; "Congressman Frank A. Barrett of Wyoming, who was present for part of the meeting, agreed that if the livestock industry *as a whole* approved of the plan, he will prepare and present legislation on the principles involved, to the national Congress" (italics added).

Barrett never did so. He used as an escape clause his proviso that the industry "as a whole" would have to approve. However, a colleague from Wyoming, Senator E. V. Robertson, a sheepman, had already jumped the gun. In the Seventy-ninth Congress, ending in 1946, Robertson introduced S. 1945, which would have taken from the federal government and given to the states for transfer to private ownership all the public domain, all the grazing lands of the national forests, and lands suited to grazing in the National Park System. As Charles C. Moore of the Dude Ranchers Association later told the Barrett subcommittee at Rawlins, Wyoming, Robertson's bill was a case of "whole hog or none, with the none left off." [13] The Robertson bill died in committee as the Seventy-ninth Congress adjourned.

The script for his wild west show was written when the livestock leaders formally asked Barrett to chastise the unruly Forest Service. This was done early in 1947, at a meeting of the American National Livestock Association in Phoenix, where the organization adopted a committee report demanding a Congressional investigation of grazing on the national forests "and appropriate legislation to remove existing evils." The Service was called a "self-made, self-interpreted, and self-executed type of bureaucratic administration," "a most vicious type of dictatorship," and "a detriment to our form of government." The report demanded transfer of national forest lands "chiefly valuable for grazing" to the Bureau of Land Management where it would, of course, be subject to the terms of the give-away legislation then being drafted.

Barrett, like Watts, is gone now. Both died years ago and cannot be asked about things that motivated them most. We must form opinion on the basis of what happened. Barrett followed the Stanfield–McCarran pattern of investigation, but with a brutality of approach that was more reminiscent of that of Ashurst and Cameron in 1925 than the polished performance given by the Bryanesque McCarran. Senator Pat had a large pink face, a head of flowing white hair, and a commanding presence. He could smile easily, even as he asked cutting questions. Barrett was stocky, of average height, with short dark hair, a face that flared brick red when his ·choler was up, and he tended to lose his tact with his cool.

Like Stanfield and McCarran, Barrett would begin his investigation in Washington, and he would operate under an equally broad charter. House Resolution 93 of the Eightieth Congress allowed him to look into just about any aspect of public land administration that happened to be brought up by a witness or a committeeman, and a Washington session did focus on public domain matters, but it was clear that the Service was his chief target. The Washington hearings [14] would be relatively sedate, as were those earlier ones by Stanfield and McCarran; he would run things with a heavy hand when he got into cow country. The script appeared as if it might have been ghost written by the staff and elected heads of the stock organizations, which would broadcast appeals to every disgruntled permittee, every rancher who thought he had a grievance against the Forest Service, to come to the widely publicized hearings. They would even specify the kinds of complaints they wanted Barrett to hear. Once in the hearing room, the organizations would decide the order in which their complaining witnesses would appear. Barrett would recognize the industry's parade marshals and let them present complainers first, and at most field hearings complainants actually were allotted so much time that when Barrett finally got around to calling defenders of the Service it was near the planned closing hour and he put a stop watch on them. This made it necessary for some of our people and unaffiliated witnesses to do little more than summarize briefly and leave extended statement texts to be put in a record that might or might not even be read. A very few defied Barrett on the time limitation; Charlie Moore was among them.

It cannot be proved, but I suspect that this matter of allotment of time was as carefully orchestrated as were the statements of complaint and the periodic public castigations by committeemen of the Service chief, his assistants, and the handful of writers who had been spreading the alarm across the nation since the first of the year.

The drumbeat of industry propaganda quickened with the adoption of that public lands committee report at the Phoenix meeting of the cattlemen. After a January 1947 announcement of its adoption, *The American Cattle Producer*, the ANLA's official journal, in February began what would become a recurring complaint that the Service was going out of its way to supply writers with propaganda "that is misleading, incorrect, and weighted, or weighted to fit the occasion."

The Denver *Post* had a custom of giving "guest editorial" space to a wide variety of articles by volunteer writers who believed they had something worth while to tell the people of the area the paper called the "Rocky Mountain Empire." The official standing of Elmer Brock lent authenticity to the contents of the long article under his byline in The Denver *Post* of February 2, 1947, about the projected land grab.[15] A review of its principal contents here seems appropriate.

The article was a peculiar mix of self-justification and castigation of those who opposed. The public lands, which had never been private since they came into the nation's possession, must be "returned" to the states and those privileged to run their domestic animals on them "if the livestock industry—the backbone of western economic life—is to survive." The industry had to be freed from "federal overlordship" that had "harassed the stockmen of the West for years and left them at the mercy of the whims and edicts of bungling officials." Those bureaus were "all predacious and most of them tinged with pink or even deeper hue" (which was a foretaste of the accusations that soon would be so widespread in the McCarthy era). Under those bureaucrats the West was being "denied the American form of government." Then Brock had these words for all who opposed in the name of conservation:

"The committee expects the baying of the pack of poolhall conservationists who will be needled into action by the threatened bureaus. Few of them have anything at stake, or any constructive ideas. They are full of misguided information and a lot of enthusiasm and don't know what to do with it except howl."

Brock used more than hyperbole and castigation, however, as he wrote. He put the objectives of the committee in plain words that had only been hinted at in earlier public declarations. The stockmen proposed to buy the grazing lands they coveted on the "basis of 10 percent down, the balance to be paid over 30 years and to carry interest at 1½ percent." He glossed over the price per acre—disclosed at other times and places to range from nine cents to $2.80 for Taylor district lands [16]—and didn't mention the fifteen years it was proposed that permittees should have in which to make up their minds, but the article plainly showed what an administrative mess the purchases would leave for the government agencies.

"Of course," Brock wrote, "stockmen would not buy all that land. Those who did not buy would continue to operate under the grazing permit system." That statement made it easy to visualize the intermingled snarl of public and private land that would ensue. The buyers normally would choose the choicest plots of ground in their allotments, and the leavings would be little more than a conglomeration of scat-

96   *Public Grazing Lands*

tered tracts; many likely would be cut off from public access, even unimpeded entry by agency personnel.

Brock's article provided the spark needed to fire the conservation organizations. It appeared, as noted, in the Sunday *Post* of February 2, 1947. On Monday, February 3, the annual North American Wildlife Conference was to start at San Antonio, Texas. These conferences drew virtually all the movement's leaders. Arthur Carhart was alert. He airmailed a tear sheet from the paper containing the Brock article to Kenneth Reid of the Izaak Walton League, who was at the conference.[17] Reid, after showing it to others, had the article reproduced on letter-sized sheets, and at the bottom, using a bit of leftover white space, he added, "If you don't believe your federal estate is in jeopardy, READ THIS!" I have in my files a marked and worn copy of the reprint from which the above quotations have been taken. In time that sheet would be reproduced by tens of thousands and sent widely across the country, mailed singly or in batches from our office in Chicago or mine in Denver, from local chapters and state divisions of the League in many states, from headquarters and branch offices of cooperating groups of many kinds, and by interested but unaffiliated individuals. It was the beginning of a great outpouring of energy in defense of the public lands that were the common property of all.

It was customary at the North American conferences to have the proceedings summed up by a prominent conservationist. At San Antonio President Gabrielson called on one of our most prestigious natural scientists, Dr. Aldo Leopold of the University of Wisconsin, a former Forest Service official, for this task. Here are excerpts: [18]

Our program here has given scant recognition to the "battle for the public lands." Perhaps it couldn't, for the opening gun was fired only a month ago.[19] I have this to say:

1. It is perhaps the biggest conservation battle since the Ballinger controversy.[20]

2. Let no man think the issue is a western affair of no consequence to other states. The defeat of public land conservation in the West would be felt by every state.

3. Let no man think this is a Grazing District fight. Disrupt the public domain and the national forests will follow; disrupt the national forests and the national parks will follow.

4. It is pure evasion to say the states or private owners could practice conservation on those lands. Neither, by and large, has demonstrated

either the capacity or the wish to do. so. To organize the practice of conservation on large areas takes decades of hard work.

5. Now is the time for critical self-examination by all federal land bureaus.

So events began to tumble upon each other in rapid succession in the early months of 1947. Barrett got his requested orders to investigate, and began to schedule hearings. First would come the preliminaries in Washington, later a carefully planned itinerary would take him and his entourage in turn to Montana, Wyoming, Colorado, and Utah, along the West Coast from Redding, California, southward, then to Nevada, and on to a grand finale in Arizona.

We in the conservation movement were ignorant of it, but the fact must be recorded that sometime in the winter of 1946–47 the elected politicians read the omens better than we did and came to the conclusion that the land grab itself could not win in Congress. No swift advance of give-away legislation through committee procedures, or victory on the floor of either house, seemed in the cards. Too many people were becoming aroused; as the year 1947 advanced delegations in Congress, especially from the East and Midwest, had begun hearing from the folks back home. And cracks began to show at the grass-roots levels of the livestock organizations as well. Barrett, it will be recalled, had only promised to push through a grab bill if the industry in its entirety wanted it so. Without the votes from the more populous regions of the country the aggressive westerners could not have their way, and the wholesale disposal proposition was quietly dropped from the agenda.

That did not mean the show wouldn't go on. It merely shifted emphasis from one grand design to another, the AUMs reduction battle and its aftermath. And the humiliation and domination of the Forest Service was the chief order of business.

9

A Ragtag Army

As a movement and a living force in this country, conservation got its first vigorous impetus in the Roosevelt–Pinchot era around the turn of the century. It faded thereafter until the emergency measures and thinking processes of the New Deal in the Great Depression gave it a shot in the arm. Government initiated and stimulated in both instances. Public involvement came with seeming reluctance. In the first instance two abrasive personalities in government dragged an apathetic citizenry into support of actions that a decade earlier would have been unthinkable. The second, despite improvisations and contradictions that at times brought harm with good, was a force intended to counter the dejection and despondency of hard economic times.

The first broadly *public* outpouring of response to the national need for an awareness of the limits of our resources and the raids upon them—accomplished fact or in the making—came in the embattled 1940s, and the organized segment of the western livestock industry may be credited, albeit somewhat wryly, with providing the alarm needed to bring about the awakening.

The conservation movement, if it truthfully could be called that, was fragmented and specialized in the earlier years of this century. The cut-out-and-get-out customs of the logging industry aroused one coterie of concerned citizens. The appeal to feminine longing for that which was declared fashionable brought devastation to plumed wading birds and other creatures, and a storm of activism on the part of militant followers of Audubon. The huge increase in industrial pollution in World War I resulted in an upsurge of interest in the early 1920s and the Izaak Walton League was born. Far out in the West mountain climbers and hikers who decried the loss of natural beauty to gold miners, loggers, and other despoilers of what had been almost pristine wilderness, had caused the formation of a small, elite group into an organization called the Sierra Club. The Wilderness Society grew because truly wild lands were succumbing to exploitation. Wholesale drainage of potholes and marshes in the north central region, followed by the Dust Bowl era, gave birth to organizations dedicated to preservation of waterfowl, with emphasis on coveted species of ducks and geese. And there were others. Generally, most of them centered their concern on one aspect of the resource scene rather than the broad spectrum Aldo Leopold would try to popularize as a "land ethic" involving entire biotic systems and the total natural environment.[1]

Individuals here and there saw the sum rather than just the parts, and as the century advanced certain of the groups sequentially broadened their outlook. As one example, the Izaak Walton League was mainly concerned at its start with polluted waters that were killing off game fish. In a few years it linked other natural factors and adopted a slogan that declared it was the "Defender of Woods, Waters, and Wildlife." In 1948 this was changed to "soil, woods, waters, and wildlife," which made it perhaps the first of the citizen groups to approach an acceptance of the Leopold preachment that the earth was a biotic unit in which what was done to this or that fraction had its inevitable effect on the whole.[2]

But by and large, conservationists with breadth of vision were few in the Great Depression, and the limitations necessitated by World War II prevented any large growth in memberships in natural resource conservation organizations. None had evinced great interest in the public lands in the sense of looking upon them in their entirety as a great national heritage to be safeguarded and cherished. The Sierra Club and Wilderness Society more or less concentrated on scenic and wilderness integrity. Others appeared more interested in the increase in numbers of creatures of the wild than in the humble forage that sustained them.

Most people, if they thought about it at all, accepted as normal the turning over of public domain to private use and exploitation. Vast acreages had been granted to new states being admitted to the Union, for such disposition as they wished to make of them so long as the proceeds went into education. The railroad corporations had been given immense tracts as incentive to open new country to settlement.

And a variety of homesteading and other devices put public land into myriads of private hands. It had been national policy to get rid of public domain as fast as possible from the birth of the republic. As recently as 1930 President Herbert Hoover had offered the remaining public lands to the western states if they would take them without title to any underlying minerals, only to have the offer refused. (In the preceding year Hoover had been awarded the title of Honorary President of the Izaak Walton League.)

Despite this, there had existed for years in the minds of scattered elements of the livestock industry a belief that no matter what their state officials thought, the grazing lands, at least, should go private. This showed up in numerous legislative measures in Congress. It had been voiced by witnesses before the Stanfield subcommittee in 1925, and speakers became more insistent as McCarran traveled about the West in the first half of the 1940s.

Elmer Brock told McCarran at Casper in September 1941 that "title or undisputed permanent control" of the ranges should be given to their users. Any further "regulation" was "unnecessary," he said.[3] Whatever "small revenues" went to the states in federal payments from grazing fees, or in expenditures for education, roads, and other things, were "in no sense a substitute for taxes" that private owners would pay after the lands were theirs. Next to the witness stand on that occasion came J. B. Wilson, long-time secretary of the Wyoming Wool Growers Association,[4] to back Brock and say his organization was officially "on record as asking that the lands be turned over to the states or sold." This united both cattlemen and sheepmen in what then should have been seen as an evolving movement. That it was not new was clearly shown in 1945, at Casper, by Wyoming's Governor Hunt when he declared [5] *"this we have heard many times before* but it bears repeating: that the federal government (1) either dispose of these [national] forests to private owners; or (2) to the respective states in which the federal lands are located"* (italics added).

Wyoming leaders of the Izaak Walton League had been urging the national staff to give greater attention to public lands matters for some time, but until the middle 1940s the League's official interest had been chiefly in the big game problem. In 1945 Charles E. Piersall and Harry L. Miner of Casper, with technological assistance by Dr. Scott, worked up a detailed indictment of the livestock leadership. Reid had been moving toward a similar conclusion and, for the first time so far as I am aware, publicly labeled the growing movement an incipient "land grab" in a talk before the Wyoming Division of the League in August 1945.[6]

Two months later an editorial Reid had written before heading west appeared in *Outdoor America,* the League magazine.[7] It urged members to bestir themselves "if you don't want to see the public lands converted into private ranges where . . . all public values will be subordinated to the demands of privately owned cattle and sheep." The league position was put in these words: "On the principle that the federal lands belong to all the people, with each citizen an equal shareholder, we are opposed to all legislation that . . . would give to individuals or groups rights superior to those of the government or the public."

Reid suffered a mild stroke two weeks after the Wyoming speech, but by January was back at his desk, where he wrote a resolution adopted by the League's executive board in January 1946, opposing any wholesale transfer of public lands to the states or to private owners. In March, at its first postwar convention, League delegates ratified the executive board action.[8] As the year wore on Reid and I corresponded with the Wyoming conservationists to assure mutual understanding of what they had written about the intentions of the land-grab clique, and to secure full documentation of their allegations.

In August, the formation of the Joint National Livestock Committee at Salt Lake City, and the publication of its mission, confirmed and supplemented what our people had written, and the public declarations of Brock, Winder, and others further reinforced our conviction that conservationists were in for a hell of a fight to keep the lands public. The Piersall–Miner indictment was published by the League in 1947 as a pamphlet,[9] *Our Western Public Lands,* in time to be used widely in later stages of the antigrab campaign.

Until about the end of 1946 we in the conservation movement believed the outdoorsmen of America were alone in their opposition to the grab. Picture, then, how we were stimulated and enthused by the publication in the January 1947 *Harper's* magazine of Bernard DeVoto's first articles on the land situation. They were his feature, "The West Against Itself," and his "Easy Chair" column, on a different aspect of the same subject. DeVoto had traveled across much of the West in the summer of 1946, and talked with people who could substantiate with scientific accuracy the evidence before his eyes of overgrazing and other range abuse. His short fuse was ignited, and his blazing entry on the scene let the nation know a new element had joined the conflict.[10]

We conservationists had few illusions about our strengths and weaknesses. We knew how small we were in numbers. The Izaak Walton League had barely 40,000 dues-paying members nationwide in 1947, and we were maintaining offices in Chicago and Denver, publishing our magazine, and rendering various services to the membership on a total budget of little more than $60,000 a year. Other respected conservation groups were seldom in better condition; few had endowments or other dollar resources of consequence. We relied largely on volunteers, and ruefully recognized that about 95 percent of all members were more interested in enlarging and extending outdoor recreational pursuits than attending to basic resource realities. The remainder looked to the fundamentals as the underpinning of our wealth as a nation, and considered the fish and game and other outdoor goodies as welcome by-products of good husbandry. With most of our members the urges that influenced them to join in the first place and kept them paying dues year after year usually were clean waters so game fish might thrive, and a verdant countryside to support abundant populations of game animals and birds to hunt as well as to delight the eyes and other senses. The chief task in our offices, as we conceived it, was to drive home to the larger mass of our people the truism that they would be guaranteed such fringe benefits only if they insisted that the basic resources upon which mankind depended for survival were appropriately used, with prudence and in a spirit of stewardship.

And we in the movement were a disparate crew. Did you ever try to reconcile the differing opinions of, say, an avid hunter of game birds with those of a dedicated watcher of all species of birdlife? As we moved toward confrontation we knew our shortcomings, but were not ashamed of our ragtag little army. The problem was to persuade more people to recognize that the battle for the public lands would be their battle, not just ours or some bureaucrat's. When Bennie DeVoto entered the fray the conservation leaders had just recently agreed on a mechanism—the Natural Resources Council—through which all major elements could collaborate to help put forward our conviction that for the well-being of the nation the fundamental resources must be saved from total exploitation or dissipation.

What I am saying is that in a period of a very few months we had seen (1) a crystallization of the determination of the livestock leaders to attempt the land grab; (2) a coming together of the once widely separated conservation organizations into a council that could help pass ammunition to and fro as obtained and needed; and (3) the emergence in the East as an advocate on our side of a formidable, dynamic, respected writer who had entree to prestigious journals and other forums we in the outdoor recreation field seldom could penetrate. This is not intended to denigrate the outdoor magazines where our writings *were* welcome. *Sports Afield, Field & Stream, Outdoor Life,* and other publications that catered to the growing millions of outdoor enthusiasts, many of whom might never read *Harper's,* eagerly published the facts about the land grab as furnished by us and our writing friends across the nation. And powerful elements of the western daily press, such as the Denver *Post* and Salt Lake City *Tribune,* were very unhappy over the land take-over attempt.

Arthur Hawthorne Carhart began his career with the Forest Service as a landscape architect—I believe he was its first—right after World War I. He was an early advocate of a national wilderness system, long before that became popular. He loved the Rockies, and in the 1930s was on the staff of the Colorado Game and Fish Commission. He was the author of several novels that had fair success as well as of nonfiction books about the outdoors, and was deep into more of these prestige builders while making enough money for daily needs by writing potboiler articles as a free lancer after he severed connections with the state agency. I had known him in the late 1930s when I first lived in Denver, but did not work closely with him until the spring of 1947.

Carhart was offered a small public relations sort of grant by eastern philanthropic sources to be used in a manner that could easily embrace combatting the entire land-grab undertaking of the livestock leadership, and we talked over how it might best be utilized. He was not a joiner, but saw the advantage of having an organizational base, so we explored ways in which the Izaak Walton League might serve that purpose. I talked it over with Reid and he agreed that we should cooperate. To safeguard our tax status and prevent possible other unpleasantnesses, I was to read and approve Carhart's pamphlet texts and so on before they might be published and distributed bearing the Izaak Walton League's name as sponsor.

This was the beginning of a fruitful relationship. Carhart was with us though not of us. We felt the same enthusiasm about DeVoto. We were sure he had a significant following, and many of his readers were men and women of considerable influence. It was nonsense to think of a merger of his friends and our conservation–recreation forces. Both could march toward the same objective but would do so to different drumbeats. Best be content to collaborate. We would imbue our people with a desire to take active part in one way or another. Let Benny's brigade move toward our common goal in whatever fashion it saw fit. So it was informally decided,[11] and so we proceeded.

For the most part, I remained in the wings in dealings with De-Voto and people he suggested we should meet or communicate with. Reid and Carhart were in touch with DeVoto more often than I. Indeed, one of my most vivid recollections is of a letter I received from Avis DeVoto, who became as concerned as her husband. She had made a rousing plea to a group of Boston women, to try to goad them to action against the land grab. Now she was back home in Cambridge sorting out her thoughts on the typewriter. She was plainly upset and angry. "Bill," she wrote, "those damned women thought conservation meant picking dead leaves off the geraniums!"

Carhart, Reid, DeVoto, and I were soon busy planning strategy. We fed DeVoto useful information. He alerted us to things he felt we could use to advantage. Some of our information found its way into more than forty articles and other writings DeVoto would devote to various aspects of western public land grazing over the years. He, on the other hand, helped Carhart get telling articles in such publications as *Atlantic Monthly* and Stanford University's *Pacific Spectator*. Carhart, certain others, and I often wrote "guest editorials" for the Denver *Post*, and seized upon clippings of articles and editorials helpful to our side in other publications. I have no records to substantiate it, but am convinced we must have printed or reprinted and distributed close to a half million pieces of literature of one kind or another between January 1947 and the end of the decade.

These would be useless unless sent to people who would read them and be impressed enough with their logic to become partisan on our side. To get them out to such people we had to have mailing lists. In time we accumulated considerable files of names and addresses that we used freely. However, Carhart's grant was so small we needed to enlist others in the mailings. While we secured lists of members of some organizations, we generally let leaders of such friendly groups know what leaflets, reprints, and so on, we had available. They in turn would tell us how many to ship in bulk to their offices to be distributed in their envelopes and at their expense.

When the Natural Resources Council of America was made operable in 1947, we assured that the general offices of all its constituent associations and societies were on our list of recipients of sample copies, and from them we received requests for large volumes of our give-away material.

Generally speaking, this was of two types. One was intended simply to inform about public land situations as they occurred or evolved. They were self-explanatory as a rule and could be employed in a variety of ways by our collaborators. Reprints often were sent with little more than a terse reference to a significant paragraph; at other times we might underline a sentence or two for emphasis. We printed a number of folders on specific subjects; two or more had to do with the Jackson Hole controversy and its relation to the land grab. The second variety was more directly concerned with the field hearings soon to be held by the Barrett subcommittee. These were directed to organizations we knew were or hoped would be friendly, some of them in or near communities where hearings would be held. We wanted to stimulate as many people as possible to become witnesses in opposition to the grab. We told them the stockmen's lobby and the association leaders had to be stopped at whatever cost, or something precious would be lost to all future generations of Americans. With our appeals for witnesses we sent background information that might or might not be used in statements by witnesses. In this we employed strategy similar to that of the stockmen in that we tried to lead our friends to say what we wanted said. We seldom tried to assign subjects, and at no hearing did we have a "parade marshal" to determine in what order our witnesses should speak their pieces, as the stockmen did at Rawlins, Grand Junction, Salt Lake City, and elsewhere. I doubt if we could have persuaded Barrett to let us do so if we had attempted it. One outcome was that a searcher could find the gist of the stockmen's complaints and arguments conveniently grouped for reference, whereas he would have to poke through an entire transcript to find our opposing testimony.

Our campaign to counter the grab soon brought association reaction. Publications of both the national stock organizations and of their state affiliates, as well as a few newspapers and magazines that favored the industry point of view, began printing defensive articles and editorials. Each one that came to our attention seemed to give us a little more ammunition for our own propaganda guns.

And we were elated in the summer of 1947 when *Collier's* magazine, with millions of readers, anticipated what did not eventuate and published a two-part article by Lester Velie under the scare title of "They Kicked Us Off Our Land." [12] How this agitated the stock lobby and Barrett!

The associations showed their muscle in several ways. At one point they persuaded several small-town radio stations in Colorado and Wyoming to keep off the air a program opposing the land grab that Dr. Albert Croft of the Denver University faculty had already broadcast from a local station.[13]

It was done in a more sinister way at Casper. Charles E. Piersall, one of our Wyoming leaders, a distributor for a large oil corporation, was boycotted and forced out of business because of his courageous denunciations of the land-grab movement. The Casper *Herald-Tribune,* which supported the stockmen editorially, nevertheless praised Piersall and decried what had happened to him. My story about it in *Outdoor America* called it gangsterism.[14] Yes, we used language as strong as any livestock leader. A recent DeVoto biography by Wallace Stegner quoted from a letter Dr. Garrett Mattingly wrote De-Voto in which this passage appears: [15]

There comes a point in writing history, as in every other activity, where conscience is just a God damned nuisance. You have to kick it in the teeth and say, "Shut up and lie down and let me get about my business."

We of the conservation community, as DeVoto was admonished, kicked our consciences in the teeth when the time came to get r'iled up, and we came out flinging at the stock lobby whatever from our vocabularies was then considered fit to print, stopping well short of libel, however. We did not believe rank and file stockmen had organized the boycott against Charlie Piersall, nor did we believe they had organized the land grab and were sure a goodly number of permittees did not support it. But in our eagerness to blast the leaders into oblivion perhaps we sometimes struck innocent ranchers unintentionally, or swung so freely that they might be considered among our targets. Some of our friends in the industry began to plead that we be more specific, saying we were giving the righteous among them as black an eye as the dastards. Thereafter we quit using the all-inclusive term "stockmen" and tried to single out specific groups and individuals whose policies we thought destructive.[16]

Carhart and I regarded ourselves as western field captains, so to speak, in the front lines of the controversy, leading volunteer helpers.

As the year wore on, local conservation leaders began to communicate with us in increasing numbers, seeking ammunition we were happy to supply. Reid, at the general offices of the League in Chicago, was our commander-in-chief, and in general coordinated League activities with those of leaders of other groups in the conservation community. And DeVoto was an eastern Patton, goading his followers incessantly and threatening the livestock lobby with apoplexy with every burning sentence ripped from his typewriter.

I still have warm admiration and a feeling of gratitude toward all those volunteers out across the land who loaded the ammunition we furnished and fired it in their own way and at the best or handiest target. I have no numbers to cite and doubt if anyone could assemble 'reliable statistics, but am confident that thousands of letters, telegrams, phone calls, and personally delivered messages against the land grab went to members of Congress from all over the United States. Much later, when we were engaged in still another contest with the livestock leaders, this time over the power grab in the Eisenhower administration, Secretary of Agriculture Ezra Taft Benson reported to the White House that letters were pouring in and ran against the industry by 100 to 1.[17] Members of Congress from districts so distant from the scene of actual conflict that it may have seemed almost alien country, learned that some, at least, of their constituents knew of the grab and wanted no part of it.

I still wear a slightly crooked smile at the memory of a visit to my home country in south Georgia in 1949. A dear lady there had never heard of the Izaak Walton League, nor did she read DeVoto. But when I spoke of the fight to prevent the land grab her eyes lighted up and she nodded approvingly. "We didn't let them take our land, did we!" she exclaimed. The odds are high that she never said or wrote a word on the subject to any member of Congress or anyone else, but the word had got to her some way, she knew the outcome, and mentally associated herself with our side. So it may have been with others, but enough did write or talk to elected officials to cause the grab to abort.

The depth and permanence of what was accomplished can be debated by any who wish to take sides, and a few did belittle [18] our efforts. Carhart and I felt we had reason to be sure the total conservation effort had got pretty deeply under the hides of the land-grab leaders. This was reflected in many ways—by the frequency with which we were criticized, by the intensity of feeling in oral or written communication, and by the stature in the livestock camp of our assailants. Our writings and those of DeVoto and others set the would-be grabbers on fire.

They were at or near the peak of their ire when Congressman Barrett of Wyoming set out on the Wild West Show circuit in the summer of 1947.

10

The Politics of Fear

Back in 1936, shortly after he was appointed director of range management for the Forest Service, Walt Dutton sent a questionnaire to about a hundred supervisors of western national forests.

"I wanted to find out," Dutton told me in 1972,[1] "why overuse of national forest land . . . continued when all of our technical knowledge indicated there was terrific damage. And practically every supervisor told us it was fear . . ." brought on by "pressure from members of Congress and influential livestock associations."

That was pressure upon officials at the grass roots, literally speaking. In the 1940s it was to be applied, as probably never before, to those at intermediate and higher levels as well, to try to instill the same sort of fear at the heart of the agency that the supervisors had said was prevalent at its extremities. And it turns out that the Service had no Pinchot in its front office, and no Teddy Roosevelt in the White House to provide the support needed by those down the line.

In this part of the present account it is necessary to travel main roads and side trails of narrative, some leading straight ahead, others going off on tangents. There are highlights and sidelights, all pertinent but needing weighted values which in some instances I don't feel fully capable of allotting. So, where such comes out, let the facts speak for themselves. I'll put my best interpretation upon them but cannot be objective for I was both participant and spectator. What did the Barrett committee do? The leading stockmen and their friends? People in the service? And we of the conservation movement? A good bit of the last named is in the previous chapter.

Dutton wrote [2] me at the end of 1971 that in all the forty-two

years he was a forester, from 1911 to 1953, "there was no real progress in stopping range destruction"; the Service, the industry, and Congress all had "failed outright to take or support corrective action."
Though he was devoted to the Service and had kept his counsel for
nearly twenty years after retirement, he must in honesty say that for
a long period the Service's policymakers were "guilty of the most
criminal neglect of the range resource."

Coming from Dutton these words were extraordinary. It was as
though conscience had burst the confines of discretion and loyalty
and a natural tendency toward peaceful coexistence and compromise
that had ruled his life for four decades. What he wrote me deserves to
be read more than once, with the former official's habits of a lifetime
borne in mind. He seemed to welcome the opportunity to unburden
himself at last and spoke and wrote freely in our exchanges.

It was as seemingly determined elements at high levels of the
Service were at last moving positively to try to halt the damage
wrought, by bringing livestock use within range-carrying capacity,
that the stock associations struck through the Barrett committee.
World War II was over. Sons were home again, and hired help was
available. Materials and supplies had begun to flow through peacetime channels of trade. The livestock industry, by and large, was
as healthy as it could remember; animal numbers all over the United
States were high, and western ranchers operating on public lands appeared to be in position to absorb needed reductions unplagued
either by a poor market or widespread drought. But the industry's
leaders were almost frantic on the subject of cuts; cuts were unthinkable, not to be tolerated under any circumstances. Yet cuts, some
deep enough to hurt, were actually being applied for the grazing season of 1946, and the Service was talking of more to come. So the
word went out to attack, to fire every gun.

It was in such an era and atmosphere that the Barrett hearings [3]
affecting the Service began in Washington on May 21, 1947. At the
start Barrett bowed to tradition. The authorizing resolution was
brought forth, and he made an opening statement. To prove that the
Service had defied Congress and refused to cooperate, he put in the
record exchanges of letters [4] between Congressman R. J. Welch of
California, chairman of the House Committee on Public Lands, and
Clinton P. Anderson, Secretary of Agriculture. The letters signed by
Welch doubtless were drafted in Barrett's office; those from Anderson
probably were written or initialed by Watts before being sent over to

the Secretary's office for signature. All was more or less standard practice.

On February 2 Welch asked Anderson to declare a moratorium on livestock reductions until Barrett finished his hearings and reported the findings of his investigation. On February 19 Anderson told Welch cuts already were being applied and should be continued for 1947; however, he would be happy to discuss 1948 adjustments at the chairman's convenience. Not good enough, responded Welch on February 21. Sorry, said Anderson on March 11; if cuts were now suspended there would be serious undesirable results, far-reaching dislocations; and plans in effect could not easily be modified at this late date. Range would continue to deteriorate; therefore, the Service must continue on course. These were firm words, indicating determination and a conviction that the actions under way were the right ones and must prevail.

Then Watts was called to the stand.[5] He was flanked at the table by Granger, Dutton, and other specialists. Watts, too, followed ritual. He read a statement that brought forward from Pinchot's time the story of range conditions, and outlined Service policy. The forests provided mostly summer range for 20 percent of the West's nondairy cattle herd and for 75 percent of its deer and elk. Most outdoor recreation in the West was enjoyed on the forests and it was growing rapidly. He considered the Service's task was to provide the largest possible total of "composite benefits," not grazing alone. Fees were low, and he reminded that all young of permitted herds and flocks grazed free of charge. Here he seemed to be telling Barrett and his fellow committeemen that in grazing costs at least these stockmen had a good thing. Though substantial cuts in grazing had been made over the years they had not yet offset the "cumulative effect" of long and serious overuse. "About half" of some ten thousand allotments required more reductions, some minor, some great; a few involved "total exclusion." Many permittees agreed with the need for cuts, but the outcry from others was loud and anguished. Watts made other points, but these describe the tenor and tone of his statement. It indicated no disposition to cave in; it was affirmative without being belligerent. Then he sat back to await committee questions.

Though some of the questions asked appeared to be the result of random thought, most showed the influence of industry complaints and covered just about all the points of consequence that would be made later in the field. I suspect, in hindsight, that Barrett wanted to get into the record at Washington policy statements that could be compared with what Service officials might say months later in the heat of debate at hearings in the West. Were Service policies intended to protect the economies of cow towns near the forests? [6] Not one word about whether they were intended to protect the resource base that made the existence of those towns possible. What was the history and philosophy of the grazing fee system? [7] Not whether the fee system gave the nation's treasury a rightful return for what the permittees were privileged to enjoy. Had the Service found it practical to increase permitted grazing anywhere in the West? [8] Ironically, this had been possible mostly in Montana, which (also in hindsight) seemed to demonstrate that the reductions ordered under Regional Forester Evan W. Kelley in the late 1930s and early 1940s, helped by generally favorable precipitation, were proving out. How extensive were the cuts being imposed? [9] Servicewide, in the West, responded Dutton, they amounted to 1.3 percent of cattle AUMs for 1947, 1.6 percent for sheep; these affected 4.6 percent of all cattle ranges, 4.7 percent of sheep allotments. (The Service often dealt in averages in its statements of various sorts, and often these looked innocuous enough. However, a small average meant nothing to the individual who found himself reduced by a large percentage figure while a neighbor on good range might get no cut at all or even be increased by a few AUMs.)

Barrett was quite upset over a Forest Service pamphlet that reproduced what others, on both sides of the controversy, had been saying in print.[10] He did not think the Service should tell both sides of the story. Congressman Robert Rockwell, from a particularly sensitive western Colorado district, hinted [11] that Service appropriations should be reduced. For daring to print such stuff it should be hit in the pocketbook—as the stock industry's publications had been demanding recently and as had been done to the Interior Department's BLM.

And, Barrett wanted to know, what had the Service done to correct range conditions other than "to continually reduce" stock numbers and seasons? Here the reply by Watts reads like a mild plea for more range improvement [12] funds, and they may have implied more than we read into them at the time. Barrett's closing words to Watts and his assistants were: *"We are only trying to keep you in line"* [13] (italics added). What line? Whose line?

About the time of the Washington hearing, the magazine *Sports Afield* published an article by Carhart titled "This is YOUR Land!" [14]

in which he drove home the realities of the land grab. He made a special point of saying something that cannot be emphasized too much. It was that the grab had been initiated and was being pushed by "a determined little group," a small band "of grasping operators" who had been allowed "to build up the impression that *they* are the industry" (italics in original). Only a "fraction" of western stockmen, he wrote, had these "greedy and predatory intentions"; while "man after man, stalwart, clear-thinking ranchers oppose transferring these public lands to private interests."

There was more than just a desire to clarify the record in Carhart's repetitive dividing of the western livestock industry into the massive majority who wore white hats and that avaricious clique on whose heads he had clapped black Stetsons. Carhart *wanted* the "good guys" to know he recognized them for what they were and that he was not taking potshots at them. He hoped the overwhelming numbers of upstanding ranchers would support a land conserving position by the land managing agencies of government and not be swayed by the rhetoric of the elected and staff leaders of the associations. Carhart's efforts in that direction may not have been the decisive factor—a sense of the-right-thing-to-do may have had more effect —but it is true that a number of smaller associations and of individual stockmen of influence sided with the federal agencies; even one Interior Department grazing district advisory board did so! [15]

The previous chapter described many things done to ready our largely uncoordinated forces for the ordeals of the hearings and their possible aftermath. One letter of instruction we sent to potential witnesses over my signature was inserted in the record [16] of the hearing at Grand Junction, Colorado, on September 5, 1947. I wanted our witnesses to ask some questions of their own, such as (1) whether the Service had been diligently protecting the forests with due consideration for their *multiple* uses, (2) whether undue pressure had been put upon the Service to favor one or another class of user or whether one or another user element had in fact been favored to the detriment of national forest resources, and (3) whether the forests in their areas were truly being administered for the greatest good of the greatest number through the years. Those questions mirrored the tack we took in our effort to buck up the Service as the hearings progressed. We hoped to start a backfire against the pressures being applied so as to provide relief from the burden. If we could demonstrate that the Service had broad public support, it might keep iron in its spine and a firm resolve to act only in the public interest. And even if we could not sway the Barrett troupe, we might influence other congressmen.

The temptation is strong to quote at length from the transcript of the Barrett field hearings, and some parts will be quoted in the next chapter. In my view nothing is more damning of Barrett and most of his subcommittee members than their own words. Nor could anything be more convincing evidence of our contentions—Carhart's, DeVoto's, Reid's, Gabrielson's, mine, and others in the conservation camp—that the bawling and bellowing came from only a small, militant, usually well-to-do particle of the generally constructive, middle-of-the-road western livestock industry.

The same names that appeared so frequently in the records of the McCarran hearings of the first half of the decade showed in the lists of witnesses before the Barrett hearings. In fact, some of the stockmen who were complaining to the Stanfield subcommittee in 1925 were noted in the McCarran and Barrett hearing records of a generation later. And as will be shown in a later chapter, some of Barrett's witnesses lived to urge wholesale public land disposal in the last half of the 1960s. Old yearnings die hard.

When McCarran and Barrett were riding the western range country the solid core of the livestock industry who disapproved of the grab usually kept quiet about it. They would talk privately with us, and Carhart assembled about twenty-five resolutions [17] of opposition from those local stock associations that were happy in their relations with the Forest Service, but that is as far as they tended to go. A fellow shouldn't stir up more trouble in his home territory than he could handle without strain. Few in this category of permittee even bothered to go to the hearings; most stayed at home to tend their flocks and herds.

An impression the record bolsters is that Barrett let complaining witnesses ramble on for pages about piddling squabbles with forest officials, some of which were comparatively ancient history, oft-told tales. He often asked leading questions and encouraged extravagant complaining language. This he gave sympathetic attention. By way of contrast, it was Barrett's custom to pounce upon real or fancied weaknesses in statements by supporters of the Forest Service and to bore in like a lawyer for the defense on cross examination in a criminal trial. I commend the full hearing record to students of political science and psychology. For this part of my narrative, the sheer volume of choice phrasemaking as well as of significant but more prosaic language limits me to impressions and highlights.

One day in my office when we were planning strategy ahead of the field hearings, Carhart telephoned Benton Stong, then on the staff of James Patton, president of the National Farmers Union, with headquarters in Denver. Art knew the union had many members in Montana, where the first field hearings would be held. We thought it would be a stroke for our side if we could show substantial opposition to the grab at the outset. So, could Stong get some of the union members, who mostly were small farmers and stock raisers who had little in common with the livestock associations, to attend at Glasgow and Billings, even to make a few statements in support of the Service? Stong didn't hesitate.

"How many do you want at the courthouse, Art? Will two hundred irate farmers do?" asked Stong.

Carhart allowed as how two hundred might be enough, and chuckled as he turned to relay the conversation to me.

I can't say whether all two hundred of Stong's "irate farmers" turned out at Glasgow on August 27 or at Billings on the 30th, but promised representation from the Montana branch of the Farmers Union was on hand at both places. Richard Shipman of Lewistown, Montana union president, put his group squarely against the land grab in his statement at Billings.[18] Several other members spoke out firmly in support of the Forest Service at both towns. And Stong testified at Grand Junction.

At no time during the hearings did Barrett himself go on record as advocating the "disposal" of national forest lands. The closest he came to anything approaching it was in his opening statement at Glasgow; [19] there he expressed the opinion that all federal grazing lands should be administered by the Bureau of Land Management, whose Taylor Grazing lands were the announced objective of the Joint National Livestock Committee. Put the national forests in Interior, therefore, and if the grab was successful no doubt they would automatically go in the pork barrel. Though Barrett had promised the Joint Committee that if it drew wide support he would introduce give-away legislation, he was careful throughout the rest of the hearings to refrain from anything that even hinted at a land grab, even when eager advocates brought up the subject of their own volition.

Nor was Barrett the only politician who had grown wary. Senator E. V. Robertson of Wyoming, the sheepman from the Big Horn basin who had introduced grab legislation prematurely in the Seventy-ninth Congress,[20] appeared at both Montana hearings, where he piously proclaimed that no land grab bills *were then pending,* which was true. At Billings [21] he voiced what seemingly had become the expedient thing to say, that favoring a land grab was "not a sound position to take." Earlier that same month Robertson sent broadcast across Wyoming a mimeographed statement in which he divorced himself completely from any grab and protested that he never, but never, had ever wanted the remaining public lands to go private.[22] As an aside, it may be noted that in the 1948 election Robertson was repudiated by Wyoming voters. Ironically, he was beaten by Barrett.

Barrett made no pretense of being objective while in the chair. The subcommittee was in the field "to hear complaints against the Forest Service," [23] so all discontented cowmen and sheepmen should come forward and tell their stories. Barrett was intensely unhappy because members of Congress from the East were complaining that grazing fees charged by the agencies were too low. When George Mungas of Phillipsburg, spokesman for the Montana Joint Livestock Committee on Public Lands, said permittees were afraid to speak out because, he alleged, threats were made by Service personnel that they might lose their grazing privileges, Barrett quickly picked up the ball. He said bluntly [24] that he would not condone that sort of thing; no way! And what did Mr. Watts have to say about it? Mr. Watts was just as emphatically opposed, he said, and would the gentleman kindly furnish him names and dates and places? The record does not show that any were supplied. And, as he often did when a complaining stockman was on the stand, Barrett led Mungas into agreeing that the only thing the Service knew how to do about a bad range situation was to cut numbers.

P. D. (Pete) Hanson, then regional forester for the area, came on right after Mungas to dispute his testimony. Hanson said the heavy cuts needed on national forests of Montana had been made back in the 1930s when Major Kelley headed the regional staff, and, in fact, the ranges had improved so much under favorable climatic conditions that increases had been granted in numbers of permitted cattle. As for sheep, yes, total numbers were down, but there were open sheep ranges vacant right then because of lack of demand. Hanson did not say so, but it is well to remember that this was the era when synthetic fabrics were making their first great inroad on the woolen textiles industry, with consequences that have continued and show no signs of a reverse trend.

Earlier in the 1940s, when McCarran carried on his extended investigations, he usually refused to hear witnesses with individual or personal grievances. He said he was there to look into matters that had a bearing on land management policies. Not so with Barrett; he often listened as witnesses recalled in biased detail episodes that had been settled years earlier.[25] The individual cases covered a variety of actions or situations. One of the more frequent was trespass, which could consist of many kinds of rule infractions. Allegations of favoritism were made, and pursued vigorously by Barrett. By far the most complaints, however, referred to cuts, which the witnesses almost invariably declared were neither necessary nor proper.

Each one brought another reminder that the chief forester who had been brought in by FDR to reorganize and tighten up the Service in the Depression 1930s had followed a far more lenient course as to stock numbers and time than the ranges could stand up under. Silcox's go-easy policy, though defended because of hard times, led to the essentiality of deep cuts here and there in the succeeding permit period, and it coincided with the crack-down on the Grazing Service, the crystalization of the land-grab plan, and a general belief by the livestock leaders that if they didn't like what was being done by the Service—or any other land managing agency—they could get relief through their congressmen. At Rawlins Congressman Robert Rockwell of Colorado, a stockman, reminded the Service that in the previous permit term he had been reduced only 20 percent, with an arbitrary limit of 5 percent in any one year. Dutton, who replied,[26] was careful not to criticize his chief's predecessor, but responded that the Service had often been in a bind because much greater reductions had been needed but could not be made because of the Silcox commitment. The statement went without comment by the committeemen at the time, but Dutton's reply was one more refutation of the stockmen's leaders that the Service's actions were capricious and irresponsible. Rather, it should have evoked new recognition that society, or some affected segment of society, must inevitably pay for even humanitarian concessions that run counter to the harsh realities of nature.

The hearing at Rawlins, Wyoming, on September 2 and 3, 1947, may have been exceeded only by the one that followed at Grand Junction for industry hyperbole, boisterousness, ranting by committeemen and witnesses alike, and excesses that never should have been permitted by a hearing chairman. It was the hearings at these Region 2 cities that caused the Denver *Post* to say editorially that they reminded of nothing so much as a Buffalo Bill-type Wild West Show. The label stuck. Carhart and I used it gleefully, spreading reprints of the editorial all across the land.

In opening statements at the hearings Barrett usually made a brief reference to the dire things that had happened to the former Grazing Service. He would then ingratiate himself still further with Taylor land users by reminding them that he had sponsored a small supplemental appropriation so the new Bureau of Land Management could provide essential services for its livestock clientele. The threat and the promise were unmistakable. The Forest Service must take notice or it, too, would be emasculated, and Barrett and his western conferees in Congress would whet the castrating knives. The promise was that if the Service officials proved to be docile, they would find Barrett their friend.

The Service could not afford to take lightly threats by Barrett and Rockwell to cut funds. The power of the western members to chop off a supply of agency money had been proved to the Forest Service that very year. For some time it had been given a minor annual appropriation for "game management," to support a small staff that studied the relationship of big game numbers to available summer and winter range, and consulted with state game officials as to seasons, bag limits, and related subjects. The item budgeted for fiscal year 1948 was only $160,000. It was killed, as was a similar sum budgeted for fiscal 1949.[27] So the threat was real. Next time something more vital might be taken away. The game management item was unobtrusively restored for fiscal 1950, but by that time range management in the Forest Service was coming to look like a whole new ball game, with the stockmen at bat.

It was a physical impossibility to move all Service records into the courthouses where the hearings generally were held. So, when a stockman told his side of a complaint the Service people responding usually refused to rely on memory for sometimes obscure facts or long ago actions. Barrett was told the files would be searched and a response forwarded to Washington to be included in the printed report. Thus the audiences heard only one side, and I suspect most of the committeemen did, too, for eventually the record ran to 1,500 printed pages, with responses to complaints in seldom-read small type. Doubt as to Service fairness and integrity planted by recitals of what in many cases was ancient history, matters long since settled except in the memories of the complaining witnesses, lingered on.

It looks to me now as though Barrett went west from Washington thinking he would have a picnic at the field hearings and was brought up short at the start, in Montana, by the strength of the public support exhibited there for the Forest Service. The Farmers Union showing was impressive, and to its statements were added a number from sportsmen's organizations and others. At Rawlins the stock associations had things mostly their way at the outset, with speaker after speaker called up in his turn to voice his grievances. Perhaps Barrett, who saw strange faces in the audience, hoped the conservationists would simply go away. They didn't. They sat patiently through long hours of testimony adverse to the Service, and of haranguing by Barrett and others of the committee. In the end, the sheer numbers of witnesses wanting to testify forced Barrett to abandon plans for sightseeing and continue the hearings through a second day.

At Grand Junction the booing and foot-stomping audience was packed for the most part with hostile stockmen from the nearby Uncompahgre and Grand Mesa National Forests, in both of which severe depletion had been allowed and where organized permittees who had repeatedly obstructed the Service in times past even then were doggedly refusing to submit to needed reductions. There the same determination not to be outwaited paid off again for the conservationists. Barrett had to run his Wild West Show until nearly midnight to hear those who stayed to speak, though he arbitrarily cut all witnesses back to a five-minute maximum at the evening session. The record indicates the night session might have been avoided if Barrett had listened only to testimony that concerned Service policy and had cut short all that was irrelevant.

Salt Lake City, on September 8, differed little from Rawlins and Grand Junction in the division of time between the competing sides, but there was less ranting and some reference to problems brought on by the division of estates over so many years in large-family Mormon country. The visible record in the nearby landscape and the foothill towns and cities of what overgrazing the Wasatch Front had brought on was striking evidence of the extent the ranges had been misused.

A marked change came over the hearings as they progressed southward in California and eastward to Ely, Nevada. At Redding the overgrazing problems of the Modoc National Forest dominated as Chairman Welch presided over a hearing by the full Public Lands Committee. At San Francisco one state official made a point[28] that no other witnesses had broached or perhaps even recognized as existing. It was that bad basic conditions on the West Coast were tied directly to the rapid growth of its human population. Though statements generally were more moderate than at Barrett hearings, the stockmen clearly were given the advantage in time at both hearings; at Redding they had four hours for planned presentations, first by cowmen, then by sheepmen, before anybody else had a chance to speak.

At San Francisco about half the hearing had to do with water matters and the rest, on grazing, was muted in tone. The Fresno hearing again saw a parade marshal take charge of presentations by stockmen, but they said little new. A complete turnabout came at San Bernardino. This was Izaak Walton League country, mostly urbanized, and the home folks had taken to heart information Carhart and I had sent them. Not one spokesman for the livestock industry appeared; our side had the floor unimpeded, for the first and only time.

At Ely, Barrett faced three hostile camps against only one that favored the livestock leaders' position. Southeastern Nevada has a large copper-mining and smelting industry, and corporation officials, union leaders, and conservation organizations all spoke solidly against any interference with administration by the Forest Service. This was not what Barrett seems to have expected. Vernon Metcalf, the knowledgeable staff executive of the Nevada Livestock Production Credit Association, was on hand and opened [29] with a long exposition of why national forest lands in Nevada should be turned over to the Bureau of Land Management. Ranch operations in Nevada were intermingled "meat factories," he said, and all that was not private should be put in one federal agency—BLM—the one that already was effectively down and hogtied and which would be the target if the land grabbers had their way.

But when Metcalf finally ran down—Barrett himself announced he had spoken for more than an hour—the copper, union, and conservation interests moved in, and did so decisively. Barrett's hearing engine ran out of steam. He abruptly cancelled the projected hearing at Phoenix, Arizona—where conservationists were also well organized—and went back to Washington. There he wrote a letter to Secretary Anderson making six demands in the name of his subcommittee. Anderson replied to the effect that five of the six already were Forest Service policy, and the last, asking again for a three-year moratorium on cuts, would not be granted.[30]

The Wild West performance was over. It looked to Carhart and me as though what had started out as a gala stock show, with everything going beautifully on cue, had come to a close much short of a standing ovation. Yet from our view something seemed oddly wrong. This came more as a feeling of uneasiness than firm conviction; there was nothing we could pinpoint. We gloated over a victory that became elusive as time passed. We felt we had more than held our own—all of us combined—especially at Rawlins and Grand Junction, despite the handicaps. We believed the Forest Service had come through the time of trial without loss, that the grab was dead, and that all would be well from then forward. We were mistaken. Something had happened, though just when is hard to say. My conviction is that at some point during the summer and early fall, top level Service will to stand up against the weight and variety of pressures it bore began to weaken, then bent and broke. I think it became obvious to the Service leaders that the conservation movement might be able to fire up its followers for an occasional all-out effort but that it could not sustain sufficient support to prevail day after day and year after year against the livestock associations, which were well heeled, adequately staffed, and skillfully represented in the field and in Washington. We were the kind who would write letters to the President which would be bucked to the Forest Service for reply, while the livestock lobbyist was sitting in the inner office of a western congressman, calling him by his first name and reminding him of favors given in the last election.

This needs further examination and will get it, for it is an oversimplification, but right now we should return to Barrett's road show and some of the individual performers.

11

Throwing Long Ropes

Something more than the fact that they were so often held in county courtrooms lent a criminal trial atmosphere to the Barrett field hearings. At the bench sat the chairman after the fashion of a presiding judge, flanked by his congressional associates. Down front at a table near the witness chair were the Chief Forester and his fellow "defendants." The hard benches were generally crowded with partisan spectators. In contrast to the decorum of a traditional courtroom proceeding, however, persons in the booted audiences were ready to stomp, boo, or applaud as on cue.

In towns where the livestock leadership had its story line well planned and its witnesses in hand, the first hearing hours were similar. A leader called his people forward in some form of order. Thereafter, as time remained, stockmen with complaints who were not in the leader's lineup, and persons with other views, were called more or less at random.

Complainants' stories often were repetitious. This was partly due to the fact that the associations had solicited the kinds of complaints they thought would be effective, partly because by the nature of range stock operations, complaints normally would tend to follow a group of patterns. At only the San Bernardino hearing, toward the end of the line, did presentations from what I have dubbed "our" side show some preparation ahead of time. At other hearings statements of the conservation group spokesmen and unaffiliated individuals seemed more spontaneous, unrehearsed.

I have attributed to earlier Service reductions in Montana the fact that so little rabble-rousing talk came from livestock witnesses at Glasgow and Billings. Most national forests in Montana had natural climatic advantages and, as previously related, much range use had been more or less amicably brought near if not below carrying capacity in recent times. Consequently, when Barrett came along permittees who might earlier have been nettled had discovered that the region's policies and practices actually worked to their advantage. We can pass over Glasgow and Billings and go on to more spectacular and significant doings farther along the road.

At Rawlins in Region 2,[1] as at other hearings, Barrett implied that there had been threats of reprisal if permittees complained, and he wanted them to be uncowed, so to speak, fearless because their champion and protector stood before them. As for those dastardly writers who stirred up so much trouble—DeVoto, Velie, and others—they were unwanted. "We can solve our problems . . . without their advice," Barrett declared. The Service had better behave, too. He would return to these themes often, and stockmen present seemed to love them.

Reynald Seaverson of Rawlins, president of the Wyoming Wool-growers Association and a sizable operator, put in the Rawlins record nearly all the standard complaints.[2] A permittee of the Forest Service had no stability and the Service had no coordinated land-use policy. Stockmen had experienced forty years of national forest range "experiments" without beneficial results, so now Congress should take control and lay down policies. The only corrective measure the Service knew how to apply was an "arbitrary and dictatorial" reduction when an "allegedly" bad range situation arose. The Service could not make a case for overgrazing when fat stock came off the ranges year after year. Service superiors or their successors in field positions repudiated or ignored commitments made by underlings or predecessors; there was "flagrant disregard" for "agreements" made with range users. Service officials were "capricious." The Service would set up advisory boards and ignore them. Little control of grass-eating rodents was done and it looked as though the government wanted big game to eat all the forage. The permittees wanted the right to appeal to the courts when there was a dispute. They wanted a total reappraisal of all public lands, with stockmen among the appraisers, after which the government would be divested of that which produced forage, leaving to it only the fully timbered regions and such other areas as were needed to protect water supplies.

Cattle on good grass, Dixie National Forest, Utah, 1941. Note streaks of snow in mountain gashes in distance. *USFS photo*

It was strange to us that in the face of testimony such as Seaverson's, so many of his associates could follow him to the stand and blandly deny that a land grab had been contemplated.

When Seaverson asserted the Service would not give permittees written grazing agreements for fear higher-ups would repudiate them, Watts broke in [3] to demand that the statement be documented.

"I'm one of the higher-ups you are talking about," he said. "Give me the names of men afraid to stand by agreements."

Seaverson replied it was all oral, done by men in the field, whereupon Congressman John Sanborn of Idaho, a committeeman, observed that if an agreement was so weak it could not be put in writing it must have been worthless from the start. Thereafter Seaverson retreated somewhat.

Soon Barrett was attacking Lester Velie again,[4] intimating that the Service had conspired with him, DeVoto, and other writers. "If the Forest Service collaborated in any way with these writers whose articles attempt to make scoundrels and crooks out of the stockmen. . . , you have done a disservice to the United States of America."

Watts replied that Velie and DeVoto made independent investigations but the Service had answered their questions just as it had those of all others who sought information, including stock association writers. Barrett persisted. "Now, I'm not afraid of Mr. Velie. . . . Any of the organizations, such as the Izaak Walton League and its Mr. Voigt, that tell me that I've got to take that nonsense from Velie or anybody else are off their base." This was prompted by the fact that Barrett had "invited" Velie to come to Rawlins to repeat before the committee what he'd written for *Collier's* and I'd wired Velie not to do so. He'd be "crucified" on the stand, I said, and I gave the press a copy of my telegram.

Senator Robertson displayed a copy of a pamphlet [6] I helped write and publish for our campaign. Its cover picture showed good grass on one side of a barbed wire fence, denuded range on the other. It made the senator very unhappy. He hinted we must have had a Service subsidy. Furthermore, the pamphlet did not display the oval logo of the Allied Printing Trades Council, which Robertson seemed to consider reprehensible. As for Velie's writings, they were no less than "scurrilous." [7] When I was on the stand later I told [8] Robertson we of the League had published the pamphlet with no help from the Service except permission to use the cover photo, which I had selected.

After Seaverson, Ferdinand E. Mollin of Denver, staff executive of the American National Livestock Association (cattle), gave the committee his organization's views.[9] Reductions by the Service were unreasonable. Every permittee he heard from complained of instability of his operations, and many believed the Service's goal was total exclusion of livestock from the forests. His people wanted grazing use of forest range recognized specifically in the law. The Service made all the decisions, even when there were appeals to the Secretary of Agriculture—which likely was true. The Service had "more generals and fewer privates than the Mexican Army." It blamed the industry for everything but "flying saucers," which "it must have overlooked." Mollin admitted in reply to a Robertson question that his association had indeed adopted a resolution advocating disposal, but it was not much and he said that the stockmen only wanted a tiny bit of national forest range.

With some exceptions, the statements and allegations by Seaverson and Mollin were typical. A great deal of committee and witness time and hundreds of pages of transcript likely could have been saved if late comers—on both sides—had merely said, "Me, too."

The associations wanted the generally favorable image of science on their side, but the outcome for the Service was at worst a

Herded sheep in good condition on Gifford Pinchot National Forest, Washington, 1949. Mount Adams in distance. *USFS photo*

standoff. Two agronomists from the University of Wyoming at Laramie said there was little overused range on the forests they studied.[10] They were countered by two Service scientists, who said that was not true. One conceded there were spots where good grass could be found, but in other areas nearby the grass "wouldn't hide a baseball" at a hundred yards.[11]

The service position was strengthened when our Dr. Scott, founder of the National Committee on Policies in Conservation Education and a national director of the Izaak Walton League, testified.[12] Before World War I, he said, cattle from the Laramie plains often topped the Denver market, but no more. The 1931–1939 drought cycle helped finish off the long continuing process of range depletion, with effects still visible. In these years, he said, "starving cattle and sheep, after eating every shred of palatable dried grass they could find, waded into the muck of drying ponds and swamps to eat cattails and other coarse green vegetation they wouldn't touch" in normal times. While vegetation densities could vary as much as 50 percent between dry and wet years, livestock numbers in Wyoming had varied less than 10 percent during the droughty decade and no more than 5 percent from one year to the next. Range had to de-

Telltale contour trails show effects of long, heavy use of this range on Wasatch National Forest, Utah. Year not given, probably in 1930s. *USFS photo*

teriorate as a result. Stock grazing should be reduced to what the range could carry in a year of minimum moisture; long-term increases in meat poundage would make it worth while. As he closed, Congressman A. L. Miller of Nebraska commented that Scott had given the committee more practical information than it had heard from all others up to that point.

The next day Dr. Olaus J. Murie of Moose, Wyoming, recipient in 1951 of The Wildlife Society's coveted Aldo Leopold Medal, author of many technical and lay writings, the country's most knowledgeable expert on elk, an outstanding wildlife artist, a scientist whose list of honors for his contributions to wildlife management would fill pages, bluntly told the committee [13] that the Service's range research findings should be followed or the entire program abolished.

My statement [14] was a plea for truly multiple use of the national forests in the public interest, favoring neither stockman, logger, miner, hunter, fisherman, nor recreationist, but dealing evenhandedly with all. I granted "there is not now any bill in Congress" for a land grab, but there was "little question" that it remained the "ultimate intention of the two national livestock associations, if they can bring it about." The committee should move with "utmost caution, before it becomes . . . entangled in any scheme to take these lands away from the public to put them in selected private hands." They were about all we'd ever have and we'd better cherish them.

Both Barrett and Congressman Wesley D'Ewart of Montana pounced on John W. Spencer, regional forester, when he spoke [15] of specific erosion conditions and stressed the importance to agriculture, industry, and municipalities of the water that originated on the forests. Barrett's comment: "Why blame it on the poor sheepherder and the little old cowboy who's trying to make a living around here on these hills? We're sick and tired of being kicked around. Maybe one of these days we'll do a little kicking ourselves."

Soon the Service was on the grill again [16] because of a guest editorial H. E. Schwan, a Region 2 range specialist, had written for the Denver *Post*, in which land conditions in the region were frankly discussed. Barrett told Watts he was in a spot where criticism was inevitable, and that the American people "reserve the right to kick the umpire." Watts replied he stood for the "right of free speech and a free press," which "applies to the members of the Forest Service as long as I'm boss, as well as to other people." If Schwan's facts were correct, he said, "I'd have authorized him to write the guest editorial on government time."

The tall, commanding presence of Charles C. Moore of DuBois, Wyoming, president of the Dude Ranchers Association, helped make his statement [17] one of the more impressive. His schooling as a lawyer impelled him to document all statements, and he was excellent in the rough give-and-take of the kind of hearing Barrett conducted. Early on he insisted that the text of Robertson's give-away bill, S. 1945, be put in the record as hard evidence that a land grab was in the making. He ended by declaring, "We of the Dude Ranchers Association subscribe to the Izaak Walton League position that the public lands belong to all and are not for the exclusive use of a few grazing permittees."

Moore quoted a letter from Mollin to Watts in which Mollin threatened to have congressional allies cut Forest Service appropriations "so there'd be fewer swivel-chair experts." He commented that up to that point the stockmen had been allotted fourteen hours for testimony as against one and a half for opponents, and all criticism by the committee had been directed at the latter, none at the former. "Never in all my experience have I attended a meeting so onesided and unfair, so full of bias," he asserted. That provoked Congressman Miller into making derogatory remarks about the dude ranching industry, and Moore demanded a retraction. Later he wrote Barrett for galley proofs of that part of the transcript, to see if anything had been deleted.[18] Nothing had.

At the close of the exchanges between Moore and Miller, Barrett said the proceedings at Rawlins had been "mild" compared with what awaited at Grand Junction two days later, and the Service officials up to then had been having a "nice time."

And Grand Junction followed, on September 5. It was a memorable day—and night, too, for the hearing ran on until after 11 p.m. The hall was crowded with from seven hundred to one thousand present, depending on which estimate of numbers one wished to accept. Though most probably were permittees, some may have been folks from nearer towns and the countryside who came simply to enjoy a good show; after all, few road companies played Broadway hits at Grand Junction. Those there to be entertained were ready to holler and clap hands at anybody's good quip, but I believe it was the cow and sheep men organized ahead of time who did the booing and boot-stomping. Yes, there was booing, though one would look in the printed record in vain for specific evidence. The nearest thing to a rebuke to the crowd for unmannerly behavior was a gentle reminder by Rockwell,[19] who then was in the chair, that "these people" were at Grand Junction as "guests of the Western Slope." The worst booing came when a spokesman for the Colorado State Grange told of the adverse effect on downstream farms of accelerated high country erosion induced by overgrazing. (It may be noted here that Rockwell as well as Robertson would be rejected by the voters of his area at the next election. I can't prove it, but suspect this was because the grabby clique he supported was indeed a minority, as Carhart and others had insisted from the start.)

Grand Junction was another Rawlins with respect to favoritism shown to complaining stockmen. Most of the morning and afternoon were consumed by detailed complaints of permittees against the way the Service tried to administer grazing on two nearby national forests, the Uncompahgre and the Grand Mesa.

In the evening session Carhart[20] was called, and afterward Benton Stong[21] of the Farmers Union testified. Carhart again emphasized our belief that the hellraising elements of the industry were small numerically but influential, and that most stockmen were as sound as an undepreciated dollar. He methodically ticked off the step-by-step actions of the Joint Livestock Committee and those who spoke in its name. Regardless of the "panicky disavowal . . . of the published objectives of the Joint Committee," he said, "the fact remains that those of us who have written on the [land grab] subject can't be accused of misrepresentation." He named the smaller Colorado stock organizations that had gone on record opposing the grab.

Stong's main point was similar to that of the State Grange spokesman. National Farmers Union members depended for their livelihood on irrigation water, originating largely in the mountains, and those watersheds must be protected. The Union, he said, wanted no climate created in Washington that would favor "divestment" of any public lands.

Perhaps the most moving moments of the Grand Junction hearing—or the entire series—came late in the evening when, after sitting through days of disparagement of himself and what he and his people were doing, Chief Forester Lyle Watts stood to speak for the defense.[22] He sketched his career from boyhood on an Iowa stock farm, to Iowa State University where he earned two degrees, through entering the Service in 1911 to start his climb to its top position. The testimony, he said, indicated grazing rules had begun to tighten up four or five years earlier (in the Clapp regime) shortly before he became chief. He agreed with his predecessor's policies. His years of work in the West had convinced him the Service had not got on top of the job that had to be done on the ranges. He was determined that the quality of range work by the Service should be lifted to equal its high levels of accomplishment in timber management and fire control. It would be easier to acquiesce in things he and his people knew were not right, but it would not be honest. He would rather have men who would go against contention such as they had encountered that day, than men who could not face up to the job for which they were hired. He and his people would continue to do the best they could for the people of America with the timber, water, range, wildlife, and all other resources in their charge.

After his defense of Service integrity, we in the organized conservation movement would have sworn Watts would stand firmly on the range reduction program until Hell became an ice rink. But something happened, surely not long after that—and Watts is no longer here to tell us what it was or its full impact. We must look to effect and other circumstantial evidence, and from them try to reconstruct cause.

After Grand Junction, with the possible exception of the Salt Lake City hearing, it was all downhill for Barrett and his field party. We of the conservation community later came to believe it was downhill, too, for the Service policy begun by Clapp and continued for a time under Watts. A new era, in which social engineering and intricate concepts of range management would take precedence, and downward adjustments to grazing capacity would become dirty words, was forming in high places of the U.S. Forest Service.

12

Crucial Policy Shifts

A question that has nagged me since the start of this undertaking is whether I have overemphasized the significance of the congressional investigations of the 1940s and associated events, which include the subjugation of the Grazing Service and echoes of that occurrence, even the land grab itself. Now it is time to examine situations I consider to have been crucial toward the formulation of policies and the enactment of laws that still are effective and are related in a real sense to the turbulent decade that was coming to an end. They may help to answer the question of emphasis.

As I see it, no changes in Forest Service policy with respect to grazing have been more critical than those which had shifted so much of the burden of rehabilitating damaged forest ranges from individual permittees to the taxpayer at large. These changes were at the heart of the turmoil in the Service that resulted in transfers that tended to sully the reputations and hamper the careers of dedicated officials. (See Chapters 13 and 14.) They brought on Service retreats in such obstinate cases as those arising from overgrazing the Roosevelt and Uncompahgre National Forests. (See Chapter 15.) Granting, for the moment, that this is legitimate reasoning, what brought on the thinking that resulted in the policy changes? What were the root causes? Doubtless there were several, and some readers may question the logic of assumptions I have considered correct.

It has been noted that range improvement undertakings in the early years of the system were almost exclusively carried out by permittees, and that many of these were devices and practices of convenience to which subsequent improvement of forage production was incidental, a by-product or happenstance if it eventuated. Holding pens or corrals and loading chutes, windmills with tanks or more elaborate water developments, drift fences, and stock driveways were among them. As personnel became more experienced and knowledgeable, or better schooled in range realities at time of employment, Service awareness of the desirability of a variety of range improvement activities grew, but funds and manpower still were scarce.

Then, paradoxically, a bonanza of both fell upon it in the depths of the devastating depression of the 1930s. The Civilian Conservation Corps had been a device through which the Franklin D. Roosevelt administration sought to keep restless unemployed young men off the streets and out of bars newly opening following repeal of the Prohibition Amendment. During the years of the CCC—1933-42—the Service had the benefit of the muscle of thousands of young men and of many kinds of equipment, materials, and supplies. It was an abundance of assistance that came with few strings attached. The Service used trial-and-error techniques as well as proven ones, and had opportunity to experiment to its heart's content on such ideas as reseeding widespread depleted areas, even total revegetative procedures. For approximately nine years the Service had range improvement resources galore; not even the often dominating demands of timbered regions on the national forests could deny the ranges a share of the outpouring from the treasury and from city streets.

Then, with the onset of World War II the cornucopia was emptied, and the Service once more experienced range improvement hunger. The war dragged on, and the Service doggedly resisted efforts to open the range gates as had been done a generation earlier. Even though it succeeded in that respect, generally adequate precipitation may also be credited with helping to sustain ranges in as good condition as they were at war's end. Chief Watts's initial determination to speed range recovery through grazing reductions followed, opposed at every contact point by affected permittees or livestock associations, or both. Even cooperative permittees who recognized that ranges were damaged and were willing to accept needed reductions were at times blocked from doing so by association action—as on the plateau districts of the Uncompahgre (Chapter 15).

Add now the persistent congressional nagging and bulldozing, most obviously in the form of the McCarran and Barrett investigations. To me it is not implausible to assume that the combination of adverse factors led more than one forest official to yearn for a way out, if only a back door somewhere through which to escape from con-

Reseeded bunchgrass on Malheur National Forest, Oregon, 1959. *USFS photo*

stant complaint, protest, and pleading. It seems inescapable that some began to cast about early for whatever would get those folks off their sore backs, and in doing so turned to the undertakings of CCC days. After all, the 1930s and early 1940s were good years for range improvement and experimentation, no matter how rough they had been in other ways. Good programs were carried out, and others tested that showed promise. Could Congress be persuaded to furnish enough range improvement money to make a large-scale continuing program feasible? If so, perhaps such a program could reduce if not supplant entirely the violently protested cuts in numbers and time. Wasn't it worth long, hard scrutiny? Why not pick up similar elements that had appeared in the ill-fated long-range program prepared by the Service in the closing days of World War II and highlighted in the chief's 1945 report and present them once more to Congress? Similar thinking must have stirred elements in the livestock industry, too.

Certain fundamental factors that affected western range areas may have had significance in crystalizing convictions for some Service officials, possibly others. Bernard DeVoto touched upon one of these in an "Easy Chair" column in *Harper's*.[1] He wrote of Utah that "the Mormon desire to hold the family together has tended to divide and subdivide the family lands, force them to support always increasing populations, and so graze beyond the safe limit, and in the end impair the land and threaten its people." Then, in the record of the Barrett hearing at Salt Lake City in September 1947, additional evidence is found that seems to support DeVoto. An official of the Utah cattlemen's organization told Barrett [2] that the *average* permit there was for only twenty-six head—which any western stockman would call a mighty small spread. Service records show that Utah's average permit, as AUMs, has consistently been the smallest in the West for a good many years, with New Mexico next. Later in the hearing,[3] a leading sheepman spoke of the "division of the estates over the years" as a reason why so many permits were small.

Upon settling Utah in 1847 the Mormons tended to huddle in villages and towns, at first for protection against displaced Indians as much as for cultural and business reasons. They farmed nearby lands they could irrigate from streams flowing down from the mountains, and sent increasing herds and flocks to open ranges within manageable distances. They were ambitious and industrious. They also were prolific. Some embraced the plural marriage practice then permitted by the Mormon church, which let a man have several wives and which was not formally abandoned until 1890. Plural marriage and the limitations of the era on family planning resulted in large families, which paralleled the proliferation of livestock and range utilization. A comparatively small number of Utah stockmen became what the West would call big operators; a proportionately large number lived at little more than a subsistence level. Many heirs and assigns have continued to do so. It will be remembered that Powell wrote of denuded Utah ranges in his 1878 report on western arid lands (Chapter 4).

In my view it is not irrelevant at this point to note that in the middle 1940s one of the rising young stars of range management in the Intermountain Region of the Service, headquartered at Ogden, Utah, was Edward P. Cliff, assistant regional forester in charge of range and wildlife administration, later chief forester. Cliff was born to a Mormon sheep-raising family, and nothing would be more natural than for him to feel deep sympathy for the squeezed small ranchers of his home state—and elsewhere in the West—when the time came to pare down excess AUMs at the start of the 1946 permit term. I have little more than deduction on which to base my assumption, but consider it reasonable to believe that sometime in the 1940s Cliff became convinced that a policy of massive range rehabili-

Broadcast reseeding on depleted and gullied hillside, Manti-LaSal National Forest, Utah, 1952. *USFS photo*

tation could decrease if not eliminate need for Service-imposed reductions, and was attractive for other reasons. Such a conviction could have been implanted during CCC days, when the benefits stemming from range improvement had a chance to become recognized, or at the time of the postwar program proposal. The precise moment does not appear important. The fact that Cliff became a leading exponent of the policy does seem so, in the light of future events.

Among the conservation groups the Izaak Walton League, in particular, looked askance at heavy involvement by permittees in range improvement undertakings. We contended [4] that this was a federal responsibility, and whatever was done should be accomplished by the land agencies using appropriated funds. To do otherwise, we believed, would only serve to support the argument of the stock associations that grazing national forests was a permittee's right instead of a privilege subject to modification or revocation. If a permittee put his own time, money, materials, and equipment into a

Ship's anchor chain dragged to rid range of big sagebrush prior to reseeding, north of Wallsburg, Utah, 1963. *USFS photo*

range improvement of some permanence such as a water development, he could feel he had a lien on it, an established use that could not be rescinded, a moral guarantee that his permit would be renewed at term end, on and on into the future. The permit would be his regardless of other actual or potential uses of the area or of what conflicting needs for it might turn out to be.

Our insistence that range improvement was a federal responsibility did not mean we believed it could or should substitute for other measures. We believed that whatever reduction in use was in order should be imposed so as to speed up rehabilitation and restore full productivity. Range improvement could be carried out concurrently with reductions, plus whatever other management techniques research and experimentation showed to be beneficial. Only the aggregate of protective and restorative measures would bring recovery in the shortest time, and we insisted that all that were feasible should be applied wherever range condition and trend were downward.

The Service leaders proved to be less adamant in the matter of who paid for rang improvement work. They wanted to control the operation, though, to approve or disapprove projects advocated by permittees, and pass on the location, design, and timing. The Service had grown accustomed to seeing range projects accomplished exclusively by permittees, for that was how it had been—in fact how it had to be done if anything was to be done at all—over many years. And it had participated with permittees in projects cooperatively, sharing the cost on a predetermined basis. The Service could live with various combinations of cooperative range improvement activities. That was a secondary consideration. The cold reality was that for a time after the passing of CCC there were no substantial sums allocated by Congress specifically for range improvement.

I am convinced that after the CCC camps were closed down and the condition of many ranges continued to deteriorate, significant divisions evolved within the Forest Service, with one group banking almost entirely on a rehabilitation policy to eliminate range troubles. The other group was not so optimistic that this alone would be adequate or that funds for range improvement could be secured in sufficient sums to accomplish what was needed in time. This group believed the first essential was range use reduction; rehabilitation techniques applied simultaneously, or when funds were available, would be added benefit.

The 1946 permit term year assumes greater importance on the basis of this line of reasoning. Watts's annual report for 1945 [5] had called for "drastic" cuts wherever needed to halt downgrading range use. Some officials moved ahead on that line with vigor, since it coincided with their convictions. Others dragged their heels. Doubtless, though I have no proof to display, Service personnel were being mentally catalogued as belonging to the cut camp or the rehabilitate camp. One beautiful side effect to those holding the latter view was that it would tend to divert rancher thinking from reductions to improvements, from a negative attitude to a positive one; it would mollify permittees and associations from which so many complaints had come. It just might bring peace to national forest ranges while these officials were still alive to enjoy it.

The rehabilitation-alone policy had another aspect that made it attractive to its disciples in the Service and in the industry. When reductions were applied, each made a dent in a permittee pocketbook. With no cuts or few cuts, and with range improvements financed from the federal treasury, each permittee dent would be infinitesmal, the part of his income tax allotted to that purpose. The bulk of the cost would be met with other people's money, extracted from taxpayers all over the country. Few from distant areas would think of that; fewer still would complain. Minimal reductions in AUMs, coupled to the local spending of appropriated funds for field work, meant improved economics for many small cow towns. It could keep some from becoming ghost towns.

Thus what was discussed and debated behind closed Service doors, on inspection rides on the ranges and elsewhere, was a difference in basic philosophy. To some, if cuts in use did not come first, or at least simultaneously with range improvements, deterioration would continue and might accelerate. They did not anticipate rehabilitative funding at a level high enough to accomplish that kind of miracle; Congress was not in the habit of appropriating so much money for such a purpose. And, if it did, where would the necessary manpower and skills be found? Followers of this belief were convinced genuine recuperation and full productivity would be delayed interminably.

In the view of this group the others, who leaned toward rehabilitation as a foremost policy, seemed more perturbed by pressures being put upon them than by pressures being put upon vital resources. Put in another context, one group appeared to want Service personnel to strive hardest to get along with stockmen while the others thought it more important that stockmen get along with the land. Which is, of course, oversimplification in both respects. The ultimate goals of all seemed similar. The question was which road to take. Cuts plus rehabilitation as funds became available would bring faster results, in the view of its proponents. Swiftness of results should make the villification and political pressure bearable. Rehabilitation alone would be slower, more costly in money, but would be conciliatory and make friends of permittees who now were adversaries. We may never know the full extent of the divisiveness that rent the Service over the issue, or the maneuvering by protagonists of either viewpoint.

In the end the rehabilitation group won the day. With it came a don't-rock-the-boat philosophy. All might still have been well if range rehabilitation could have been carried out as a crash program, properly sustained and maintained, but that did not eventuate. Again there was overoptimism on the part of high level officials. Congress was persuaded to authorize a large-scale program,[6] but never did appropriate all funds authorized, and the use of such appropriations as did come along were weighted in favor of regeneration of forested lands rather than ranges.[7] We are still paying the price, in wide expanses of substandard range, less than optimum livestock productivity, loss of soil mantle through erosion that contributes unnecessary sedimentation to irrigation reservoirs downstream, and a less even yearlong outflow of water from high range sources.

Hints of changes taking place in Service thinking show up in the annual reports of the chief, but do not clearly disclose the underlying reasons. The call for reductions in the 1945 report had been dramatically phrased, and included a threat of total exclusion in some places.[8] Surely that would lead any reader to believe a firm policy of quick, decisive reductions had been adopted. In 1946 the report said [9] much the same thing and reminded that cuts in seasons and numbers "should have been made long ago."

The 1947 report undoubtedly was written while the Barrett subcommittee was already in the West or headed in that direction. It was issued as of September 18, which was after hearings had been held in Montana, Wyoming, Colorado, and Utah. In it we find,[10] "Some of our employes have been subjected to unusually severe and often unfair criticism," yet Service morale "and a spirit of public service is strong." Those criticized in strongest terms were the ones who imposed reductions. The report added that "about half" the ranges "need further corrective action," some of which doubtless could be other than downward adjustments. In total context the report seems to have been written more defensively than its immediate predecessors, but I detected no open symptoms of surrender to demands that cuts be outlawed, or of any bending of the earlier will to achieve needed reductions.

One must read the 1948 report closely and tie it to other evidence to find significant changes in attitude. In fact, upon looking back in 1971 as he replied [11] to a question I had submitted on the subject, Chief Forester Cliff could find no noticeable difference in report "tone." He granted that 1947 and 1948 had been turbulent years, but then, "as these events subsided I'm sure the reports reflect the situation as it appeared to the Chief. Pressure as such would not have been a unique experience at that time, nor any more disturbing than it is today." The 1948 report did say [12] the Service must take "decisive action" where there were "serious problems"; it did not define "serious," nor did it say where such problems existed. It said some permittees were "loath to accept" reductions, which was under-statement. Then 1949 brought a report that today reads like total abandonment of the stern line followed as recently as 1945 and 1946. It was devoted largely to research and range improvement, as if to prepare its readers for policy and other changes to come. Where range conditions and needs were noted, the report [13] said only that "certain unsatisfactory range situations *should be* cleared up" (italics added), which was a far cry from the call for "drastic" action only four years before. But even as that report was being written, large sums of range improvement money were being dangled be-fore Service eyes.

As echoes of the Barrett declamations faded at the end of 1947 and the politics of the 1948 election year began to heat up, Clinton Anderson resigned as Secretary of Agriculture to run successfully for the Senate from his home state of New Mexico. The average Forest Service permit in New Mexico was almost as low as that of Utah. Anderson was sensitive to that situation. My rationalization has not been accepted by some with whom I have consulted, but it seems difficult to believe that the merits of range rehabilitation pro-grams versus reduced grazing privileges was not the subject of more than one discussion in his years as Secretary, when visiting his home state and when in Washington. The benefits accruing from the work done in CCC years certainly were not lost to this astute individual. Whatever the truth may be, one of the first bills Anderson intro-duced [14] called for a comparatively large outlay of federal funds for forest and range rehabilitation. A companion bill was introduced in the House by Congressman Mike Mansfield of Montana.

Ordinarily a piece of major legislation takes several years to gain acceptance and be enacted into law by the Congress. The Anderson–Mansfield Act was passed in October, 1949, before the freshman sena-tor from New Mexico had been in office ten full months. Parts of it should be quoted:

> Whereas, the national forests . . . contain approximately . . . eighty-three million acres of the nation's important grazing lands; and . . .
>
> Whereas, these lands are the sole or main source of summer range for ten million cattle and sheep grazed by thirty thousand livestock permittees whose livelihood is wholly or partially dependent upon livestock grazed on national-forest ranges; and
>
> Whereas, these lands contain over four million acres of . . . seriously depleted range lands; [15] and

Collecting gama grass seed for revegetation project, Cibola National Forest, New Mexico, 1959. *USFS photo*

Bulldozer with special bar to push away juniper treetops in range clearing prior to revegetation, Magdalene District, New Mexico, 1960. *USFS photo*

"Stump jumper" plow used in stumpy or stony ground to prepare range for revegetation, Boise National Forest, Idaho, 1948. BLM also uses this type of equipment, as well as chains, 'dozers, and so on. *USFS photo*

Whereas, these lands will not . . . revegetate satisfactorily or within a reasonable time except through . . . revegetation and other measures . . .; and

Whereas, it is practical to . . . revegetate these seriously depleted range lands *in a period of fifteen years;* and

Whereas, it is necessary to provide reasonable continuity of . . . economical operations: Therefore be it

Resolved by the Senate and House . . ., that it is the declared policy of Congress to accelerate and provide a continuing basis for the needed . . . revegetation . . . [italics added].

The bill authorized up to $133 million to be appropriated for a combination of reforestation and range revegetation through fiscal year 1965 and "thereafter such amounts *as may be needed* for range revegetation" (italics added), but it did not specify how the funds should be divided between timber and range, which may have been a mistake. National forest range acreage outnumbers primary timber producing land considerably, and western national forest timber takes a long time to mature. However, the uninitiated would assume, I believe, that the division would be approximately equal as between the two. Whether this actually was the case does not alter the hypothesis that range managers might expect about $65 million to become available for revegetation if Congress appropriated what it had authorized. Since the act did not prohibit permittees from undertaking approved improvements at their own expense, or in cooperative actions with the Forest Service, one could assume that the total sum actually to be expended on range work would exceed the funds appropriated under the authorization.

I consider the Anderson–Mansfield Act a tremendous victory for the Forest Service group that wanted much range improvement and very little livestock grazing reduction. It was a victory also for the livestock interests that had contended for so many years that cuts were unnecessary, that all the West needed was a little rain now and then and better range management by the Service. With Anderson–Mansfield operative, the associations looked to a time when reductions would come, for the most part, only when a rancher went out of business without succession, or voluntarily surrendered part or all of his permit. They were seldom disappointed.

Conservation forces paid little attention to Anderson–Mansfield. No mention of it is found in *Outdoor America,* magazine of the Izaak Walton League. The League was then more interested in bills to give legal status to national forest grazing advisory boards, and an abortive effort it made to try to reach accord with the national cattlemen's organization through intergroup meetings; two inconclusive conferences were held in the spring and summer of 1949.[16] The conservation forces as a whole had been united against statutory advisory boards, agitation for which had been going on for many years. The stockmen won that one, too, with the passage of the Granger–Thye Act of 1950.[17] We let Anderson–Mansfield go by with scarcely a whisper of interest. Indeed, at present I am at a loss to understand why the official magazine didn't disclose enthusiastic support by the Izaak Walton League. The new law seemed to assure that the preponderance of the range improvement accomplished would be federal instead of private, which we thought was right. It occurs to me now that we were looking for burglars under the wrong bed. We visualized the forest advisory boards as ruling cadres on individual national forests throughout the West, or in the local ranger districts, just as we considered them to be in Taylor Act districts. Instead, through Anderson–Mansfield and succeeding efforts yet to be discussed, the industry wanted control over the central structure of the creature, the central nervous system at its headquarters, far more than the separate parts far out in the field. And, so far as I have

Helicopter sprays 2, 4-D on brush sprouts in 1959 revegetation effort, Angeles National Forest, California. *USFS photo*

learned, the activities of the forest advisory boards up to now have not seriously hindered administration.

The House Report of the Anderson–Mansfield bill [18] is revealing. The traditional excessive optimism found in Forest Service policy shows clearly in the letter reproduced in the report, signed by Charles F. Brannan, Anderson's successor as Secretary of Agriculture, and doubtless written for him by Watts or a member of Watts's immediate staff.[19] The letter, addressed to the Congressional Committees on Agriculture, was enthusiastic. It spoke of the four million depleted acres mentioned in the bill, a figure it doubtless gave to Anderson in the first place. Many of these were on important but unnamed watersheds. There was "pressing need" for an "enlarged program . . . to check the present downward trend . . . and to restore the depleted areas to maximum productivity." Then this:

"The depleted range and watershed areas can be restored to productivity within 2 to 4 years and made to support from 5 to 10 times the number of livestock now being carried." (italics added).

All that was needed was for the Congress to give the Service the millions the bill would authorize. An inconsistency appears here that seems to have gone entirely unnoticed. The Service, through the Department, declared that range miracles could be accomplished in from two to four years, yet the bill called for an accelerated spending program to span fifteen years, plus whatever funding might be required thereafter—which presumably would be mainly for maintenance or replacement of depreciated improvements. The promise of increased capacity has proved to be wholly false.

The Service's appropriation bill for FY 1949—just ahead of Anderson–Mansfield—provided a line item of $543,000 for range improvement including reseeding, and the House generously added $250,000 by floor amendment. Brannan's letter dutifully acknowledged the generosity but said more funding was needed; it declared the Service had proved reseeding could be successful, having already replanted some 200,000 acres of depleted range. Appropriately enough—and, I might say, traditionally as respects things of this kind —the letter hedged a little on the universality of revegetation as a panacea. It said overgrazed ranges in a good many national forest areas "require drastic reductions in livestock use." In this way the Service retained its options if, at some future time, the pendulum should swing in the other direction. And such words should quiet ahead of time any qualms conservation organizations or more knowledgeable members of Congress from eastern constituencies might have.

Without revegetation, the letter read, "in some areas decades would be required to restore vegetation," and "even then the results would fall far short of what could be accomplished" through employment of man's newfound reseeding skills. Relying entirely on nature's recuperative powers would be "insufficient and wasteful," and would defeat the worthwhile objective of doing something practical to provide more forage for stock in an era when the world was in process of coming back from war's desolation and urgently needed all the food that could be produced. "The more constructive approach" was one of range improvement "along with a somewhat less drastic reduction in livestock numbers." Doubtless the stockmen would have been happier if the letter had said flatly that AUM reductions would be wiped out entirely, but the Service would not go that far. We conservationists should have read the omens better, but at the time we had no true conception of how much "less drastic" the reductions would become in a short while.

Experimental reseeding in early stages, Pike National Forest, 1949. *USFS photo*

Same area five years later, showing good stand of grass. *USFS photo*

When the bill was being considered on the floor Senator Anderson remarked that the Barrett subcommittee had "visited . . . areas that complained that stockmen were having their grazing . . . reduced, *and suggested that this would not be necessary* if the Department of Agriculture would undertake a replanting program" [20] (italics added). This was additional warning language that at the time went right over our heads. I doubt if any of the men and women in leading positions in the conservation movement of that day even read that passage in the *Congressional Record;* I am positive it was not then brought to my attention.

Thus, as I see it, the groundwork was laid for an almost total abandonment of mandatory grazing reductions by the Forest Service. Did this also make it easier for higher-ups to agree to demands by association heads for the scalps of field officials who had especially irked the industry through insistence on AUM cuts to meet demonstrated range needs? Pressures on the Service eased off therafter except where those individuals were concerned. The word had gone out from Washington that field men should not "make waves" or in other ways anger the livestock leaders. It took another couple of years to render impotent the officials who thought range productivity was more important than accommodation, but it looks from here as though their doom was sealed when Anderson–Mansfield was signed into law. There is no question as to which policy won and which lost that October day in 1949. The Service became committed to a slower, more prolonged, and more costly era of recovery for damaged, eroding, ranges. This was one price of détente with the industry's grabbers and hotheads. The humiliation and exile of a few individuals seemingly was considered a side effect.

It is tempting to look beyond cut-versus-improve reasonings and rationalizations, not so much to form judgments as to try better to understand policies and policymakers as well as underlings under compulsion to abide by established new policy.

The permittees whose stock grubbed grass to the roots and chewed shrubbery shoots to stubs and stumps in the late 1940s were not the original ranchers on what became forest ranges. If they had been, the question of whether the general treasury should be drawn upon to bring about correction of abuse might bring a different answer. If they had been, if it was their stock that had caused the original harm and was continuing to do so, they could be held directly responsible and could be compelled to pay the full cost of restoration if the Service wished to force the issue. But this was not the case.

True, in some instances old timers still active in the 1940s had been running cattle or sheep for decades. A few had been there in the devastating years of World War I, a handful even earlier that that. More had survived the Great Depression with its concurrent drought, both of which were critical in their impact on the forage producing areas. There were mitigating circumstances in both the First World War and in the Great Depression, deplorable though the results on the ground were bound to be. Doubtless a reasonable defense could be made for most of the veteran ranchers, and the younger ones could well plead that the bulk of the destruction had occurred before they came on the scene. They had an alibi.

The substance of this recitation is that relatively few of the thousands of national forest permittees could be held directly responsible for the bulk of the deterioration that had come about over the previous half century or more. Too, the Service was not faced with a single resource situation, isolated in this or that ranger district, but with a large number of them. No two allotments are alike. No two forests or regions are comparable. Lands of varying degrees of suitability for grazing, or carrying capacity, were or are intermingled with land in other categories. One permittee's allotment might contain range in a half dozen stages of condition or trend. Pockets of range of naturally poor quality often were interspersed with areas that would respond fairly quickly to one or another kind of treatment. Where deterioration could be laid positively to overuse or abuse, the cause might conceivably be traced back to a specific era, or it might be obscured by time.

Under these circumstances would it be fair to penalize present users of such intermingled lands for blameworthy events perhaps brought on by persons long dead or departed? Instead of correction of a situation being somebody's business, had it become everybody's? In relevant fashion the situation is reminiscent of the huge task of rehabilitation we face elsewhere to heal land and water wounds inflicted in other ways by people no longer here to be confronted. A parallel I have mentioned [21] in another context and place that comes readily to mind is the older coal country of such states as Pennsylvania, West Virginia, Ohio, and Kentucky. There millions of scarred acres and thousands of miles of poisoned streams are crying for restoration to a semblance of their former beauty and productivity. Instability and insecurity are chronic in those areas. Destruction in some coal regions has been going on far longer than most western ranges—certainly those in the interior West—have been overgrazed; coal was first mined in Pennsylvania in 1769. Long gone coal operators cannot now be subpoenaed and forced to pay reparations for damage their actions brought about. States and the federal government are facing up to corrective reality where coal was a wastrel king. It is to be hoped that they will take preventive measures in newer coal mining areas, including large parts of the stockraising West, that are now driving toward increased coal output to help meet national energy wants.

Similar parallels may be found in other fields. This one seems to make the point that the entire blame for range conditions of the 1940s could not be pinned to individual permittees. On this reasoning, given the urgency of the need for restorative action, a case could be made for the federal government, as the landowner, to underwrite revegetation and rehabilitation. Even if this was the reasoning of those who wanted to abandon reductions in AUMs, with their punitive overtones, it still left unanswered one vital question. It was whether those who were running stock on federal lands in the 1940s and thereafter should be allowed to aggravate the existing damage by continued excessive grazing. Those who have guided the destiny of the Forest Service from the late 1940s forward seem to have so believed.

One would think the momentous policy switch from reductions plus range betterment to rehabilitation without reduction or with minimal cuts, would have been victory enough to last the livestock industry for a generation or more, and that the leaders would now relax to savor the sweet taste of what had been accomplished. This was not to be. Emphasis shifted and outright ownership of the public domain, national forest ranges, and other federal forage lands dropped out of common communications. But backstage maneuvering to gain ever more "rights" for their clientele never slackened in the councils of the associations. And while they were going about that, they would have the blood of those Service officials who had dared to advocate quick cuts as the fastest way to restore deteriorated western range. So, fuel the fires and heat the irons and put a smoking brand on every one! Those people wanted to smell burning hair and hide, and wasted little time getting started.

13

The Expendables

Shifting people around in an organization can have many purposes. It is used to promote the worthy. Even if no immediate increase in prestige, responsibility, or salary is involved, it can be used to move a capable individual laterally to a spot where his talents are needed more than whence he came. This can be praiseworthy. On the other hand, a transfer can be disciplinary, a form of rebuke short of discharge, for errors committed in line of duty or otherwise. It can be a put-down for what higher authority might consider overzealousness. It can be appeasement of a customer or client who was merely antipathetic to the actions of the individual being transferred. This kind I consider wrong, even if expedient.

Transfers of personnel have been routine in the Forest Service. As no two personalities are alike, so it is with transfers. The transfers to be detailed here differ from the laudable kinds. I contend *they punished individuals whose major crime was doing precisely what they had sworn to do when they took office.* They believed the Service meant every word of that famous policy sentence of 1905 about "the greatest good to the greatest number in the long run." They thought they would be upheld, even commended, by their superiors for following that policy explicitly.

Here one must move cautiously, for in every instance someone has to decide what the "greatest good" means and who the "greatest number" are. Human judgment enters. The reader must decide whether these disciplinary transfers were correct, or were intended to appease.

The federal Civil Service system is specific. Unless an official in-

After 30 years of protection, a start toward recovery, right of fence, Pike National Forest, Colorado, 1949. USFS *photo by F. Lee Kirby*

volved has overtly violated complicated rules set up mainly for his or her protection against arbitrary discharge or discrimination, removal can be a tedious, complex procedure. An inefficient official can be punished by being given adverse ratings that hinder pay increases or promotions, or even be demoted under certain circumstances. These disciplinary measures are not as easy to bring about as is a simple transfer from one agency area to another or to work in a different field of activity. Some disciplinary transfers have been given the label of a promotion that, in fact, they were not.

My research has not disclosed which Forest Service official was first shipped from range management to some other kind of work because he dared confront livestock permittees who were violating permit terms or resisting needed reductions. One fact stands out, though, in each of the transfers to be recounted. It is that to the affected officials condition and trend of rangeland came first. They were committed to protect and enhance the growth and vigor of the vegetation that constitutes the life-support system of the earth's living creatures. These men were convinced that acceding to demands for

Exposed root systems backed by overused aspen grove, Pike National Forest, Colorado, 1947. *USFS photo by F. Lee Kirby*

more than the land could safely carry, or bowing to permittee resistance to needed reductions in use, were wrong, could lead only to further deterioration and ultimately the destruction of national forest ranges. Their problems, in the last analysis, stemmed from their conviction that their duty was clear wherever or whenever a healthy range was at stake.

If a case is examined in one light, the commitment of the individual affected may be judged to be rebellion in the ranks that topside fears it must halt if it does not wish to find its authority challenged on every hand. If it is looked at in another way one sees human beings humiliated or knocked out of the cherished fruits of a lifelong climb to career heights because they had the guts to protest policies they considered out of line with the high principles enunciated by the creators of the Forest Service. This line of reasoning may require refining, but it seems to contain at least a smidgen of logic. It is unlikely that either side will be found completely alabaster or stygian. My bias will show in this account, for the evidence I have seen convinces me that the expendables to be written about were victims, not villains. I raise questions of the rightness or wrongness of policies at high levels.

The Lee Kirby Case

Since F. Lee Kirby took his lumps before Barrett's hearings, the question may be asked why it is included here. I do so for several reasons. In a sense Lee Kirby's superiors had some reason for their action; as will be shown, he was goaded into what could be called insubordination. But the Kirby case is prototypal in some essentials, and he has left a record that should be examined. The forces of conservation should have paid more attention to basics and less to comparative superficialities when he was under fire so as to be able to guard against repetitions of similar sequences of events where no insubordination could be alleged.

Kirby's troubles began when he was supervisor of the Tonto National Forest in Arizona in the late 1930s and climaxed in the mid-1940s. His headquarters were in Phoenix, the state's capital and largest city, most of whose municipal water originates on the Tonto. So does the flow that irrigates fabulously productive farmland retrieved from desert by the availability of Tonto water.

Kirby retired in the 1950s. He was interviewed in 1963 by Arthur Carhart, and the resultant tape recording, now in the Conservation Center of the Denver Public Library, is the source of much of the material used in this account.

Kirby's Service career began in 1909. He told Carhart that as he grew older and more observant, he became increasingly aware of the extent to which the range in general had been impaired by excessive grazing. He considered overstocking in World War I significantly responsible for its sad condition in the dry thirties. By that time the ranges on the Tonto were producing only about 10 percent of their potential.

Range deterioration, said Kirby, "is somewhat like growing old. You always feel about the same as you did yesterday, or even a year ago, but there comes a time when you realize something of a cumulative effect has been taking place, and the changes are very great." On the ranges "the changes have not been sudden. It would have been better if they had, as in the form of a blast or an earthquake . . . so the results . . . and the causes could be easily seen. But it has

Four years of total protection gave results at left of fence, Tonto National Forest, Arizona, 1945. *USFS photo by F. Lee Kirby*

been gradual, insidious, over a lifetime, and the people generally have not been conscious of what's been happening."

In early times in his part of Arizona the soil cover consisted largely of grasses and forbs that were highly palatable, and the livestock naturally ate first what they liked best. Heavy use of the more palatable varieties of forage reduced their vigor. "The only way to maintain fertility" in that region, he said, "is to leave a substantial part of the vegetation . . . right there on the land, to go back into the soil. . . . We need to be sure the plants are not cropped to the point where the root systems are damaged. . . ." Eventually the plants lost so much vigor that when it did rain, in an area where rain itself was a rarity, plants used most of the moisture just to get back part of what they had lost. In his region unimpeded nature required anywhere from five hundred to a thousand years to replace an inch of lost topsoil. When the desirable bunch grasses began to go they were replaced by inferior vegetation, such as snakeweed, which had originally constituted only 2 to 3 percent of the plant cover but came to occupy as much as 90 percent. The invading plant types in their way tried to heal the land but, Kirby said, "*You can't heal it over with the cause of the damage still there*" (italics added).

So Kirby undertook to get his ranges on the road to recovery. He did so in large part through reductions in AUM use by the permittees. Small plots had been fenced off for experimental purposes for some time, and he increased both their number and size, so they would be more representative of natural biotas, as demonstration areas. No matter that they showed his premises right; an influential minority of the stockmen he had reduced began "agitating" trouble for him.

"I decided I had to work on the big outfits, cut them down and not have the little fellows ask why pick on me," said Kirby. "I thought if we could get their ranges started shaping up we could then proceed on down the line toward the smaller permittees. We soon found we were going to have to put out facts and figures, do educational work to people other than stockmen. . . . We had to show they had a stake here, that it was not just a fight between the Forest Service and permittees."

So, starting about 1938, Kirby began writing articles for newspapers and making speeches telling of conditions and trends. He went to community and state leaders. The president of a large bank was on a four-day show-me trip with him. The governor went out for one day of inspection. Newsmen and others indicated interest. Labor leaders went, too.

Kirby said a stockman had two motivations: First, ranching is his living; second, a national forest grazing preference had a cash value because fees were low. Therefore, cuts meant loss of money from having fewer animals to sell, either on the market or in a transfer of base property. Kirby considered some of the permit values fantastic; grazing preferences on the Tonto sold for as much as $400 to $500 a cow.

"They'd come to see me and say they'd paid good money for preferences and cuts were taking money away from them," Kirby continued. "Finally, stockmen were protesting clear to Washington. Once when the American National Livestock Association [met] in Denver, five of them chartered a plane to go to Washington on this situation on the Tonto. . . . Their attitude was that range condition and the need for reductions had become an obsession with me. . . . I'd made reductions up to as high as 60 percent—and they should have been 100 percent in some cases."

Severe effects of overuse, Big Horn National Forest, Wyoming, 1932. *USFS photo*

Same hillside 17 years later; slow recovery on way after stock trail was abandoned, Big Horn National Forest, Wyoming, 1949. *USFS photo by F. Lee Kirby*

Often, he went on, practical aspects of range recovery were obscured by "the human angle." He "went out on ranges with permittees, and often had someone from the Division of Range Management in the Regional Office with me for the benefit of his judgment
along with my own. I tried to avoid mistakes as to range condition."
At times the regional office man would agree to the need for cuts but
say, "This is not the time to do it." His answer, said Kirby, was, "I've
been up against the problem for thirty-five years and have yet to see
a *right* time for corrective action."

Kirby: One rancher I had to hit hard was a four-time president of the
ANLA; he had two outfits on the Tonto and in addition had excess numbers
on his allotments . . . We had to eliminate that man entirely.
Carhart: How did you get by with that?
Kirby: Well, it made the regional forester sore. In other cases this rancher
forced the removal of various forest officers; he used to boast about it.
Carhart: What was his leverage?
Kirby: Well, being president of the ANLA was part of it; and he'd gotten
the support of various forest advisory boards. Even when he was no longer
president he was at all the meetings, and so on.

To bolster the competency of his ranger staff, Kirby took them on
trips of several days' duration, complete with chuck wagon and camp
cook; they had long discussions in the evenings about ranges they
had inspected during the day. "We were studying conditions right on
the ground; . . . I was highly complimented for the innovation." However, as he pressed on with his campaign of education and AUM
reductions, things got hotter.

We finally had an investigation down here. The affected permittees
tried to make me compromise some of these adjustments. The investigation
was by the regional forester and two assistants. They couldn't find I was
wrong, but thought I should have gone at it more carefully, and I was
criticized for doing so much preaching to so many different groups. . . .
Well, we had a [reduction] case come up on the Pine District [in 1945],
in which I had the full cooperation of the ranger [who had been called to
meet superiors in Kirby's office.] I met the ranger before daylight and we
talked it over. . . . I told him he'd be under much pressure, as I had been
for more than three days, and I'd like him to just take it if he still thought
the downward adjustment right. He sure didn't yield. Frank Pooler was
regional forester and Alva Simpson was personnel chief; they had come to
my office.
I finally told the regional forester he was asking me to compromise my

judgment. I told him it would be all right if he took the case out of my hands or overruled me or if he gave me written instruction; but he'd have to take full responsibility. . . . After a while I . . . asked Pooler how much longer this was going to go on; we had been repeating ourselves a couple of days, saying nothing new. . . .

They were getting scared to death of stockmen pressure. . . . They told me maybe I didn't realize that relations with stockmen were never worse than then. I replied I was the man at the end of the line, getting the pressure the strongest. . . . I told him there never was a time when the Service had better support than then, and reminded him of the people I'd taken on show-me trips. Pooler said something about my being a martyr and thought I liked the situation. . . . I didn't like that too well and said, "The trouble with you, Pooler, is that you don't have what it takes to face this." He wasn't the kind of man to take that and I knew it, and he started to tear into me and I fired right back at him that he'd dig into somebody working for him but wouldn't face this bunch of stockmen. . . .

You don't talk to your boss like that unless . . . you're just backed into a corner. I didn't want to lose my retirement privileges . . . and I did know Civil Service would give me a little protection. I knew it would take them [Pooler and Simpson] sometime to get back to Albuquerque and write their memorandum to Washington, so I stayed up that night and beat them to it. I had inside information that the regional forester had instructions not to move me or make other commitments without first consulting Washington. I wasn't supposed to know that, but it was a pretty comforting thing. Before they could get their memorandum written mine was there [in Albuquerque] with an extra copy and a request that it be forwarded to Washington along with what they wrote. I was going through channels, . . . not violating Civil Service rules. What I wrote was about what I'd said orally: Give me written orders and I'd follow them, but I wouldn't compromise my judgment.

The result was that Kirby was transferred to Washington for a brand new job that seems to have been created solely for the occasion.

Carhart: In other words, they were moving you away from an area where you knew the whole situation, away from the battle lines; they were going to muzzle you.

Kirby: Well, put it this way: They felt so much ill feeling had been stirred up that someone else might better take it up at that point and carry on. I was assured they'd stand pat on all adjustments I'd made and that my information and education work would be carried on. . . . I thought my program of land recovery would continue. What I . . . finally learned through a stockman himself was that they were promised, if they laid off pressure and let things quiet down, they'd remit my actions. And that's exactly what happened.

At about the same time, in May 1945, Pooler, the regional forester, said at a McCarran hearing [1] that the main concern of the Service on the Tonto was "maintenance of vegetative conditions that will best serve large farming developments depending on its water. . . . Unless we attack the problem . . . realistically we are going to . . . continue to damage that watershed." Further, the livestock people were "difficult" to work with on it.

Two weeks earlier Pooler had written [2] Henry G. Boice of the Arizona cattle growers organization a five-page letter in which he said criticisms of Kirby "stem fundamentally from cattlemen opposition" to the Service's program of cuts and conservation. He could not take action against Kirby, he wrote, because of Kirby's "sincere efforts" to do the job for which he was hired.

Ostensibly, Kirby was shipped out for insubordination, whereas his refusal to subordinate the needs of the range to the demands of big permittees seems to have been a more compelling cause of his departure from the Tonto in official disfavor.

After eleven months in Washington Kirby was transferred to Denver in charge of watershed management—and the special spot created in the Washington office thereafter remained vacant.[3] Kirby felt watershed management went hand in glove with range management, but had little opportunity to prove much, for about this time a wave of Interagency Basin Committees came into being as river basin planning for impoundments, irrigation works, and such grew to full postwar flower; Kirby was assigned to attend basin committee meetings and shuffle water resource planning papers, in which capacity he ended his career in the Forest Service. Before the Carhart–Kirby interview ended, these other points regarding range management in relation to the Service were made;

Kirby: By this time I think you know we made our full share of errors. I think some of the biggest mistakes have been made in high places. I think a lot of field men—I got a lot of letters when I was transferred to Washington—wanted to do the right things and were watching what was happening to me. When they saw, they decided they'd better just sort of swim with the current. So, . . . the facts are written on the land; if put to use they'll knock out the effectiveness of these organized minorities, and an aware public will respond and back the defenders of the resources. . . . It is a mistake to remain on the defensive as the Forest Service has all through the years. It isn't necessary; I don't think we can meet our responsibility that way. . . . We've got to get the big shots to realize there's no quick or easy or painless way of getting the range job done. It won't get easier by postponement; also, recovery potential is gradually being reduced. I don't think some ranges can be brought back in the lifetimes of anybody now living, to anything like what they were when white people began using these lands, but we ought to bring them back to the maximum of which they are capable; most range lands today are still on a downward trend. . . . What I did I've done conscientiously. I gave it the best I had. Guess I made my full share of mistakes; I just hope someone else will have more success than some of us who pushed the trail through in the first place.

The Roy Williams Case

In his last two field assignments, Roy Williams was either in the frying pan or the fire—and the searing that resulted must be labeled the accomplishment of stockmen and association leaders with whom he dealt, and their ability to influence higher officials of the Forest Service directly or through political channels.

I became acquainted with Williams in 1947 when he was supervisor of Grand Mesa National Forest in western Colorado, but much of this case study comes from the files of E. D. Sandvig, and communications between Sandvig and me, now in the Conservation Center of the Denver Public Library.

The Mesa had been a hot spot for a long time. Dan Hughes of Montrose, chairman of the Joint National Livestock Committee in the Great Land Grab era, revived memories of troubled times— caused by overgrazing—as far back as the 1920s when he testified [4] before the Barrett Committee at Grand Junction in September, 1947.

In the winter of 1946–1947 there was talk of merging the Grand Mesa with the adjoining Uncompahgre National Forest for more efficient administration. The Service had merged several national forests about this time, and in general the joinings appear to have been beneficial. In this instance, stockmen speaking out in favor of the merger did so mainly because they wanted Williams replaced by a supervisor who would be more amenable in grazing matters. [5] Precisely because he felt the firm hand of Williams was needed there, Sandvig, chief of range management in Region 2, opposed the merger at that time. He was not averse to moving Williams, but wanted his transfer delayed until a man of his caliber would be available to take command of the newly consolidated forest area.

The reason for livestock people's eagerness to have Williams sent

packing was really quite simple in its essentials. He had been pursuing a policy of reducing grazing to fit the condition of the ranges,
especially those of stream valleys at the western end of the Mesa
whose waters fed the municipal lines of the City of Grand Junction
and the irrigation canals of a regionally important fruit- and
vegetable-growing area. East and West Divide Creeks and Kannah
Creek were vital drainages. The Mesa is high, around 10,000 feet
above sea level, and nearby Grand Junction sits at about 4,500 feet.
The creeks in question pitch down rather steep slopes and their valleys generally are narrow. Yet their basins had been heavily loaded
with livestock for years. There was considerable erosion. Streams
tended to flow with a muddy rush during spring runoff, to be followed by low levels later in the year. And the stock numbers raised
questions in the minds of city folks and irrigation farmers as well as
Service officials. E. B. Underhill, testifying at the Barrett hearing at
Grand Junction, said [6] that at times the streams resembled the
effluent emerging from the back side of a barn—which may have been
exaggeration.

People of the area were divided. Some, such as Underhill, approved sizable grazing reductions so there would be less question
about the availability and the quality of the city's drinking water;
purity was less at issue than taste and appearance. Others sided
with the stockmen. In time there would be highly publicized show-me
rides, with the stockmen's leaders wanting to go to areas still in good
condition while the Service's people were equally insistent that badly
overgrazed ranges be inspected.[7]

It was in this sort of atmosphere that Williams carried out the
multiple duties of forest supervisor which, in the face of rising hostil-
ity, he felt had to include decisions to cut livestock use where needed
to conform to grazing capacity. That is, he made such decisions until early 1948. In that year Chief Watts approved a three-year moratorium on reductions that Grand Mesa permittees had clamored for,
in and out of the Barrett hearing room.

Being overruled by the chief's office in Washington is no small
matter to a field official. It becomes known quickly all over the forest,
the region, and the entire Service through the "grapevine"—and the
effectiveness of the official is inevitably affected adversely. Consequently, Roy Williams was glad to be moved to Wyoming in late
1947, when he learned that the moratorium ruling was to be issued.
He went to the Big Horn National Forest as supervisor, succeeding
lenient William Fay. And he went knowing that range conditions on

Forest Supervisor Roy Williams on range rated poor to depleted, with severe erosion and soil scalping, Big Horn National Forest, Wyoming, 1948. *USFS photo*

the Big Horn were just about as bad, and permittees he would have to deal with were at least as onery, as any he had faced on Grand Mesa.

Williams did not go unattended. The livestock leaders of Colorado sent a dossier of Williams's alleged bad traits ahead of him so he'd be assured of a belligerent reception on arrival, and harassment during his tenure. He was alleged to be irascible, hard to get along with, would side with recreationists against stockmen at every opportunity—that sort of thing.

I have not seen the dossier, but its contents may be gauged by these lines from a letter Mollin of the American National wrote [8] to Senator Joseph C. O'Mahoney of Wyoming in October 1950:

> . . . In four years time he [Williams] has torn the livestock industry of the Grand Mesa country completely apart, forcing many stockmen to withdraw from the forest completely and in general just simply raised Hell. He was then sent to the Big Horn. Apparently for the same purpose and *unless you intervene with the top officials in Washington* to save the permittees of that area, they are going to be subjected to the same disgraceful tyranny . . . [italics added].

On the other side, here is an excerpt from a letter Sandvig[9] wrote me in May 1971:

> Of the many of us who got our necks wrung, . . . Roy Williams probably took more punishment than anyone. . . . He was dedicated in every sense of the word in trying to stop the terrible abuses that were occurring on the range. I never heard Roy speak one cross word in his discussions with ranchers. . . . The Forest Service should have given Roy a Superior Service Award. . . .

The recipients of the dossier about Williams included J. Elmer Brock, vice-chairman of the Joint National Livestock Committee, former president of the American National, and one of the industry's more intransigent spokesmen. Williams needed experienced men badly for at least two ranger districts; Brock ran stock on one of them. Raw recruits could not be expected to stand up under the strategies and tactics ranchers such as Brock could employ; they knew the rules as well as the Service people, and tricks of the trade for getting around or negating those they didn't like. Williams also needed an assistant in his office to handle range details; again an experienced hand was required. In time he got rangers, but not the needed headquarters help.

And the permittee leadership kept the pot of discontent boiling. Every downward adjustment, in numbers or time, was considered a personal affront. Two techniques of protest seem to have been favored. One was to find ways to discredit Forest Service judgment as to range condition or trend. The other was to persuade the state's congressional delegation to bear down on the Service through political pressure applied in Washington.

The stockmen had no difficulty getting a team of agronomists from the University of Wyoming at Laramie to make a study of Big Horn range conditions. The study team came from the same group that had appeared before the Barrett Committee at Rawlins in September, 1947.[10] It was notable that nearly everything the Forest Service had to say about deteriorated or depleted range conditions was disputed by the university team. Williams got range research help to counter the stockmen's experts,[11] but in the adversary atmosphere that prevailed it was a rare permittee who would concede that the Service findings were correct.

Senator O'Mahoney wielded the hatchet for the livestock lobby in Washington. Mollin provided him with material from the ANLA's offices in Denver, and political supporters from the Big Horn country filled him in on local details as they saw them. Letters I have seen were saturated with misrepresentations, some blatant, others containing rather nicely phrased nuances instead of blunt accusations. O'Mahoney was inclined to be direct and to apply a crusher when he acted. Here is the text of a letter he wrote [12] to Chief Forester Watts on October 11, 1950:

I note your statement that the provisions of the Act of April 24, 1950, relative to the establishment of local advisory boards, have not yet been implemented since the necessary regulations and policies, though now being formulated, have not yet been issued. Technically speaking, of course, the policies were announced in the law itself, and the rules and regulations to be issued are for the purpose of effectuating those policies. I know that we are in agreement with respect to the importance of establishing the best possible public relations between forest management and the livestock industry, upon the one hand, as well as with the members of wildlife and conservation associations and the general public upon the other. The sooner the local advisory boards are established and the rules and regulations promulgated, the sooner it will be possible to bring about the mutual understanding and cooperation which is so essential.

The enclosed copy of a letter I have just received from Mr. F. E. Mollin, . . . together with the other communications we have already discussed, emphasize the importance of the problem. The Senate Appropriations Committee, of course, is interested in facilitating the management of the national forests in the public interest, and it occurs to me that it might be helpful if I should undertake to arrange a public hearing for that committee in Sheridan, perhaps some time before the Congress assembles. After you have reviewed the enclosure I shall be glad to have your comment.

Although only two paragraphs long, the letter contained these four admonitions or threats that Chief Watts clearly understood:

1. The Service must speed up the work of establishing the new type of advisory board authorized in the Granger–Thye Act.
2. The Service was not following a course of getting along with the stockmen; it should at once pursue better "public relations."
3. The Senate Appropriations Committee was in position to reduce Service funds if the stockmen didn't get a better deal.
4. The threat of another public hearing, which was a powerful weapon.

The ordeals of the McCarran and Barrett hearings were still fresh in the memories of all affected Service personnel, from chief down to ranger's assistant. No official wanted any more.

When the lid blew off for Williams, however, it came in the course of what ordinarily would have been a minor aspect of the total situation, the extent of predatory animal control work to be carried out on forest ranges by the U.S. Fish & Wildlife Service. During and after World War II chemical corporations everywhere were developing powerful poisons to use on whatever was considered a pest or a hindrance to what men wanted to do. Among these were devices and poisons calculated to rid the ranges of predators. There was the cyanide gun, for instance, which fired deadly poison into a coyote's mouth when it bit into a tempting piece of meat set out as bait. The poison would, of course, kill whatever carnivorous creature might happen along, including valuable dogs. There was a highly toxic poison formula known as "1080"; and there were other materials and methods.

Under an agreement with the Interior Department the Service had power to approve when and where such poisons might be used on the forests. At a meeting of the Wyoming Wool Growers Association at Worland in November, 1951, Williams suggested that the poisoning program the sheepmen wanted for the following year was unnecessarily severe. A letter from Williams to Sandvig dated November 20, 1951, is revealing:

"I felt my position was sound," Williams wrote [13] his then regional range superior, "since the losses were so low in 1951 as to be hardly noticeable, . . . and I attempted to defend my position."

Ed Cliff had by then been promoted first to the position of regional forester at Denver succeeding John W. Spencer, and quickly thereafter to be C. M. Granger's successor as assistant chief forester in charge of administration, which had jumped him over the head of Walt Dutton, ostensibly next in line. Cliff attended the Wyoming meeting and, Williams wrote, because Williams stood his ground, "was mad as hell" saying "I'd win a battle and lose a war."

At Cliff's suggestion the predator control matter was referred to a committee where Williams was forced to back down. "The entire committee including Cliff was hostile toward me," the letter continued, and the association secretary, J. B. Wilson, said "if there is only one coyote on the Big Horn we are going to get it." Despite this, after the meeting Williams worked out an arrangement with Interior's wildlife officials whereby the program would be kept under control and not expanded to the point of total eradication of predatory animals.[14]

That was not the end of Williams's problems, however. He wrote that "just before Cliff left on Friday morning he called me into a corner and let me have it." He said Cliff accused him of having contrived the poisoning controversy for ulterior purposes; that he was "out of sympathy with the livestock industry and will not cooperate with them"; that he spent "too much time with other groups who antagonize the stockmen" (which apparently referred to the Sheridan chapter of the Izaak Walton League, as it was the only conservation group in the vicinity at the time); that his "usefulness as a supervisor on any western national forest had ended since my reputation would follow me wherever I might go"; and that his transfer had been under consideration ever since the controversy a year earlier over the university range study.

Then, "after many other remarks as to what a poor range administrator I am, he began to build me up as an organizer, a planner, and a damn' good man." "I saw the light," Williams said, when Cliff followed by denigrating the regional officer at Denver then in charge of forest fire control activities. "No question as to whether I wanted it or not, I move to Denver February first and start fighting fire."

"I see myself in about the same position as [Lee] Kirby," Williams went on. "I have only five years to go [before retirement] and with Cliff in Granger's spot and the political picture as it is and the animosity existing here, I am going along with the move rather than be forced into it. I don't like it, but with the hook-up between Cliff and O'Mahoney I can see where he expects to capitalize on my transfer and possibly yours. . . . With [Cliff] in Washington I can see where O'Mahoney's office will become the clearing house for Wyoming stockmen."

A story in the Denver *Post* of December 16, 1951,[15] quoted Cliff as saying Williams's transfer was a "promotion," and that he told inquiring reporters neither it nor the impending transfer of Sandvig to Oregon "ordered two weeks ago" meant "a retreat from sound range conservation or a 'purge' of advocates of . . . programs mapped" by Sandvig during his tenure as assistant regional forester for range management.

But C. A. (Andy) Anderson, who had been a range conservationist under Sandvig until he, too, was shipped elsewhere, saw it differently. Anderson wrote Sandvig [16] on February 6, 1952, that Williams's "eyes reflect the beating he took."

Roy Williams stuck it out in forest fire control at Denver until retirement. He died not long afterward.

Three years and two supervisors later Lee Spatziani, a ranger on the Big Horn, wrote [17] Sandvig that the "new policy" there seemed to be "to hell with natural resources but just don't make the cowboys mad. . . . We have no control over [them]. They just tell us to go to hell and that is it. Most of us don't even bother to count the cattle or inspect the range or anything. There is no use because there is nothing we can do about it. . . ."

He quoted a story brought by the grapevine from the Routt National Forest in Colorado. It seems some Washington officials were there on an inspection visit and the local foresters had been told that before they could move in on overgrazing permittees they'd have to "line up our ducks so we'd be ready when the time was right." A bold ranger was said to have asked, "All right, which of you ducks do I start lining up first?" Then, back to the subject of Big Horn problems, Spatziani wrote that the University of Wyoming agronomists had finished a four-year range survey and "I imagine it will take us twenty years to disprove their findings and meantime the cattle and sheep men will be assured of their preferences. . . ." The study ploy had been "a nice move" by the livestock leaders, he said.

Was Spatziani's letter just the griping of a disgruntled ranger or was he airing conditions as they really were at that time? The Williams case record makes one wonder.

Other Expendables

The "purge" denied by Cliff in the Denver newspaper story at the time Roy Williams was shifted from the Big Horn to the fire control desk did not end with him or with Earl Sandvig, whose story is told in a separate chapter. Others who had been identified with the Sandvig–Spencer team in Region 2 also were on the "hit" list. Spencer had taken retirement before reaching mandatory retirement age partly out of frustration, for his health and other faculties were sound, and I have no doubt others did so also.

H. E. Schwan, range specialist under Sandvig, was offered a spot in the technological aid program launched in postwar years and secured a foreign assignment; he did not return to the Forest Service. Schwan's name was on a list of purged men Sandvig furnished in 1972, compiled from memory.[18]

Art Cramer, staff assistant in range management, Denver, was ordered to take a timber "bug control" desk job after Sandvig had been shipped out. He soon retired for disability and died shortly afterward. His file of photos in the Denver Public Library's Conservation Center constitute a revealing record of the damaged, even depleted, condition of much of the range in Region 2 in the years Sandvig and Company struggled to bring about corrective reductions in stocking. Some of Cramer's photos help illustrate this book.

C. A. Anderson, range management assistant at Denver, was shifted to Region 4, Ogden, Utah. He, too, quickly secured a foreign aid assignment and, like Schwan, did not return to the Forest Service.

Joseph Radel, range and wildlife staff assistant on the San Isabel National Forest in south central Colorado, made higher-ups unhappy because he failed to "cooperate" with one George Everett, an influential permittee near Salida. At about that time—late 1940s, early 1950s—Joseph W. Penfold of the Izaak Walton League, my successor as western representative in Denver, learned from the Colorado Game and Fish Commission that Everett had filed a large claim for alleged damage to range by antelope. Penfold discovered that the antelope damage, if any, was on state-owned land leased by Everett for grazing purposes at pennies per acre per year.[19] Radel, who had nothing to do with Penfold's disclosures, was nevertheless accused of having conspired with him and was shipped to San Francisco and a desk job in personnel management, which was far removed from his range specialty.

Gordon Van Buren, ranger on the Salida District, San Isabel National Forest, was deemed tainted with Radel in the George Everett case. He initiated reductions on the forest allotment where Everett's stock grazed. Washington officials were furious because Radel and Van Buren cooperated with newsmen who wrote stories published in Pueblo, Colorado, papers about range conditions on the allotment.[20] Van Buren retired after being shifted to a staff job on the Rio Grande National Forest, a job that had nothing to do with range management.

The C. K. Collins story is a goodly part of Chapter 15, the story of years-long domination by stockmen of the Uncompahgre National Forest.

Those listed above were few in number, in a sense, but they did not have to constitute a regiment for the message to take effect. I have read and later will quote from a number of letters from field men to Sandvig,[21] all of them telling how swiftly the word spread that all who had worked closely with him had been purged or would be unless they fell docilely into the mold shaped by the new policies of Watts and Cliff. They appear hard to discredit. They are a good part of the reason why I am convinced that most of the Service's men in the field felt they had no choice other than to acquiesce in the new go-easy policy if they hoped to advance in their chosen profession.

14

A Hide On a
Corral Fence

The cynical expression, "Let him hang there and slowly, slowly twist in the wind," lingers from the aftermath of Watergate. Cowboys on the western range might use different terminology with similar meaning. They would hang his hide on a corral fence.

In this instance the hide to be hung was that of Earl D. Sandvig, assistant regional forester for range and wildlife management in Denver 1944–51. But it is not true to say that livestockmen stripped the skin from Sandy's living flesh. They provided whetstones to sharpen knives, but the skinning was done by Sandvig's superiors in the U.S. Forest Service.

In July 1971, Sandvig wrote[1] me from his retirement home in Portland, Oregon, that since he no longer was in the Service he felt he could speak freely so his story might be told "just as it happened." Now, several years and many manila folders and other containers of letter exchanges and documentation later, I am setting down facts as official files, personal recollections and records, and other information, much of it furnished by people who were there, disclose them to be.

The Earl Sandvig I knew in Region 2 might not be called handsome in the classic western movie hero sense, but had all the other required attributes. He was medium tall, lean, and weathered. To another westerner meeting him for the first time it would be obvious he was an outdoorsman, probably spent many hours annually in the saddle, likely could handle camp gear or rifle well, and even pass the acid test of casually throwing a double diamond hitch on a pack horse. Sandy's recent pictures indicate the lean look remains; the features have mellowed, the lines deepened through the years.

Sandvig was reared on a northeastern Montana ranch, and a taste of forestry on a summer job in 1920 while a student at the University of Montana persuaded him to make a career of it. He led a range survey crew on Helena National Forest when graduated in 1923, did more of the same in 1924, and was at a desk in the regional office at Missoula in 1925. Very soon he went out for another year of range surveys. In 1927 he was assistant supervisor of Custer National Forest, and moved to the bigger Beaverhead in 1930 in the same capacity. Four years later he became its supervisor. In 1936 he carried out a special study of the ranching–grazing industry, with emphasis on setting up limits on numbers of stock that might utilize forest allotments, in which he explored economic justification for such action. When the report was finished he became assistant to the regional range and wildlife chief. For a year, 1937, he was forest inspector for eastern Montana, and in 1938 was promoted to assistant regional forester for range and wildlife at Missoula. Six years there, and then on to Denver, Region 2, with the same title. At the end of 1951 he was ordered to Portland. This had the appearance of a simple lateral movement similar to that which had brought him to Denver. In fact, it was a repudiation of what he had undertaken and stood for in Region 2, and I doubt if any personnel shift in its history has brought the Service quicker or more intense public and private criticism. Shortly, Sandvig took a foreign aid assignment. When that ended he returned to the Service, and retired as soon thereafter as possible. He sat for a time at the personnel desk in Portland, and his close-out title was deputy regional forester for Hawaii. He and his wife Dorothy then came back to Portland.

Here we are chiefly interested in the period from 1944 through 1951, seven of the most turbulent years the range managers of the Service have gone through. The Sandvig story is pertinent today because fundamental aspects of the ongoing administration and operation of our great National Forest System are involved. Two diametrically opposed philosophies of national forest range management clashed. One favored by the livestock lobby won. The subject is worth closer examination than it has been given heretofore. Years ago a forest officer told me that when there was a tough problem to unravel he'd lay the facts on the desk of a superior who would ask, "What is the right thing to do?" No question of what was politically expedient, or what might let the service off with minimal criticism by

Forester Earl Sandvig examines shrubbery (cinquefoil) in depleted wet meadow, Roosevelt National Forest, 1949. *USFS photo by Art Cramer*

its livestock or other clientele; just, "What is the *right* thing to do?" This may be the crux of the matter.

In Chapter 12 we examined the clashing philosophies that brought on a radical change in Service policy. Sandvig and Ed Cliff were leading field-level exponents of the opposing philosophies, and when the critical time arrived in Sandvig's career Cliff had moved on to a high spot in the Washington office, where the views he favored prevailed. Sandvig got shipped out. Cliff stayed on and in due course became head of one of the most prestigious agencies in our government. Was the shipping of Sandvig the right thing to do? Was it expediency, to move away from a sensitive administrative area an official who was making political constituencies unhappy by his advocacy of reduced grazing use as a range management method? Were there scientific or technological reasons why Sandvig's approach to curing range disorders—which, it must be recalled, had also been those of the entire Service hierarchy a few years earlier—wouldn't work or shouldn't be applied? I suspect the beating Sandy and his supporters took was administered because to let him stay on the Region 2 range job would continue to irritate industry leaders and obstruct the chosen change in Service policy. In other words, hanging Sandvig's hide on the corral fence was a *quid* by the Service for which the industry moguls pledged a *quo* in the form of peace on the range. It is undeniably true that, coincident with the purges of Sandvig and others linked to his policies, the Service retreated almost all the way from AUM reductions plus rehabilitation to range betterment alone.

I do not promise an unbiased narrative, for at that time I believed Sandvig was traveling the proper route. I was involved in more than a fringe way. And I consider myself among the gullible who were flummoxed by the actions and end results of happenings at high levels in the Forest Service. Yet removing Sandvig from an effective role in the management of public range resources was, I think now, the lesser of the injustices perpetrated. I believe the long-term victims who have suffered most are the rank and file of permittees on the one hand, and the taxpaying public on the other. For despite the millions spent since 1949 on rehabilitation, forest ranges today appear actually less productive overall than in that earlier year, if AUMs of grazing are a fair yardstick. Grazing has declined and, because that is so, permittees have been forced to look elsewhere for the feed required to put flesh on herds and flocks. This has been costly to the ranchers, has consumed cereal grains that might have been used to advantage elsewhere, and in the end has been a loss to the American public.

Mentally I can see Service hackles rise over the implication that declining forage resources may be the sole or principal reason why fewer animal unit months of grazing are had nowadays than then. There certainly have been additional reasons, as is made clear elsewhere, why stock numbers and grazing units have declined. No argument there.

Sandvig's story ought to be an exception, one rare enough to be called unique, but it isn't. Files drawn upon show that a number of foresters received similar treatment. One roll was called in Chapter 13. Others were not purged but their morale was shattered. Sandvig at the time received more than 150 letters,[2] and the majority that were from Forest Service personnel are eloquent testimony to the despondency his going brought to range men in the field.

As Sandvig put his feet on successive rungs of the career ladder in Region 1 he had the guidance and example of one of the Service's truly dedicated officials. Regional Forester Evan Kelley, a major in World War I, had high leadership qualities. He was determined to bring livestock use of Region 1 forests to within safe grazing capacity.

He moved steadily in that direction, even in the Great Depression years when Chief Forester Silcox was ordering a slack policy that, while humanitarian, was hard on the ranges. Kelley believed the nation could not enjoy maximum benefits from the land if it was allowed to produce at only a fraction of its capability. Man's suffering from quick corrective action would be temporary; the benefits would be lasting. This is a truth essential to the whole thrust of this book.

The years under Major Kelley's leadership had a profound influence on Sandvig. In Region 1 he saw that the ranges responded when moderately grazed. The results have persisted. In 1972 I was urged by Service people to visit Montana forests to see for myself how wounds of earlier years had been healed. True enough, those ranges received their fair share of the appropriations for revegetation and related work since enactment of Anderson–Mansfield, but it seems incontrovertible that today's healing began when Kelley was regional forester and Sandvig was with him. Meantime, forest ranges to the south, in Region 2, had not fared so well.

Frames of time and circumstances when Sandvig was moved to Denver are important. World War II still raged. He kept at hand a copy of the orders Acting Chief Earle Clapp had sent to the field in April 1942,[3] to hold the line against such abuses as had devastated the ranges in World War I. Officers in the field could interpret those orders as reversing the soft Silcox line enunciated in 1936. Major Kelley had already done so, and it rubbed off on Sandvig. Lyle Watts, when he succeeded Clapp in 1943, gave every indication that he wanted the Clapp policy continued. This is a vital point, for I have not found any orders from Watts telling the field to back away from a policy of firmness against overuse of range. Not until 1949 did Watts publicly display weakness in that regard.

At Denver, Sandvig's judgment was trusted by Regional Forester Spencer, who gave him much leeway as preparations began for reaching 1946 permit term decisions. Spencer believed firmly that signals sent from Watts's office indicated that Washington was dedicated to the proposition that range condition and trend were to be basic guides to reaching those decisions. The two acted accordingly, and instructions to staff and line officers were to that effect.

The developing land-grab movement in the livestock industry was worrisome and ominous. Leaders among the permittees and in the associations were growing assertive and aggressive. This attitude was in part a result of the McCarran investigations—what it was achieving for the industry in general, and specifically what was befalling the administration of the public domain under the Taylor Act. The industry and the federal agencies were traveling fast toward a confrontation intended to show once and for all time who was boss.

In Region 2 Sandvig prepared to meet the challenge willingly, even eagerly. Soon after arrival in August 1944, he wrote Major Kelley that the contrast between "the waving bunch grass of Montana" and "the oakbrush of Colorado" was so great as to be hard to describe. "The grass has long since been chased out of much of the country—so long that present-day inhabitants seem to have forgotten its importance to a happier and more abundant life on the range." He was perplexed that forest officers apparently had not seen what was happening many years earlier, for evidence of deterioration was on every hand, with better forms of plant life destroyed or on the way out.

Earlier I likened the oncoming of depleted range to the insidiousness of drought. Sandvig's comment that "present day inhabitants seem to have forgotten . . ." brings the added thought that each new generation tends to accept what it sees or experiences as normal. Faced with a depleted range, it might assume that was its nature, that it had always been so—unless it was taught and brought to realize otherwise. Sandvig considered his a teaching assignment as well as a managerial task, and he drew freely on the research staff for assistance to drive home the truth about Region 2 ranges.

The process of adjustment is going to be a difficult one [his letter to Kelley read]. First there is the orientation of Forest officer viewpoints regarding proper conditions. I'm afraid . . . optimism in grazing capicity and complacency bred of long association with a bad situation will not yield to easy treatment.

Second, there is well-organized resistance to change on the part of stockmen, and what appears to be good support from livestock publications. Third, the climate is severe, extending the length of time it will take for corrective measures to show up favorably. . . .

The boys here tell me I haven't seen anything so very bad yet—that the worst is yet to come.

A few days later Sandvig wrote J. N. Templer, a friend then in the Washington office, that "It has been my unpleasant lot in the last four weeks to initiate . . . revocations of more preferences than I did in more than five years in Region 1. . . . All of them stem from flagrant and repeated trespass. Some of them may dribble into the Chief's office before they are finally settled."

Big-game-proof fence at test plot, Deerlodge National Forest, Montana, 1947. *USFS photo*

Test plot fence removed at same area and moderate grazing allowed; maintains range quality. Deerlodge National Forest, Montana, 1967. *USFS photo*

I doubt if Sandvig was as prescient as his words hinted, but the two letters gave the essence of the existing situation, the overall dimensions of the task ahead, and a glimpse of the frustrations and final defeats that lay only seven years in the future.

Sandvig viewed successful correction of past abuses not as a dreaded duty but as a challenge to his ingenuity, diplomacy, and technological capacity. The time to announce to permittees the conditions under which they must operate in the 1946 permit term was only a few months ahead. Determinations had to be made of range needs and usage for the next decade in an area that encompassed two national forests in the Black Hills of South Dakota, those in the eastern two-thirds of Wyoming and all of Colorado, plus small acreages in Kansas and Nebraska that are not important to this narrative. Field personnel who figuratively were expected to tip their hats when an influential permittee or association official passed, had to be inculcated with new or renewed pride in their profession. Innumerable meetings with permittees and others had to be attended, with sometimes tense periods of questioning after frank disclosures of conditions and of what should be done to reverse downward forage trends.

If we liken the land-grab turbulence to a servicewide hurricane, it is right to say that its eye passed across Region 2, which was pounded with both the leading cumulus outriders and the gusts and torrents that followed. Many of Region 2's permittees had had their way so long it had become habit, and habit usually is changed with difficulty. Vociferous and influential leaders lived in or worked from Region 2 bases. With the exception of Nevada's McCarran, it would be members of Congress from Region 2 states who would apply the strongest political pressures.

With Spencer's blessing, Sandvig and his range specialists worked closely with their people out on point, the forest supervisors and district rangers. He wanted to learn to know his men, discover their varying talents, rouse those who were just hanging on, wondering if they would see the day when regional headquarters would get some iron in its backbone. As many as possible of the field people must become imbued with new assurance, new determination. For three years most of them moved purposefully ahead under his leadership, with growing confidence.

Working carefully on the basis of inspections on the ground backed by opinions of range specialists, the field staff, often accompanied by Sandvig or an assistant from the regional office, gave permittees the prospects for the new term. They rode the ranges with them to show reasons why in cases where cuts were needed. The advisory board on the Uncompahgre National Forest was stripped of management powers an earlier administration had wrongfully given it. (See Chapter 15.) Untoward sheep numbers on high ranges of the Routt in northwestern Colorado were sharply reduced. The growing Denver metropolitan area was encroaching on the Roosevelt, which lay to the north and northwest abutting Rocky Mountain National Park on three sides; recreation had become dominant there and lingering herds should be removed from remaining allotments on national forest lands lying between the city and the park. Excessive grazing use of the Big Horn in northern Wyoming and the Medicine Bow to the south had to be curtailed. On Grand Mesa in western Colorado, problems affected the basins of Kannah and East and West Divide Creeks. In south central Colorado there were difficulties over grazing on the San Isabel. All needed, and got, Sandvig's attention.

As far as surface indications are concerned, things seemed to be going well for the new regional leadership at the beginning of Sandvig's tenure. Here and there symptoms developed that in a different context might have given more concern. They were considered isolated instances at the start, but that could not and did not last. At a date not well defined, Region 2 learned it must be on guard. It was nagged by implications of the 1945 surrender by Region 3 and Washington in the case of Lee Kirby, and by official weaknesses in handling problems on the Modoc National Forest in northern California. There was an increasing chorus of dissent among permittees. Their spokesmen put repeated complaints and demands to western congressmen, after which both took them to the offices of the Chief Forester and the Secretary. We can look back upon them now in the way we view pictures in time lapse photography, which speeds up processes, and see various linkages.

The formation of the Joint National Livestock Committee came as a jolt. Put another way, it was a warning light that flared in intensity as its spokesmen paired national forest ranges with the public domain for the coming land grab attempt. The emasculation of the Grazing Service was real, and the excesses of the Barrett Subcommittee were burdensome in the extreme. Both were still hot memory when evidence surfaced of the effect of the increasing pressures on those officials in Washington who mattered most to the range men in the field. Sandvig watched the changes warily. He wrote [5] me on July 3, 1971, in part as follows;

"When Watts became chief many of us were elated over the positive stand he demonstrated in getting on top of the range problems. We held several strategy meetings in Ogden and Washington on the necessity of taking action to halt what we all knew was a disgrace in land management. *He began to weaken at Grand Junction . . .*" (italics added).

The degree of Watt's determination affected, or was affected by, others close to him. Leon Hurtt, a range inspector out of Washington and a Watts intimate, gave evidence of the weakening attitude in a report [6] that was sharply critical of the Region 2 program of grazing reductions. C. M. Granger, assistant chief for forest administration who had overall charge of range management, made an inspection trip to the Black Hills under the guidance of Ed Cliff after the latter had succeeded Spencer as regional forester. Granger showed both bias and technological weakness in his report [7] of that trip.

Granger's report said he had seen no erosion, no overgrazing, no conflict between livestock and wildlife on the Black Hills forest ranges. It reached Sandvig's office while he was away, but was read by four of his assistants who scribbled comment for his attention when he returned. An August 3, 1971, letter [8] to me from Ralph R. Hill of Denver, then Region 2 wildlife biologist, now retired, contained the following:

> I was the only one in the office at the time the Granger report reached Region 2, and wrote a note to Sandy saying what I thought of it. Later Herb Schwan, Art Cramer, and C. A. (Andy) Anderson came in and each added his notes to the memo. One said we might as well fire all ecologists. A second said that Chris Granger must have been wearing dark glasses. The third note was along the same line. *Sandy was the last man to see the memo.* Later . . . Sandy . . . [was accused of] putting us up to writing the notes. I fear the Washington Office got some poor analyses of Sandy. Later Chris said he hoped I wouldn't hold the memo against him" [italics added].

The "poor analyses" would naturally go from the regional forester, Cliff, to Washington, not from an underling. Hill wrote that Joseph W. Penfold of the Izaak Walton League had to apply pressure himself to get a glimpse of the Granger report, and that thereafter it was locked in Cliff's files.

Spencer's retirement in 1949 was a blow to Sandvig, and the promotion of Cliff to regional forester was a capper. He was convinced that chances for continuation of the corrective stocking program with which he was so closely identified had gone to zero. He felt he and Cliff had little in common in their approach to range management, that it would be only a matter of time before there was a confrontation, and that he, the subordinate, would be the loser. He determined to ask to be transferred to range management elsewhere, was called to Washington to confer with Watts, and was talked out of it.

A year earlier Sandvig and Cliff had shared a room while attending a public lands conference in Cody, Wyoming, as part of a meeting of the Wyoming Wool Growers Association. Sandvig was there as range chief for Region 2's forests in the eastern two-thirds of the state, Cliff in the same capacity for Region 4 at Ogden, with jurisdiction over western Wyoming forests. Sandvig commented on happenings there in a letter [9] to me of September 9, 1971:

... I was the center of attack by the Wool Growers' spokesman, Byron Wilson. When Cliff was called upon, ... he told the group that the Ogden Region ... would be glad to have ... range plants that we [in the Denver Region] considered ... indicators of a downward trend.

In our room that evening Cliff said we should take it easy in making reductions, that it took 50 years to ruin those ranges and we ought to go slow in making any changes, that the stockmen were powerful politically and the timing wasn't right to oppose them.

The Cliff comments comparing range vegetation in the two regions might have been no more than a wry wisecrack born of envy of a region better endowed by nature, or a wishful commentary on climatic differences. I heard a somewhat similar comment in July 1972, when I visited Deputy Regional Forester Basil K. Crane in Denver. Crane had come to Region 2 from Utah, in fact, had followed C. K. Collins as supervisor of the Uncompahgre National Forest in 1953. Crane told [10] me the Great Basin country, including much of Utah, "had the most fragile cover to start with," and so "went quickest" under heavy grazing use. Things "never got that bad here in Colorado and Wyoming." Sandvig interpreted Cliff's comments at Cody as denigrating, which may have been a correct assessment or a gauge of a growing clash of personalities, increasing antagonism. Cliff was ambitious, and he may have seen Sandvig as a threat to his own future progress in the Service. Or, the conversation in the hotel room could be interpreted as indicative of a political reaction to what in essence was a technological situation.

I was drawn into the schism between the two before the end of 1949. I wrote [11] Sandvig from the Izaak Walton League office in Chicago on December 31, 1949, saying Dutton and Cliff had recently been in and Cliff told me "you had just about reached the limit of what any human could take," which I construed to mean from the livestock industry, certainly not from Service superiors. They told me Sandvig was "thinking of asking to be transferred," and hoped I'd write and urge him to hang on. My letter to Sandvig was the result of the request:

I feel the loss of [retiring] John Spencer keenly enough. If you were to go, too, I am confident the entire situation would simply explode into something approaching chaos.

I recognize, to my regret, that your activities and situation have been affected by orders from [your superiors]. I think I know how difficult this has made your position. I suspect it will be tough for some time to come, *despite the assurances I had in this office this week that there'd be no further retreat and no appeasement* within the limits of existing authority. . . . I hope you will stand firmly and sweat it out where you are, *at least until we can see beyond doubt the direction your higher authority is traveling* [italics added].

Watts had written Sandvig a letter [12] on December 19, 1949 (which I first saw in 1971), in which he obliquely admitted he had failed to complete the corrective range program he had embraced when he took office. The Region 2 portion of the program had raised "sharp issues of far reaching importance," Watts wrote, adding they had "caused many equally sharp differences of opinion," for which there might not have been any ideal solutions. Then:

"*Some issues have become sort of complicated and decisions have had to be made accordingly. This has resulted in some disappointments personally, to you and to us as well*" (italics added).

The political meanings in that passage were clear, and disheartening to Sandvig.

Watts went on to say he believed Sandvig and Cliff would make a good team and "in time" eliminate "many of the difficulties that have beset the earlier stages of your work in Region 2." He wrote that "Ed, I know, wants you to stay and plans to talk this over with you," at which point Sandvig wrote, in a marginal note to me on a copy of the letter, that no such talk with Cliff had occurred and that, on his visit to Washington he had "the promises of Watts, Granger, and Dutton to support my program on the range." Those promises had persuaded him to stay on, a decision he later would call [13] "a tragic mistake."

It was much later before I realized the extent to which I had been gulled by Dutton and Cliff, and came to believe they were a large part of Sandvig's problem; Cliff the activist, Dutton the silent partner. The question must rise of why, if there were such irreconcilable differences between Cliff the superior and Sandvig the subordinate, it took another two years for Sandvig to be removed. I am convinced it was because Washington officials were still a bit uncertain as to the strength or weakness of the conservation community; it could have been a simple question of whether they could get by with Sandvig's ouster without an overwhelming upwelling of indignation and outrage.

Few of us in the movement had seen and acknowledged how far topside in the Forest Service had shifted from the Clapp and early Watts policies. We had not grasped the significance of the Anderson–Mansfield Act, nor had we linked it to the increasing softness developing in Washington.

I no longer am familiar with what others in the conservation movement felt and did in the years when the bold, brave determination of the Service to bring grazing under quick control reached its apex and then slid downward and in part degenerated into a purge of officials who had believed the course of the mid-1940s was the right one. My recollections are clearest of efforts Joe Penfold and I made to bolster the morale of Region 2's Sandvig and others, and to try to swing Washington away from capitulation. I was in close touch while in Denver, and Penfold quickly picked this up when I was moved to Chicago. He and I were in fairly regular touch with Watts, Dutton, Assistant Chief Edward C. Crafts (who specialized in legislative matters and other liaison with Capitol Hill), and later with Cliff after he moved on to succeed Granger.

Did our efforts have what we should now consider a wholesome effect? Did we egg Sandvig into taking an obdurate stand, or would he have remained as firm if we had never been on the scene? I may never know for sure.

We told the Service's Washington officials what steps we were taking or planned with respect to bills in Congress, and kept them informed of our activities related to those of the livestock associations. We received soothing words to our faces and in letters, even as the wheels turned toward almost total reliance on Anderson–Mansfield appropriations to right range wrongs. Now Penfold is gone—he died

in 1973–and there is no record available of his activities; the Izaak
Walton League's general offices allowed his files to be destroyed or
dissipated when the Denver office was closed in the late 1950s and
Penfold became the organization's conservation director in Washington.[14] Memory tells me our strongest and most persistent efforts were
employed against the procession of bill drafts that emerged from
livestock association offices and committees, in the hope that our defense of the Service's previous policy would persuade it to hang on.
We were convinced that in that aspect of the controversy between
the industry and the Service—as we conceived it—the Service was on
the verge of total victory, that it would take only a little more firmness and persistence to cause the stock leadership to capitulate. It
was not to be. Sandvig must go, and his going was symbolic.

His departure from Denver loosed a flood of comment that reflected bitterness against the officials who brought about his downfall
or stood silently by while it was taking place. The following[15] are
typical of comments in the letters and cards to Sandvig now on
library shelves in Denver:

"I wouldn't give a thin dime for the morale in Region 2."

"I'm glad I have only a few more years until retirement; you
were right all the way."

"We feel lost without you. We felt sure of ourselves because we
knew you'd back us when we were right."

"Your leadership breathed a little life into some of us older ones
who'd slept peacefully for so long. . . . You backed us loyally. . . ."

"I'm fearful the rangers will fold with you gone."

"I've never before so hated to see a man go."

"I'm horrified by the purge. There's a deepseated unrest, tension
in the service."

"It was a good, . . . clean fight all the way. You made man-
sized tracks. . . ."

"It seems we must now throw away the stick and get an um-
brella."

"The whole business was pretty low."

"Without you we'll have no true conservation, just nice sounding
words. Its too expensive to work for posterity."

"I'm thoroughly disgusted with the Washington Office."

"You should have been made Regional Forester long ago."

"Our heads are sore and bloody without your support."

"Policy now is to let the resources go; just don't make the cowpokes mad. We don't even bother to count the cows on and off the range."

Even part of the opposition was disturbed. The Denver *Post* quoted [16] a Colorado Wool Growers Association official as saying "We could sit with Sandvig. We'd argue and then we'd work together afterward. We admired him."

After his removal was ordered in December 1951, Sandvig wrote [17] me a moving letter, parts of which summarize what I have been trying to convey in this chapter.

Two years ago I took a new grasp on myself after reading your splendid letters [he wrote]. I thought I saw coming the disaster that has arrived, but took a chance that I might be wrong.

Few people knew as I did that when John Spencer left here the Forest Service was going to pull the rug from under its campaign to restore its range lands. John and I were faced with stiff opposition from within; a much bigger obstacle than we could handle. *It was a happy day in the upper levels of the Forest Service when John retired. Then it would be relatively easy to take care of me with a new Regional Forester. If our philosophies didn't . . . coincide it would be me, not the Regional Forester, who was wrong* [italics added].

I asked for transfer . . . after considering the risk. . . . I knew Cliff wasn't going to stay in the groove. He had already given me the idea he was not in sympathy with such stout pluggers for conservation as Carhart, DeVoto, yourself, and others. It was OK to use you fellows, but the main effort would be to improve relationships with stockmen. . . . Above all, do not tell the public about range conditions as that would antagonize the stockmen. Granger strongly subscribes to the same philosophies and I have every reason to believe Watts does to a somewhat lesser degree. The theme of our supervisors meeting when Cliff arrived [to succeed Spencer] was "we must improve relations with the stockmen." I go along with the idea if it can be done without selling our resources down the river. My relations with most of the progressive ranchers have been excellent, as recent protests over my transfer testify. I've only tolerated [certain association officials], and some others. Their lives are dedicated to gaining advantages for their clientele contrary to . . . public interest. They've fought the Forest Service by foul and fair means on every issue. We've suffered intolerable indignities at their hands. I resolved long ago not to associate with them more than was absolutely needed. Seems I was wrong and I should have practiced some kind of political hypocrisy. If so I'd probably be an assistant chief, but if it takes that kind of double crossing to get there I'm perfectly happy beside the Kirbys, the Roy Williamses, Collinses, . . . and others who failed only because the props were cut from under them. . . .

Of his 1949 visit to Washington and being talked out of leaving Denver, Sandvig wrote,

> I was told my leaving would be interpreted as surrender to the stockmen and that I owed it to the personnel of Region 2 to stay. . . . Fourteen months later they made the first pass at me. I'd be sent to the Columbia Basin to be some kind of chair arranger [as service representative on an interagency committee]. I didn't go because then they seemed afraid of the reactions of the Izaak Walton League and others, but 24 months later I was served with an irrevocable ultimatum. . . . This time they had no fear. [Senator] O'Mahoney had told them it was OK.

Sandvig reviewed other correspondence between us, and commented that he had wrongfully believed Watts "was sincere when he told the Barrett Committee [at Grand Junction in September, 1947] he would "much prefer to have a man who'd go up against battle, . . . than men who'd not face up to the job for which they were hired." All of which was set forth, he went on, "to back my belief there is no chance the Forest Service brass will change its existing philosophy of sacrificing field forces to quiet someone. I am convinced the conservation groups backing the Forest Service had better become realistic. The stockmen gained concessions with rough tactics, yet we can't even use the criminal code when they flagrantly violate regulations. . . ."

There was much more to the letter; it was fifteen pages long, handwritten. Near the end Sandvig wrote:

"In furnishing this material, Bill, I am disloyal to the service. . . . I have chosen to throw in with a group of conservationists . . . because I believe in them and the objectives they are trying to achieve. I am in a precarious spot with the Forest Service. Only by the grace of God and the help of fellows like you and DeVoto and Carhart can I expect square treatment."

Sandvig ended with a request that I be cautious in any public use made of his letter. This is the first time it has been put in print. Was he truly disloyal—in a larger sense—in writing as he did? To the Service, probably yes, but to the country as a whole? Or for taking such writers as Lester Velie of *Collier's* and newspaper reporters on show-me trips so they could see the condition of the ranges through the eyes of a schooled and experienced range manager? These were his major crimes, according to the best information I have secured. His actions had been similar to those of Kirby of the Tonto, who went to the public, even took Arizona's governor out for a ride to

Earl Sandvig in 1975, the facial lines deeper, but still fit to straddle a horse or throw a double diamond pack hitch.

inspect range. That had been Kirby's basic sin; that he "sassed" his superior was topping on the cake. As I have been told on pretty good authority, Sandvig committed the unforgivable by not maintaining a tight lip when people not on the Service payroll were in hearing distance.

In the summer of 1972 I interviewed Walt Dutton, director of range management in the Washington office most of the time from 1936 until he retired in 1953. Thus Dutton was in the thick of things in Washington that had to do with range in the years of Sandvig's triumphs and defeats. Dutton corroborated [18] Sandvig's assumption that his principal wrongdoing had been to seek public support for the Region 2 program of reducing range use to grazing capacity. He said the policies for which Sandvig fought were "right as right" as to what should have been done.

"God knows that. I know it, and if you look at the facts you'd know it," Dutton told me. "And [the Chief Forester's office] didn't fire him, but they didn't give him the regional forester's job which he should have had in place of Cliff. You see, I know all the details. . . .'"

Dutton's line of thought shifted. He said, "Sandvig . . . was smart enough to know he couldn't make them change their policy. Well, he was awfully stubborn, and he goofed. He went outside, and talked to outside people and agencies. Now, Sandvig shouldn't have done that. He should have quit." Dutton paused, then continued: "I should have. I felt like doing it year on end over this stuff but never—. And they all know it. I never went outside and told newsmen. . . ."

Dutton's closing sentences are worth reading again. He was heartsick over "this stuff," but he "never went outside." He kept silent for nearly twenty years until our quiet but intense conversation in a private room of the Kennedy–Warren Apartment Hotel in Washington that steaming August day in 1972. Once he determined to talk he seemed to relax as though a load had shifted, and the words tumbled from him as we got deeper into the subject of the Sandvig years and "this stuff" that went on in them. At the end, though Walt seemed perfectly willing to continue, I stopped him, fearful that second thoughts later might cause him to repudiate his words.

Yes, until mid-1972 Walt Dutton locked his innermost thoughts tight inside himself. Should Sandvig, too, have remained silent while he was still on the Service rolls? His letters to this day reflect lingering unhappiness, though if bitterness remains he conceals much of it. I'm sure he sleeps well at night and, working from his home base in Portland, in 1975, he was still crusading for what he considered a more direct and realistic approach to healing and rebuilding the ranges of the public land West.

15

"When you Walk in Cactus..."

In any discussion of the combinations and variations of strategy and tactics used so often in the western livestock industry to prevent or delay reduction in grazing on deteriorated national forest range, the Uncompahgre Plateau is bound to be mentioned. For most of sixteen years it was the scene of struggle between grazing users and Forest Service officials over the numbers of stock and the seasons of use that might be allowed, a struggle that culminated in questions—still not fully answered, in my opinion—as to parts played and attitudes assumed by high-ranking Service personnel.

The plateau is a rugged, high-elevation segment of the Uncompahgre National Forest (now combined with Grand Mesa National Forest), in western Colorado southeast of Grand Junction. The plateau is the most spectacular natural feature of the region. It contains wildly beautiful scenery topped by Uncompahgre Peak, which rises to 14,314 feet above the sea. The survey team that found Yellowstone said Uncompahgre forage was excellent in 1876. The area was brought into the National Forest System in June 1905, some twenty-four years after the Uncompahgre branch of the Ute Indian Nation was "resettled" westward. Whites entered the Uncompahgre in 1882; cattle followed in 1888. In twenty years the ranges showed deterioration from overgrazing.[1]

The historical record I have seen is on the sketchy side, but doubtless grazing the Uncompahgre went about the same route followed on other western national forests. That is, from 1905 until World War I there likely was a fairly small increase in allowed stock and numbers of permittees. During the war the numbers rose to a point far above grazing capacity, and heavy damage to the soil resource resulted. In the early 1920s the Service began to try to trim AUM numbers to a more realistic level; was lenient again in the 1930s because of drought and depression, and more deterioration followed. That efforts to hold grazing to grazing capacity on the Uncompahgre were inadequate is indicated by the fact that a survey in depth was ordered in 1937, to gauge and pinpoint prevailing depletion before taking steps toward better control. The survey was completed near the end of 1938. Early in 1939, ahead of the grazing season, the forest supervisor and his rangers began to describe the results of the survey to the permittees. Group meetings were held, followed by personal communication with individual permittees that specified in detail what conditions had been found on their allotments and what action was needed to correct those that were bad. The supervisor sensed trouble ahead, for in a letter to the Denver regional office he said,[2] "By this time the fireworks will have begun."

They had indeed. The principals in setting them off were leaders of the Uncompahgre Valley Cattle and Horse Growers Association. Here and there permittees agreed with the Service's findings as to range condition and trend and were perfectly willing to go along with sound management practices and reductions in both total stock numbers and seasons of grazing use so as to restore the area to greater productivity, but the association presumed to speak for all and obstructed wherever, whenever, and however it could.

Typically, the initial action by such an organization would be to try to soften the Service officials in the field with arguments that their findings were wrong. And, traditionally, there never has been a "good" time for a forest officer to impose a reduction in grazing. A rancher naturally would want to fend off as long as possible any action tending to reduce the cash value of his holdings or his immediate profit potential. An adversary position was sure to develop when the forest officials felt duty bound under the law to protect the ranges from deteriorating use. It made for situations where those on both sides needed wisdom, vision, and tact for long-term results beneficial both to the user and the public owners of that which was being used.

Failing to persuade the Service to retreat from cuts through debate over whether they were needed, the next step often was to adopt a resolution of protest. This, sometimes with supporting material, would be passed along to the state association for concurring action, and at times to other groups having an interest. The state organization just as often took the matter up with the national. The intent was a common one: to get as many people as possible to back their play so as to bring to bear on the Service the total weight of pressure of all groups enlisted.

If that should not prove successful, various not very subtle techniques could be applied to weaken individual Service officers. This might be political, with elected officials taking part whenever they could be persuaded to do so. They would be at local community, county, state, or federal levels, right on up to the congressman from the district or either or both of the state's senators. The social ostracism treatment might be given to a local ranger and his family, or the forest supervisor. The wives might have the cold shoulder applied each time it might be expected to leave an inward chill. The goal, of course, would be so to dishearten the target official that he would back down or ask for removal to a more congenial locality.

Personal abuse and villification were commonly employed at meetings rangers and supervisors were obligated to attend. Perhaps the strategy tried most often was to persuade an official's superiors that feelings were running so high against him in his jurisdiction that his usefulness there had come to an end. As a rule the man would not be fired; Civil Service regulations protected him against discharge unless he had in fact been grossly derelict in handling his official duties. Instead he'd be shipped somewhere else "for the good of the Service," and the public usually would never learn the real reason.

The Uncompahgre Cattle and Horse Growers Association was adept at persuasive techniques. When the supervisor's meetings ended in 1939 the association adopted a resolution [3] which read:

"We emphatically protest the enforcement of the proposed cuts. Instead, we urge a spirit of tolerance and cooperation as best adapted to meet the situation; and insist that further study of conditions and conference with the local [advisory] boards should be made before final action is decided."

That sentence contained more than the standard protest. It urged compromise toward continued excessive grazing. It requested the ages-old delaying device of "further study." It wanted additional debate with the permittees who comprised the advisory boards that already had refused to countenance reductions.

The supervisor of the Uncompahgre at the time was, in fact, eager to bring about improved forage conditions, but he was no match for the association. In 1940, after three years of futile effort to achieve results in friendly communication with the livestock leadership, he reported [4] to the regional office that "the situation . . . is hopeless." He said the association "has done all in its power to confuse the issue and to influence people against remedial measures that embrace reduced grazing use." Everything he proposed was opposed. He was transferred and succeeded by a more complacent supervisor.

In January 1941, the stockmen made a proposal of their own. Under it the Service would not change grazing seasons or reduce stock numbers, and the Uncompahgre National Forest Advisory Board—consisting of members and nonmembers of the association —would make management decisions, not the Forest Service. Regional Forester Allen Peck attended a sizable meeting to discuss the proposal and its implications. The outcome was extraordinary.

"It appeared the [Service was] on the verge of winning, . . . but the regional forester . . . threw in the towel and agreed to give the management of the ranges to the advisory board. . . ." [5]

This was the situation in 1944 when Sandvig was brought to Denver as regional range chief. As time went on and matters failed to improve, Sandvig cast about for leadership on the Uncompahgre that was not associated with the Peck regime's concessions. Montezuma National Forest in southwestern Colorado was to be divided between two other forests and its supervisor, C. K. Collins, would be available. Collins knew range realities and had the fortitude to stand fast when that was the thing to do. He accepted the hard job on the Uncompahgre when Regional Forester John Spencer and Sandvig pledged their unequivocal backing. Shortly after he moved to the forest's headquarters at Delta, he was visited by Earl Loveridge, assistant chief forester for operations.

"He came into my office," Collins told me,[6] "closed the door and said he had a personal message for me," presumably from Chief Forester Watts. "He told me my job was to get the reductions needed to correct the overgrazing. . . . I was told to use any method I deemed necessary. . . . He also told me the Forest Service at the regional and Washington levels would not back down again and I would have . . . full support. . . . I did have that support for as long as Spencer was regional forester and Sandvig was in charge of range management. . . ."

He also was visited by some of the association leaders, who "told me they would oppose any range reductions to anyone, even if needed, *because it would set a precedent*" (italics added). Under such circumstances a showdown had to follow.

Three ranger districts on the plateau were hot spots. There were far fewer difficulties in the other two forest districts—one lying be-

Overused range at left of fence, properly grazed area at right. On plateau allotment, Uncompahgre National Forest, Colorado, 1948. *USFS photo by Art Cramer*

Same Uncompahgre National Forest plateau area, downstream from overused area; banks of stream undercut by excessive runoff, 1948. *USFS photo by Art Cramer*

tween Ouray and Lake City and the other south of Norwood. "The permittees there, with few exceptions, would discuss their problems in a rational way," but this "was not the case with the ranger districts on the plateau."

"We had no good cattle allotments on the plateau while I was there," Collins said, adding that by 1973, when he dictated his statement to the recorder, some of them, where adjustments had been made in spite of stock association protest, "should be showing signs of recovery. . . ."

When I visited him in July 1972, Basil Crane, deputy regional forester at Denver and a former Uncompahgre supervisor, told [7] me that good range could now be found there, which would tend to bear out Collins's statement. I judge, from later information, that the recovery areas were spotty and scattered, for grazing use of the plateau ranger districts has come down considerably. Part of the reduction may be attributed to the fact that grazing seasons are about two months shorter now than then.

In March 1975, information [8] from the service at Denver included a table showing grazing use of the plateau districts at ten-year intervals since 1940. The totals that follow are in cow–months;

1940	1950	1960	1970	1974
339,762	242,372	273,556	171,492	124,783

Collins's account said other allotments on the plateau needed cuts of from 30 to 60 percent if ranges were to be able to begin to come back, and others at lower elevations were in worse shape since they usually received less moisture. "The key areas, with few exceptions, were poor to depleted," Collins said, and their condition and trend constituted the crux of the issue.

At one point in my communications with him at his retirement home in Albuquerque, New Mexico, I asked Collins about his ranger staff. They were under the gun, so to speak, and I wondered if many, or any, "finally sort of quit bucking the current in order to get the permittees and associations" to ease their pressure. Here is C. K.'s reply: [9]

My staff and rangers were exceptional people. In spite of livestockman pressure they never gave in to what may have seemed the easy way out. They were dedicated people who knew their jobs and deserved more than normal credit for their efforts in spite of attempts of some of the stockmen to discredit them. They tried their best to find fault with our every move. They tried to find things on which we [Service people] might not agree so they could be used to show we were not consistent in our thinking. They found nothing. They resorted to rumor, and tried every method of character assassination. . . . At hearings they would counteract statements made by . . . us with witnesses who would swear to anything so long as they thought it hurt us. . . . In 1948 we rode the plateau ranges with permittees, always accompanied by members of the association. We rode for four solid months, sometimes seven days a week. Very little was accomplished. . . . Permittees on each allotment were present. The association representatives prevented the allotment permittees from agreeing to any realistic range program. We could have had a fist fight any hour of any day we rode. We were forced, due to our positions, to tolerate oral abuse that no one should have to take.

The businessmen of Delta . . . told me that some of the cattlemen talked of "getting" me in hunting season and making it appear an accident. . . . This did not stop me from hunting. In 1953, when it was announced that I was going to be transferred, the president of the Delta Chamber of Commerce told me, "We wouldn't have given 15 cents for your life; we expected to pick up the paper each day and see where someone had shot you."

When Collins was moved out of the Uncompahgre in 1953 the Delta Chamber of Commerce gave him an appreciation dinner at which he was presented a plaque commending him for "outstanding and lasting contributions to the future welfare and growth of this community."

That administration of the Uncompahgre ranges by the Service was first to get adverse attention when the Barrett subcommittee held its hearing in Grand Junction in September 1947 does not appear coincidental. Collins had been supervisor for only four months at the time and presumably would be less able to answer hard questions as lucidly as one who had been longer on the job. At any rate, the Uncompahgre association led the accusers at Grand Junction,[10] and after each witness Barrett or Rockwell, whoever happened to be wielding the gavel at the moment, would ask the standard question, "What have you got to say to this, Mr. Forester?" If Sandvig or some other higher official did not step in, Collins offered to search the record and send the committee the facts. In my study of the Barrett record, I came to the conclusion that the Service position had been sound far more often than otherwise, and that many of the complaints were made of flimsy stuff.

With Barrett gone and the responses in the mail, Collins and his staff, supported by Spencer and Sandvig, pressed efforts to cut Uncompahgre grazing to an approximation of grazing capacity. The old agreement with the advisory board had been abrogated by Spencer and Sandvig much earlier. The four months of range riding in 1948, with their unsatisfactory results, have been recounted. It turned out that local obstacles to reduction were not the only roadblocks Collins and the regional range staff faced.

Once, when asked to comment on the merits of a proposed change in range policy, Collins wrote,[11] "When you walk in cactus, wear shoes." That was excellent counsel for one tramping amid the vegetation of certain regions of the United States on or off national forest land, and especially so when dealing with thorny permittee problems. But what if cactus characteristics are brushed against in a Forest Service regional office or its Washington corridors and offices? How does one prepare for or guard against that? I have only the declarations of field men of that era, plus circumstantial evidence and inferential material of other sorts, to indicate that so strange a growth was to show up in Denver and in the venerable South Agriculture Building on Washington's Independence Avenue, but am convinced my facts are on straight. The time was at hand when officials dedicated to the proposition that the good of the land was the prime consideration, that its condition must dictate actions taken, would discover that both boots and chaps should be standard wearing apparel.

After they failed to subdue Collins, Sandvig, and Spencer with traditional methods, the Uncompahgre association appealed to higher authority.[12] Spencer had turned down the local appeal before he retired at the end of 1949, and it went on to reach the desk of Charles F. Brannan, Secretary of Agriculture, in April, 1950.

The nub of the appeal lay in the question of when permittee stock should be allowed to go on the forest ranges in the spring and when the animals must be removed in the fall. For years the opening day had been May 1, the closing date October 31 (in a few cases November 15). Service field forces argued that both dates were wrong, the opening far too early, the closing late. On May 1 there usually was snow here and there, and the ground was soft where tender young forage was just coming up. They held that grazing cattle at that stage caused harmful trampling and accelerated erosion was sure to accompany the spring rains. Available forage would be reduced in future years because of lowered plant vigor. Likewise, they held that grass should be left to reseed naturally in the fall; it should not be cropped to the roots, and some forage should be left to help build new soil to replace that eroded away in the past.

In the summary of the Uncompahgre case, Sandvig described the intransigence of the stockmen's leaders:

The ideas of the stockmen regarding grazing capacity, and other conditions concerning range condition and range use, remained the same in 1948 as expressed by them in 1938. Their protests against [reduced] stocking and [shorter] grazing seasons were just as vigorous. . . . After ten years of continuous, patient, and tolerant educational effort on the part of the Forest Service, there was obviously no closer agreement . . . as to what needed to be done. The Advisory Board in a meeting at Montrose on December 6, 1948, addressed this statement to the Forest Service: *"We the undersigned reject your orders for any reductions"* [italics added].

In this, the 14th year since an attempt to correct Uncompahgre range conditions was started, the Forest Service is very little closer to solving the problem. Methods employed by the cattlemen have successfully prevented necessary action at the expense of public resources during all these years.

A hearing on the Uncompahgre case was scheduled in Denver at the end of February 1951. Before 1950 ended, the field officers learned [13] that Washington had decided in favor of permittees in an appeal from orders to cut grazing on the Roosevelt National Forest, despite overwhelming evidence at the time of the hearing plus the results of a yearlong study by a team of range scientists. It was a jarring decision, and convinced Sandvig, on whose shoulders would fall the major burden of presenting the Uncompahgre case, that his testimony and documentation must be complete and decisive in every respect.

The hearing lasted five days. Sandvig was backed solidly by Supervisor Collins, by specialists from his Denver office, and by scientists from the Service's range experiment station staff. Much of the testimony concerned the length of the grazing season; the early spring start was believed more damaging than the late closing.

In May 1951, three members of the Board of Appeals returned for a weeklong inspection of the plateau ranges, to see for themselves what they were like in early spring. They were accompanied on the ride by Sandvig, Collins, and other Service personnel, as well as by groups of permittees and association leaders. The show-me trip clinched the case against the appeal. The board reported [14] to Secretary Brannan that in only three small portions of the plateau allotments, including two where reseeding was under way, could ranges be classed as "holding their own or improving." Ranges in two other reseeding tracts and in "scattered and relatively small areas . . . along and below the plateau top" were in such delicate equilibrium that it was moot whether the trend was up or down. Then came this straightforward declaration:

"Except for the areas mentioned, . . . practically without exception all the more open parks and more accessible aspen areas in the upper portions of the range *show evidence of downward trend*" (italics added).

That surely should have resulted in a clear-cut decision for Region 2 findings, but it was not to be. Brannan's ruling came in a letter [15] of January 3, 1952, addressed to Kelso Musser of Delta, president of the association. Only in the less important matter of the fall closing date did Brannan uphold the Region. The spring opening would be on a date that was "generally acceptable to *both the stockmen and the Forest Service*" (italics added), and it already was certain the livestock leadership on the Uncompahgre was opposed to any deferment.

Brannan's letter pinned hopes for improvement on future range management practices, while the going practices the Region had tried so hard to modify would continue. As the department head, Brannan took responsibility for the language of the letter that bore his signature. It is a virtual certainty that Brannan signed without so much as changing a comma of the draft that came to his desk from Watts's office. I am sure he did not question the propriety of the letter's contents, in terms of the Service's long-boasted philosophy of acting in behalf of "the greatest good to the greatest number in the long run." Why should he?

I visited Brannan at his Denver office in July 1972, and our talk was tape-recorded. This later was transcribed and, after making minor changes in ink, he signed a copy. In our discussion Brannan said: [16]

> We must remember that in the period we are talking about I was much involved with other things, matters of high policy and importance. . . . I could not and did not divide my time equally between all the agencies in the Department. This tended to cause me to rely more on the heads of certain agencies and bureaus than others, and I must say that I relied a great deal on the recommendations of Lyle Watts and his staff, . . . and don't think this was a misplaced confidence.

Further in the interview, Brannan rather emphatically said, "I just don't believe we ever yielded much" to political and related pressures to go easy on the stockmen. I have no doubt Brannan firmly believed he told me the truth as he sees it, and what he said may be unassailable as it was phrased. The critical point does not seem to me to be whether there was a yielding to specific political pressure so much as whether the ruling had not been a result of basic change in the high councils of the Forest Service itself. I wonder just who in the Service gave the order to override the appeals board. Watts may himself have carried the letter to Brannan for signature, but who sat in on prior discussions? And how was the decision to override arrived at? The record I've seen doesn't say.

We still thought that, based on Secretary Brannan's letter to the association, we might have a chance to make needed reductions," Collins told me on tape. "Cattle permittees had started to come in to determine how the reductions might be handled. About this time the region decided that, since we had been successful in getting reductions in grazing seasons, we would make no more until there was time to see if there was any range recovery. *The seasonal reductions amounted to less than half the total needed* [italics added].

This was followed by a letter from the regional forester stating I could not make any further reductions *unless the permittee agreed to them*. . . . Ed Cliff [had been] promoted to the Washington Office and Donald Clark became . . . regional forester. Things began to happen fast. Clark informed me that he and his staff were unhappy with my performance, so he was lowering my performance rating [italics added].

Collins rebelled, demanding a statement in writing presenting specifics of unsatisfactory performance. Clark backed down, but friction remained. Collins said he was accused of "disloyalty to the organization."

I had no time to polish Forest Service personnel, especially those who had supported appeasement and compromise [said Collins]. The right and the wrong of the range battle on the Uncompahgre was as clear as black and white. . . . Whoever had heard of it being right to compromise key issues where the soil and its resources were at stake? I had come to the Uncompahgre with instructions to correct a grazing problem that had already been sabotaged by the Forest Service itself [through the previous agreement giving the advisory boards administrative powers]. I was promised full . . . support, with no further backing down by either the regional office or the Washington Office. After about six years I, my headquarters staff, and rangers found ourselves isolated and surrounded by hostile permittees and the so-called "organization" within the Forest Service. How do you think we felt?"

And a year later he found himself no longer in range management, which was his primary love, but holding down a desk job in the Region 3 office at Albuquerque. He retired when he reached sixty-five.

And the Uncompahgre? The Service insists its ranges are in good condition now, but Sandvig wrote me that in response to repeated requests for facts about specific Uncompahgre allotments with which he is familiar, he has received only generalized statements that were not truly responsive.[17] Sandvig said that he'd gamble that the answers were readily available to the Service, "down to the last cow or sheep," within "arm's reach" of the Service officials. Much as I want to believe what Basil Crane and Frank Smith told me about the Uncompahgre, I wonder what the results of another survey would be, compared with the one out there in 1938.

The Uncompahgre story has been told at some length. Those of other areas have been just as stormy, and doubtless are of equal significance. The Tonto in Lee Kirby's time, for instance; later the Roosevelt. Then, consider the Modoc, in northern California.[18] It has had more than its share of turmoil over grazing, and the excessive use does not appear to have been matched by recuperative medication administered by the Service.

The Modoc came into the system in 1905 also, and its Warner Mountains area already was in bad shape. In grazing the Service seems to have followed the typical course described previously for other national forest ranges. The truth of this range's illness was disclosed after a detailed survey and analysis conducted in 1934. It showed that the Service was annually selling about 50 percent more forage than could be delivered to the customer–permittees without accelerating damage to the soil and its vegetation. The survey report recommended that grazing be halved to bring it in balance with the production of forage.

Russell Beeson was appointed supervisor with orders to act on the survey findings, and for three successive years he made systematic reductions, in which he survived repeated demands for his ouster. Things quieted down a bit, until 1940, when the Service began to apply maximum upper limits for grazing there. Three of the Modoc's larger permittees started agitating to have the forest transferred to the Grazing Service, Department of the Interior. The regional office in San Francisco "panicked"—Beeson's word—and tried to placate the complainers. Beeson was transferred and softer supervisors followed over the next five years. Pat Thompson, a new regional forester, determined to bring things under control again. He installed Charles M. Rector as supervisor in 1946, at the start of the new ten-year permit term. Rector began making headway toward reducing the overgrazing. Thompson and his assistant for range management, Charles A. (Chic) Joy, backed him determinedly. Rector recalled, in a letter to Sandvig years later,[19] that the permittees were suspicious of him from the start, knowing he was a skilled range man, but progress was made. Then came the aftermath of the McCarran investigations, and the Barrett hearings. The Modoc was on the agenda when the full House Public Lands Committee sat at Redding on September 20, 1947, and at San Francisco two days later.

The stockmen brought on an Oregon attorney to organize their presentation of complaints. At rebuttal time the Service witnesses lacked legal guidance and "from the regional forester on down, were made to look like dummies." [20] At San Francisco a state game specialist described the complications caused by a large resident deer herd; ranges had been "gutted" by livestock, with most of the perennial grasses destroyed and followed by low-value annuals such as cheat grass (*bromus tectorum*). I recall getting complaints from members of the Izaak Walton League at the time to the effect that permittees had put up posters declaring no hunters would be allowed on their private lands until the Forest Service quit calling for livestock reductions. The state scientists testified that even if every deer was slaughtered or removed the Modoc ranges would continue to go down under existing livestock use.

Rector persisted, and inaugurated a five-year program of cuts tied to a range improvement program, then moved on in 1951. Beeson wrote Sandvig that range conditions had improved on the Modoc over the next twenty years, but at an excessive cost in range improvement funds. He said he was opposed to "welfare for cows." The inference was that the Service had bought peace on the Modoc with a procession of range vegetation jobs.

Sandvig inspected the Modoc in company with Frank Smith in the summer of 1971 and afterward wrote him a gloomy report.[21] The gist was that with the exception of a few small meadow areas that had been given special protection and treatment, and one sheep range, "I saw no allotment that I could give a higher rating than poor. . . ." On the other hand, Smith felt much progress had been made which, from the copy of his letter I saw, seemed mainly to have occurred in areas where high-degree range rehabilitation and management practices had been carried out, including the fencing of allotments to keep stock from running loose. On the thrust of Sand-vig's comments, Smith wrote: [22]

"I am sure that no one is ever completely satisfied with what has been done or the rate of accomplishment. . . . I want to assure you that the present generation of Forest Officers are not content to rest on the laurels of the many accomplishments made by their predecessors, but continue to work at the problems."

As I interpret written and oral communications from both camps, the Service position appears to be that both the Uncompahgre and Modoc National Forests are in better condition than in the era of such great stockman discontent, but need more improvement. Sand-vig seems to feel that after sixty-five years or so on the job the Service should long since have eliminated nearly all but maintenance problems in the management of forest ranges. Witnesses before Mc-Carran and Barrett in the 1940s voiced somewhat the same sentiments, but that hardly means they and Sandvig share the same philosophy.

16

Toward an
Authority Grab

As the turbulent 1940s drew to a close the western stock industry leadership seemed to have gained about all it could hope for, short of having the federal lands handed over as a gift. The public domain had long been under industry domination, and the still new Bureau of Land Management was not likely to mount a successful confrontation. The Forest Service now seemed snugly tucked into a hip pocket of its Levis. The policy of "drastic" reductions had been abandoned, succeeded by one in which publicly financed range rehabilitation techniques would be accelerated to try to show they could substitute for cuts. The long-sought goal of statutory recognition of theretofore permissive advisory boards was just ahead. Fees remained so low, under the Depression-era formula tied to last year's market prices of livestock on the hoof, that a permittee could command a handsome bonus for each animal unit month of grazing he enjoyed, if or when he wanted to sell. The Roosevelt case was giving evidence that even an adverse ruling by the Secretary's Advisory Board of Appeals need not be feared, for the now trepidatious Forest Service would nullify its recommendations on demand. In another year the Uncompahgre case would add more proof of service timidity in the face of association intransigence. John Spencer, who had been such annoying gravel in their boots, had given up at Denver and retired when he learned he would be undercut on the Roosevelt appeal. Sandvig, and others who pitted their wills and skills against the industry on range management matters, had come under new officials whose policy was to avoid confrontation and to get along with the stockmen.

All this had come about in the last half of the decade, or was imminent. The association leadership still was not satisfied. The recent dream of outright ownership through the attempted land grab had faded, but a committee similar to that of 1946–48 began drafting new legislation not long afterward. Up to that time control by the industry had been largely through the persistent application of various kinds of pressure. It had used influential individuals and organizations outside the stock industry as well as elected officials as persuaders, and relentlessly employed the wearing down effect of a constant stream of complaints, evasive actions, and delaying tactics. Now—far from least of the developments—new leadership rising in the Service seemingly could be counted on to think as much like permittees as it did like managers of public range, and be sympathetic to industry points of view. That kind of attitude might not last forever, though. Therefore, this time around the livestock interests involved would try to rivet their Service domination into the law. We in the conservation movement began saying an "authority grab" was in the making.[1]

Committee drafts of legislation surfaced from time to time. The first, dated October 24, 1950,[2] was labeled "Suggestions For an Act" of Congress. It would (1) allow "advisory" boards of permittees to rule on standards stockmen would have to meet to get or retain grazing permits; (2) make permit renewals every ten years mandatory, as under the Taylor Act, if the permittee had a bank or other loan on which his stock had been pledged as security; (3) prohibit reductions in use of range upon transfer of title to livestock or base property through sale or inheritance; (4) freeze existing low fees pending another study to determine if there was need for an increase; (5) create a pyramid of advisory boards to hear appeals from service rulings; (6) allow appeals to the federal court system after Service and other departmental procedures had been exhausted; and (7) in case of title transfer, require the Service to reimburse a permittee for any range improvement partly or wholly installed at his expense. Finally, the most horrendous of all in our viewpoint, the draft provided for merger of the Forest Service with the Bureau of Land Management and selection of the two chief agency officials from western livestock country.

The adverse implications of the bill's language seem obvious enough to require little elaboration. Surely advisory boards should not be given administrative powers; the fact that stockmen did so function under the Taylor Act and for a time on the Uncompahgre, did not in our view make it right. Such responsibility belongs to government. As to the section dealing with collateral, any permittee could guarantee there would be no reduction in allotted AUMs, no matter how worn the range or desperate the need, so long as his herd or flock was put up as backing for a loan. The bigger the permittee's operation, the easier it would be to get such a loan. The provision for another study of the fee structure was a delaying device to try to head off any contemplated increase. It recalls a remark by Lee Kirby, one of the martyrs of the 1940s to Service flaccidity, when Carhart interviewed [3] him.

. . . you'd have a range that needed adjustment, in fact needed total rest, and we'd argue back and forth a while and finally decide we'd better make a study before we acted. I've seen many needed things postponed by a study. Takes three or four or five years . . . and before that's over you kind of forget what started it in the first place.

The stack of advisory boards was almost a sure guarantee that a damaged range could go to pot before an argument over a diagnosis and a prognosis ended in decision, and appeals thereafter to already overloaded courts could assure still further delay while improper grazing use continued unabated.

The initial "Suggestions For an Act" drew a blast of adverse reaction. Much of it came from our camp, part from inside the industry. Some of its own leaders felt the language was too coarse, the approach too overt. Better give a degree of concealment to some of the objectives with legislative doubletalk. So the initial draft was worked over several times. A "Proposal For an Act" was produced as of January 12, 1951, and still another six weeks later. In the last of these, the idea of choosing men from the public land West to head the combined grazing agency was dropped.[4]

In April the Granger–Thye Act became law.[5] This was the statute that gave legal status to national forest advisory boards consisting of stockmen, which we had opposed for a decade for fear such status would tend to give them as much power as the Taylor boards had. It also gave statutory legitimacy to livestock grazing on national forests. The industry presumably would now settle back to see how this new fulcrum for leverage would perform. But, not entirely so. It would keep its spokesmen active, trying to assure as much public support as possible when the authority grab drafts become bills and were introduced.

One whose oratory was utilized at frequent intervals was Far-

rington Carpenter, the Hayden, Colorado, rancher who had inaugurated administration of the Taylor Act in the 1930s. The *Pilot*, daily
paper published in nearby Steamboat Springs, would not be beguiled
by what it called Carpenter's "high sounding phrases," and his promises that the bill, if enacted, would provide true democratic administration of the forest ranges. The editor, Maurice Leckenby,
wote that "Ferry is just too liberal when it comes to giving away
something that belongs to somebody else." [6]

And collecting a war chest for the coming events on Capitol Hill
went on apace. State associations of stockmen were given dollar
quotas to meet. Carhart obtained a copy of a letter that told of the
fund-raising campaign in Montana. [7]

As 1952 approached, Chief Forester Watts decided ten years of
absorbing the brutal punishment that went with the job in those days
was about as much as a man should endure. He had reached retirement age after thirty-eight years in the service of the National Forest
System's many publics.

I had admired and respected Lyle Watts, and am sure I was not
alone in so doing. I had watched from the sidelines as the pummel-
ing by the livestock associations, or stimulated in their behalf, began
smothering the flame of his earlier resolve to bring forest grazing
down to limits commensurate with the condition and trend of the
ranges. Watts had taken over in 1943, a critical time. The war years
made extraordinary demands for all the system's varied products. By
fortunate coincidence, the fighting ended ahead of the forthcoming
new permit term scheduled to begin in 1946, for reductions of any
kind would have been most difficult with it going on. The firm way
Watts spoke out in the annual reports of his earlier years has been
recounted. Nineteen-forty-six would be a testing time, but Watts gave
every appearance of meaning every word in those reports.

Then the pressures were built up, poured on in all the ways described, and who knows what others. The outcome of the McCarran
hearings on the Grazing Service was not lost on Watts or his chief
associates. They were proof the livestock lobby had clout, and
showed willingness by westerners in Congress to do industry bidding.
With Interior beaten down, could Agriculture be far behind? The political heat was intense, and Watts worried. He pondered conflicting
advice and suggestions by trusted aides, and embraced the intent of
the Anderson–Mansfield Act. One of his finest moments had come at
the Barrett hearing in Grand Junction. There Watts stood, after all

the oral abuse, the foot stomping, the booing, the vitriolic complaining, and defied whatever lightning Barrett could bring down on him and the faithful public servants in his beloved Service. He looked and talked invincible.

We on our side did not recognize it as such at the time, but that ringing defense of his integrity and that of Service subordinates was a swan song for the 1946 range program, and his leaning and bending lay just ahead. Under the continual thrusts and poundings, Watts gave a little here and found it was but a beginning, as he had to follow by giving more there. The Roosevelt and Uncompahgre cases are revealing in this respect. Later, in retirement, Watts regained some of his former vigor when in a letter he strongly protested the form of the industry's bill that nearly got by Congress [8] in 1954. (See Chapter 16.)

But, as 1951 wore on, some of us wondered why the associations dallied on the actual introduction of their bill. Then came light. Next year, 1952, would bring a national election. President Truman was not popular in many quarters, and that unpopularity would rub off on other Democrats. The Republican nominee might be more amenable. The decision appears to have been to work on leaders of both parties to try to get public land planks to their liking in the party platforms. They would try to commit both parties to their program, but if they persuaded only one, then it would get the bulk of their support and carry their hopes in the next Congress.

In this the Democrats disappointed. Their platform [9] simply pledged the party to continue "effective conservation and use programs," which included improvement activities, on public range. On the Republican side they were more successful. The GOP plank [10] would provide "opportunity for ownership" of public lands by private landholders to "promote" their "highest use"—which had a familiar ring. It favored a study of "tax free federal lands" to judge what effects their status had on the "economic and fiscal structures" of states and communities. It pledged the party to eliminate "arbitrary bureaucratic practices" and, to that end, to enact laws to define the "rights" of livestock grazers and to provide for "judicial review" of "administrative invasions" of such "rights"—which were more familiar words. While the plank contained few specifics and was couched in traditionally fuzzy language, its intent appeared parallel to those of the last form of the bill we had seen.

Shortly after the Republican plank was made public the Salt

Lake City *Tribune* editorially declared [11] the "arbitrary bureaucratic practices" referred to were in fact "courageous efforts" to protect watershed lands from being despoiled, and it believed the party had made a mistake. We held a similar view but were more restrained in the pages of *Outdoor America*. Although we believed our members were conservationists first, and Democrats or Republicans somewhere after that, we tried to be even-handed in presenting [12] without special comment what each said in its platform, and printed gist paragraphs side by side. We did emphasize, however, that the Democrats' plank called for "sound harvesting to promote sustained yield," language far different from that used by the GOP.

That fall General Dwight David Eisenhower was elected President, and the Congress had a Republican majority in both houses. Now, if party platforms meant anything—which some skeptics have doubted—the time had come for a showdown, and the livestock leaders wasted little.

Congressman Wesley D'Ewart of Montana, who had been a member of the Barrett Subcommittee, was chosen on the House side. He had been warned that back home there were interests other than livestock grazing, and in March 1953 agreed to introduce [13] the measure, numbered H. R. 4023, only "by request." The stockmen's committee found more eager sponsors on the Senate side. They were Senator Hugh Butler of Nebraska, and Barrett; their bill was S. 1491. Barrett wanted a senator with more seniority to be the principal sponsor.

The introductions set off about as fast and furious a period of political maneuvering as any I remember from my participation in the national conservation movement. Nearly all we did about the two bills had to follow certain niceties involving governmental customs and regulations. Most conservation organizations enjoyed a cherished status with the Treasury Department's Internal Revenue Service. Under it they were exempt from federal income taxes and contributors to their causes could deduct their donations when making personal or corporate returns. We could not lobby as freely as we liked for or against specific bills, for that was one of the limitations put upon us by the IRS. The Sierra Club, which grew increasingly aggressive in legislative matters after David R. Brower became executive director, lost its tax-exempt standing in the late 1960s as a result of overt lobbying against a high dam proposal affecting Grand Canyon National Park and vicinity.[14] We of the Izaak Walton League made arrangements with most committees of Congress to be notified when legislation in which we had an interest would come up for hearing. We would then be "invited" to present statements. With such an invitation, we could take a bold position if we wished to do so.

Hearings were scheduled quickly in the House and Senate on the new stockmen's bills. Both were to be held in the same week of May 1953. Before this, Ezra Taft Benson of Utah had succeeded Charles F. Brannan as Secretary of Agriculture, and we centered early attention on him with regard to the bills. Joe Penfold took the lead for the League. He urged that the Department oppose the bills, which, he wrote,[15] would entrench one user group as dominant and controlling in public land country regardless of other uses and values equally as important as grazing. Interest was lively throughout the West. Joe and volunteer League workers there sent me what became almost a daily supply of newspaper editorials that indicated overwhelming opposition to passage of the bills. On April 2, Sam Hyatt of Hyattsville, Wyoming, in the Big Horn basin, then president of the American National Livestock Association, sent a long "confidential" telegram to Secretary Benson in which he complained of adverse editorial comment in the Denver *Post*.[16] He accused the Forest Service of supplying the paper with "propaganda." One of the *Post* editorials, dated March 31, 1953, said H. R. 4023 was "a slick rights grabbing scheme on behalf of special interests. In promoting it, the stockmen have overplayed their hand. It deserves a quick death."

I analyzed the bill in *Outdoor America* [17] for the guidance of Izaak Walton League members; certain a goodly number would echo headquarters opinion in communications to their state delegations in Congress.

These interim days also were busy ones in the Washington office of the Service. Dr. Richard A. McArdle, who had succeeded Watts on July 1, 1952, sent a directive [18] to the field in April 1953, decreeing that thereafter there would be no more reductions in permits for redistribution purposes and no more transfer cuts except to comply with upper-limit standards. Thus, nearly a half century after its inauguration, the distribution reduction policy died its lingering death. Born when the West was still capable of sustaining new agrarian settlers if they were careful in choosing the land to homestead and were situated geographically so they could use national forest grazing privileges to advantage, it had long since outlived its practicality. Watts was the last chief to cling to it; he did so not so much to utilize it to significant extent, but because it might be considered a deterrent to overambitious livestock operators clamoring for excessive permit privileges.

A hint of how much internal dissention the outmoded privilege–distribution policy had caused within the Forest Service is given by the fact that Walt Dutton waited until twenty years after retirement before disclosing that he had written a poem on the subject in 1953, right after McArdle's decisive action.[19] A covering letter in 1972 told recipients that Secretary Benson had ordered it killed. A few representative stanzas follow:

> Back in nineteen hundred five
> Was born an institution
> With dedicated leaders
> All hipped on DISTRIBUTION.
>
> Successive Chiefs then followed
> And ordered prosecution
> Of more and more devices
> To enforce DISTRIBUTION
>
> Back in nineteen thirty-five
> This misled institution
> Ignored most protection needs
> But increased DISTRIBUTION
> . . .
> Nineteen hundred forty-five—
> A stockman resolution
> Bared a Forest Service Plan
> For still more DISTRIBUTION.
> . . .
> All these years this absurd scheme
> Intensified confusion,
> Neglected conservation
> And played up DISTRIBUTION.
>
> Nineteen hundred fifty-three
> Brought final retribution—
> 'Twas the tolling of the knell
> For dying DISTRIBUTION
> . . .
> So the writer hopes the Staff
> Adopts a resolution
> Exonerating all who
> Resisted DISTRIBUTION!

McArdle's instruction also indirectly recognized that permits had dollar values to their holders. It ordered that buyers and sellers of properties related to a grazing allotment be given fullest information on its estimated grazing capacity. Another April directive by Mc-Ardle told [20] field forces to let the permittees know they would be given any increased grazing capacity resulting from range improvement work done by them, provided the work had been approved by the Service and did not conflict with other uses of the forests.

One theory I had held before I saw Dutton's verse and letter was that McArdle was trying to lay groundwork for a Service and departmental stand in opposition to H. R. 4023 and S. 1491. The two directives amounted to considerable concessions. They affected Service practices that had been the subjects of numerous complaints from many western regions. I had believed McArdle wanted to soften the blow of opposition by the Department. In fact, unknown to outsiders, formal letters and statements in opposition were even then being put laboriously in draft form by McArdle subordinates. Early in May these were sent over to the Office of the Secretary of Agriculture for approval.[21]

Secretary Benson already had written President Eisenhower that mail was running heavily against the legislation.[22] This undoubtedly reflected the independent writings of DeVoto, Carhart, and others as well as the appeals which conservation organizations sent to their constituencies. On May 14 a "route slip" from Bureau of the Budget Director Rowland R. Hughes to Harry McKitrick, chief of the bureau's Division of Resources and Civil Works,[23] disclosed that Hughes had promised Senator Barrett "this morning" that he would be told when the department reports on the bills were received, so Barrett could "come in and state his case before the hearings."

There is no question in my mind but that Barrett was notified and did see the drafts of opposing statements. The combination of congressional and Eisenhower administration forces favoring the legislation succeeded in completely muzzling whatever resistance flourished in the Forest Service. The opposition material never got beyond a preliminary written stage. A brief statement intended for delivery by Assistant Secretary J. Earl Coke in Benson's behalf, a longer one to be read by McArdle, and a letter addressed to Senator Butler, ostensibly to be read by Coke when the Senate Public Works Committee hearing was held on S. 1491, all were squelched. Copies I have seen [24] all bear a scribbled notation, in Walt Dutton's handwriting, that they were "turned down" in the Secretary's office.

The evidence I have seen seems to indicate that McArdle did indeed oppose the stockmen's bills. It had been the custom for years for heads of the Department of Agriculture to defer to the expertise of the Forest Service on such matters as timber and range management. Why the deviation this time? And why did it succeed in such total suppression without a murmur of Service dissent? One answer that appears plausible lies in a political device created in the early years of the Eisenhower administration called "Schedule C." In earlier administrations, officials under Civil Service rose to be heads of bureaus as large as the Forest Service without losing their job protection. When Eisenhower became President and Schedule C was adopted this was changed selectively, putting more high and middle echelon federal positions in the patronage grab bag. How heavily did the threat of having the Chief Forester put under Schedule C, so he could be fired at will if he didn't toe the administration mark, hang over the head of Dr. McArdle? When I approached him for an interview in 1972, nearly ten years after he had retired, McArdle's response [25] caused me to believe he would rather not talk of those days. They were far behind him and he had not thought of their problems in years. He did not refuse but surely was far from enthusiastic. I took the hint and did not intrude further.

Marion Clawson of Resources for the Future, Inc., Washington, a former director of BLM, wrote [26] me in early 1975 that Schedule C was not as great a threat as many believed at the time, saying that it would be difficult for a bureau head to resist a request to resign or accept a transfer if it came with sufficient urgency from the secretary of his department. Nevertheless, we had seen Schedule C applied in other agencies and knew it was effective.

Then, there is the question of how staunchly the McArdle opposition was supported within the Service. Just what would have happened if McArdle and a solid phalanx of his senior associates had stood firmly on principle in an effort not to have his views vetoed in the office of Secretary Benson, or by even higher authority? I doubt that it is practical at this late date to get definitive answers.

When the House hearings were held on May 21 and 22, no one identified as being from the Forest Service or any other agency in the Department of Agriculture was in the hearing room, not even as an unofficial observer. This was unheard of when legislation directly related to an agency's activities and operations were being considered. The muzzling of the Service was specific, complete, and inescapable. This was noted [27] on the floor of the Senate by Senator Mike Mansfield of Montana on May 26, when he severely criticized Benson. He also took to task Douglas McKay, Secretary of the Interior, who later, when it did not matter much, told [28] the Denver *Post* in an interview that D'Ewart's had been "a lousy bill."

Charlie Moore of the Dude Ranchers Association sent [29] the President a stinging letter of complaint over the administration's handling of the situation, saying the clamp put on the Forest Service had "made a farce of the hearings."

There is no printed record of the hearing on D'Ewart's bill by the House Public Lands Committee. There is a typed copy in the National Archives. Before I could see it, I was told, the copy would have to be retrieved by the chairman of the Interior and Insular Affairs Committee and I would have to go to the Committee's offices on Capitol Hill to read it. The red tape involved, and the fact that my time in Washington was limited, made it impractical for me to see the official record. However, from memory and other sources I can reconstruct the essence of what occurred.

As is customary, the proponents of the bill were heard first. Among them was Farrington Carpenter. Asked if the bill would not freeze national forest grazing permits in the hands of the relatively few stockmen who then held them, Carpenter replied, "It sure will— just like a homestead." [30] William B. Wright, head of a large ranching operation at Deeth, Nevada, and president of the American National in the land grab years, supported the bill not as a stockman but as the official spokesman for the Chamber of Commerce of the United States.[31] He was tangled badly by Congressman Eugene McCarthy of Minnesota, who asked how the Chamber could fight so strenuously against the closed shop in industry yet favor it for livestock permittees.

That evening several men from the conservation movement huddled in a hotel room to discuss statements we would present the next day and whether to try to answer the industry's arguments extemporaneously when we got in the witness chair. Former Judge Robert Sawyer, publisher of the Bend, Oregon, *Bulletin,* representing the American Forestry Association, would lead off for our side. I was to follow, and then would come Chester Wilson, Minnesota Conservation Commissioner, who would speak for the International Association of Game, Fish, and Conservation Commissioners.

Next morning Judge Sawyer read his statement in full and was excused without a question. I asked that the text of the Izaak Walton League statement be put in the record, then gave its gist orally—

and the roof feel in on me. I was sharply questioned by Congressmen Clair Engle of California, and John P. Saylor of Pennsylvania. They soon had me snarled up worse than McCarthy had Bill Wright the first day. Engle, I wrote in a recap of the hearing sent to League leaders shortly afterwards "attacked my statement as violently as he could without using cusswords." He said, among many other things, that I was "intemperate." Maybe so; my orders from the League executive board were interpreted by me to call things as I saw them and to speak as vigorously as I felt proper. In that case I had no doubt whatever as to the course I should follow. Saylor, later honored as one of the strongest conservationists on Capitol Hill, challenged our opposition to the part of the bill that would let complainers go to court for redress under the Administrative Procedures Act. Judge Sawyer had opposed this as stoutly as I without committee reaction. I can only conclude that Saylor hesitated to take on a knowledgeable lawyer and preferred to tackle me, a layman.

Wilson, also a lawyer, followed me to the stand and, like Sawyer, was allowed to step down without a question. Other conservation organizations were heard, including the National Wildlife Federation, which opposed this bill but would veer over to the affirmative side when a less obnoxious successor bill nearly passed in 1954. Congressman Lee Metcalf of Montana, former Chief Justice there, made a telling statement against the bill.

Hearings were held on S. 1491, the Butler–Barrett bill, on May 25, 1953. At the offices of the Senate Committee on Interior and Insular Affairs in 1972 I was told no transcript was available, but happened upon a typed copy at the National Archives, in the Bureau of the Budget files on the bill. The line-up on each side was nearly the same. Senator James E. Murray of Montana argued against the measure, reinforcing Metcalf's House position. Murray said enactment would be a "grave mistake," and it would give permittees "automatic and perpetual renewals." He had received "hundreds" of communications on it, but not one in favor of passage. Barrett debated with Murray for several pages of transcript, and neither would give in to the other.

Testimony of a director of the National Association of Soil Conservation Districts brought back memories of the previous winter's convention of that organization in Cleveland. I attended. Ferry Carpenter did, too. He tried his best to sway Waters S. Davis of League City, Texas, NACD president, but Davis and a majority of the directors stood firm and refused to approve the bills. The director said the subject "practically caused a riot in our convention."

Within days after the hearings both bills were put in deep freeze, but this is not to say the issue had been killed and the Forest Service freed to administer its ranges without further interference or new legislative forays by the livestock lobby. The Anderson–Mansfield Act, with all its implications for the benefit of the permittees, was not enough. The Granger–Thye Act, granting statutory status to the forest grazing advisory boards, did not satisfy. The new submissiveness evidenced in so many ways by the Service only whetted industry appetites. Its leaders still yearned for more. They were determined to drive ahead until they had won every shred of privilege they could read in the Republication Party platform plank. They still had strong administration support. To them the setback on the authority grab bills meant merely that they should go back to the drafting tables and try again. This they did. Their efforts would be climactic in 1954.

A Sly Bootleg Play

The door had hardly closed on the D'Ewart–Butler–Barrett bills of 1953 before work began on their successors. The livestock leadership was determined to pursue the authority grab, and the Eisenhower administration showed an equal insistence on making good the promise in the 1952 public lands plank of the party platform. Notes, often scribbled with pencil or in ink and difficult to identify as to authorship, now in old files in the National Archives,[1] hint at much scurrying around as between Capitol Hill, the Department of Agriculture, and the office of Sherman Adams in the White House. Judging from these files alone, one would come to the superficial conclusion that the major part to be played by the Forest Service was to supply technical information, if or when it was requested, and to submit to decisions made by others.

"On Saturday," begins a copy of a memorandum[2] for Adams from Budget Director Joseph M. Dodge,

you handed me a draft bill on grazing the national forests and asked if we would go along with it. I assume you had the draft from Senator Barrett. This bill grew out of conferences on the senator's earlier bill which was objectionable on a number of scores. It is a considerable improvement over the earlier bill and, on balance, it is probably something which we can support. However, USDA has not yet commented on the bill *but Assistant Secretary Coke is ready to support the bill when it comes to the Department for comment or recommendation* [italics added].

Agriculture informs us as follows: Senator Aiken [George D., of Vermont] expects that you will do nothing on the bill except after talking with him; he wants the bill referred to the Agriculture Committee [of which Aiken was chairman] and Representative Hope [Clifford R., of Kansas, chairman of the House Agriculture Committee] agrees. Most important, Aiken wants to hold off introduction and hearings on the bills until next year. The Bureau of the Budget strongly supports this position.

Aiken and Hope prevailed only in part. The bills got to their committees, but were introduced in 1953. Before Congress adjourned that summer, Senate Resolution 127 was adopted under which an Agriculture subcommittee chaired by Aiken would tour the West and hold hearings on the new form of the bills. Aiken was the chief sponsor of S. 2548 in the Senate; Hope sponsored the identical H. R. 6878 in the House. This time around there would be plenty of preliminary congressional action; the groundwork would be laid carefully in an effort to assure public acquiescence if not enthusiastic support.

And the bills themselves? They would authorize the Service to "promote and encourage" range improvements by permittees "to the maxium practicable extent"; would have the Service agree that permittees would get the benefit of any increase in grazing capacity brought about by the improvements; would provide compensation to any permittees whose grazing was terminated for any reason before full amortization of range improvements installed by them; and would let a permittee sell his interest in such range improvements if or when he should sell his ranch. It would outlaw reductions made on the basis of transfer of property alone. Several sections were required to detail the tedious appeals procedure. Finally, it stipulated that the Service still possessed the authority to reduce or eliminate grazing if need be for range protection or to accommodate higher uses—which the Service had already shown it was reluctant to do.

To us in the conservation movement the new bill was an improvement but not much better than the old ones, and we reacted accordingly. I have no records to refer to for details, but recall a number of letter exchanges between my office and that of Congressman Hope. Joe Penfold wrote him from Denver, too. In these letters we stuck with our views as he tried to get us to come around to the administration position—which would have aligned us with the livestock associations and the administration on features we considered basically wrong. However, Hope's letters had reasonable aspects and we believed his mind was open to constructive suggestion.

That year the Izaak Walton League convention was held just after the H. R. 4023 and S. 1491 hearings. Our banquet speaker was

Dr. Gabrielson, president of the Wildlife Management Institute and retired former director of the U.S. Fish & Wildlife Service. Gabe was a shrewd assessor of the natural resources scene. He told [3] our delegates he didn't think the peeple in power in the administration would "deliberately give away the nation's resources," but went on:

"The . . . danger . . . is that some of these supersalesmen will sell them a bill of goods in the name of conservation. You'd be surprised how many good reasons can be developed for a perfectly lousy project with a little ingenuity, . . . and I don't think the 'gimme' boys were ever as thick [in Washington] at any one time as they have been . . . in the last few months."

Coming specifically to the grazing bills that had been killed and the ones then in the making, Gabrielson said, "In my opinion it would be the greatest [conservation] mistake the American people ever made to give any such small group any vestige of legal right to these lands within the national forests." We applauded.

The summer passed with the industry leaders and the administration adamant about living up to the platform commitment, and the conservation community equally firm in its opposition.

The Aiken committee would be in the West from September 11 through 17 to get grassroots sentiment.[4] This was fine, except that the grassroots where it listened were those being grubbed by the stock owned by those who had initiated this whole series of legislative drafts in the first place. No hearings were scheduled in the East, the Midwest, the South, or any other neutral area. However, even in the camp of the numerically small clique leading the authority grab, the conservation side was able to assemble a sizable array of witnesses. The hearings followed the usual pattern; the stockmen's leaders were up first and our people and others speaking on their own initiative came along afterward. But Aiken knew something we didn't, for he had in his pocket a letter in which Secretary Benson had already committed the department to support the bills in their original form. This was not disclosed until hearings were held in Washington several months later on S. 2548.[5]

In opening remarks at Albuquerque on September 11, Aiken said [6] the bills would merely fix in law what the Service already was doing—which should make one wonder why all the fuss, why there was such a tremendous drive to get the bills enacted. Surely there must be something else deep in their wording that gave them special significance. We in the conservation movement believed this was the case.

First to testify at Albuquerque was Oliver Seth,[7] a lawyer and spokesman for the New Mexico Woolgrowers, the New Mexico Cattlemen, the New Mexico Farm Bureau affiliate, and a smaller grazing association. His statement was typical of what the committee later heard from stockmen at Salt Lake City on September 15 and at Helena on September 17.

Seth recalled the "new, different, and disturbing atmosphere" of the earlier years of the Watts regime, failed to refer to any changes in Service policy and practice that had occurred since the Barrett hearings, and insisted there still was a "general feeling of insecurity" in the industry. He ticked off types of actions that he did not like, mentioning a good many that no longer existed, such as the cuts McArdle had abolished the previous April. The Service, said Seth, simply didn't "understand" the "everyday problems" of the range users. And all that talk about the quality of the range having deteriorated was to him so much hogwash; he had the word of old-time ranchers that it wasn't so. Finally, he liked S. 2548, and so did all those for whom he spoke.

What Seth and other proponents complained of in 1953 sounded much like what Stanfield's colleagues had heard in the 1920s and what had been told to McCarran and Barrett in the 1940s. A non-rancher who spoke for the New Mexico Farm Bureau [8] wanted to impress upon the committee that the word it was getting from him could be repeated in many other places, for he said his parent organization, the American Farm Bureau Federation, with political power in nearly all forty-eight states, also supported S. 2548. Nothing startling was put in the record until a spokesman for the New Mexico Association of Soil Conservation Districts testified in support of the bills. The previous chapter told that the National Association of Soil Conservation Districts had refused to endorse H. R. 4023, and we wondered if this was an isolated thing or if there had been a widespread change in attitude. It apparently was a final fling by one of the NACD's western affiliates that had participated in the warm discussions at Cleveland in support of Ferry Carpenter; nothing further was heard from the NACD or its state subdivisions.

At Salt Lake City, Don Clyde of Heber City, head of the Utah Wool Growers Association, said [9] S. 2548 wasn't good enough to give stockmen "the rights and privileges" they wanted, but it was better than nothing because "now they don't have anything." Vernon Metcalf of Reno gave [10] a long statement that to me seemed as biased in favor of the livestock associations as I have doubtless seemed to be toward the other side. John W. Noh of Kimberley, president of the Idaho Woolgrowers Association, injected a bit of wry humor into his statement,[11] declaring that "in ancient times they called us 'good shepherds'; now its 'damned sheepherders,'" which recalls the bitter wit of DeVoto once when he said [12] he had come to the conclusion that "Cain got a dirty deal!" Clifford P. Hansen of Cheyenne, president of the Wyoming Stock Growers Association, later U.S. senator, said [13] implementing "the ideas back of this legislation" would go a long way toward making the country the sort of "place we like to think it should be."

At Helena, S. E. Whitworth of Dillon, president of the Montana Woolgrowers Association, told [14] the Aiken committee he didn't think S. 2548 was slanted enough in favor of the sheepmen, but approved it nevertheless. Other statements in behalf of the bill at all three hearings were much like his and the others quoted.

Typical of the arguments against S. 2548 were statements at Albuquerque by Hugh B. Woodward,[15] local attorney and a director of the National Wildlife Federation; and at Salt Lake City by Dr. Walter P. Cottam,[16] professor of botany at the University of Utah. Woodward later turned sharply and favored an amended form of the bill, but at Albuquerque that day he opposed it with vigor.

Woodward's chief dislike for S. 2548 was that it was "solely beneficial to one class of users" of the national forests. The high market value of permits—ranging in his area then from $150 to $200 per cow—was excellent evidence that ranchers were not being harassed or treated unfairly by the Forest Service.

Dr. Cottam commented on the "amazing array" of legislative proposals by the industry over the previous decade, ranging from outright sale of public lands through granting a statutory right to forage, which could "be bought and sold as property," to the present which, in the end, would vest final decisions in the court system instead of the "scientific judgment of a well-trained forest personnel." The "only encouraging aspect" of the "continual flow" of bills was that the ranchers "seem to be progressively lowering sights." Still, though S. 2548 was not as offensive as the earlier bills had been, it was bad enough. As to the frequently heard complaints by permittees against reductions in grazing, Dr. Cottam said the crux of the matter was whether Service grazing estimates were "founded on scientific fact," and if cuts proposed were "in the public interest." He opposed this bill, he went on, because it was unnecessary and would weaken the Service by "delay and intimidation"; because it was undemocratic in that it favored only one class of national forest user; because it was unsound in assuming that the Service could separate the grazing function from the protection of watersheds and other uses; and because it was dangerous in giving "at least a semblance of vested rights" in public watershed lands.

Deep in the record of the hearings there appeared the letter to the chairman from Lyle F. Watts, mentioned earlier. Watts recalled his many years in the Service in stating his qualifications to comment on S. 2548, then pointed out its failings, as he saw them, section by section. He feared the effect its enactment would have on the men in the field, saying it would surely cause "the forest ranger to countenance any but the most flagrant violation" of the law and the regulations. The bill also "would just about lock the door against any further redistribution of the range privilege to deserving, qualified ranchers," and "those who now enjoy the privilege, and their successors, would continue to do so indefinitely." He still believed, despite the fact that distribution had been abolished by his successor and there would be exceedingly few "deserving, qualified ranchers" adjacent to the forests from then on, that the situation should be reviewed every ten years before new term permits were issued. He seemed to say that he refused to believe the distribution policy had been irrevocably killed. The "need to watch for needed redistribution" was there, Watts wrote, "so long as 3.7 percent hold permits to graze 16.9 percent of the sheep, and 7.3 percent . . . hold permits to graze 40 percent of the cattle" on the national forests. I doubt if Watts really believed the old policy would be revived, and it may be he used the hearings as an opportunity for a gentle rebuke to McArdle for his action in ending it. I lean somewhat to the view that Watts was taking advantage of an opportunity to strike back at ranchers whose blows he had absorbed for so long.

Aiken returned to Washington convinced that the bill should be softened further. The more insistent among the stockmen would have to be convinced that this would be good strategy, and efforts would have to be made to turn the conservation movement's position around or the bill still would be in trouble if it came to a floor fight. So in the fall months the bill was revised once more, and Senate hearings were held on the amended version in Washington on January 21 and 22, 1954, House hearings in February. Barrett was invited to sit with Aiken and take part in those on the Senate side. The new language provided that there would still be forest boards to advise the Service on grazing subjects, but now they would be called "multiple use advisory councils" [17] and their composition would be broadened. Also, the bill had been changed to allow any user of a national forest to appeal if he had a complaint against the Service.[18] The old Section 5, which had provided for a new fee study, was killed. This was a steep descent from the outright controls in H. R. 4023 and S. 1491.

The softening was adroit enough to cause searching examination of the legislation by both sides. The livestock people's testimony at the hearings was generally favorable; the attitude seemed to be that if they could not get all at one whack they would take what was offered at this time—and probably be back in another year or two for the rest.

I don't believe I had yet fully grasped the extent to which the will of the Service to resist livestock industry pressure had been eroded, and the printed report of the hearings, replete with expressions of admiration for the record of the Service over the years, shows clearly that this was true of spokesmen for other conservation groups as well as ours.

Eight months earlier the Service had not even been allowed to have an official observer at the hearings on H. R. 4023, and the Department of Agriculture had gone into a deep silence on its contents. Now came total reversal. Chief McArdle would tell both committees [19] that the Service would be happy to have the bills enacted into law. The record already contained Benson's September 3, 1953, letter [20] approving the earlier version of the same bills. And Schedule C could still be applied to the office of Chief Forester if McArdle refused to go along. I believe administration pressure as strong as any ever applied by the livestock industry was bearing down on McArdle.

The stockmen divided their forces for the hearings, sending one team to those held by Aiken, another to that held by Hope, but there was little new in their presentations. Fairly typical was that before Aiken of Frank C. Mockler of DuBois, Wyoming, a member of the state legislature who represented the American National. His major points: [21]

1. The stockmen wanted whatever range improvements they might choose to install themselves, and to be repaid if for any reason they went out of business before improvements were fully amortized. My view is that this would simplify things for stockmen concerned but would not at all guarantee that what was done would be what the ranges needed.

2. The stockmen wanted no fee study for fear it might conceivably result in a different formula and higher charges. Mockler made a

statement in all sobriety that in 1975 looked strangely naïve and old fashioned. He said, "We've completed, we think, a period of high prices which we will not soon see again." If what he envisioned came to pass and a new formula should be put into effect, it might do away with the low fees enjoyed ever since the then existing formula had been worked out at the depths of the Great Depression when all prices were at rock bottom.

3. He opposed the idea of multiple-use advisory councils on the forests, contending that they and the advisory grazing boards still in existence might make conflicting recommendations; which those speaking for our side believed was exactly the reason why they should be inaugurated.

4. According to Mockler a *"new era of good feeling between the permittees and forest officials"* was "in the offing" (italics added). I consider this a true statement, but not necessarily because of the "feeling of mutual respect and esteem" to which Mockler attributed it. My view is that resistance to livestock lobby demands had already largely gone from the backbone of most Service officialdom, and the bill would seal the tacit new pact—existing or in the making—whereby the stock associations could almost write their own tickets. The Service today would no doubt disagree violently with me, as doubtless will the associations, but I am convinced the total weight of evidence favors my assertion.

Vernon Metcalf of Reno, a perennial witness at congressional hearings on grazing matters, told [22] the committee that if the stockmen did not get the "definite protection" of tenure the bill provided "against the day-to-day whims of the landlord," then it would be better not to have any grazing use of the public lands at all. His reasoning was that without unlimited tenure, permittees would follow the course history made clear and ruin the lands through overuse. He phrased it slightly differently, saying that history showed that injury to soil and water resources was sure to result from lack of tenant tenure. Either way, to me it read like a threat, a demand that the permittees be given all the rights and prerogatives inherent in the bill, else, with limited or uncertain "tenure," the public lands would face further deterioration.

He deviated somewhat from the fee position assumed by Mockler, saying that a study would be quite satisfactory, provided it was tied to "the ability of the users to pay" fees and also pay all other costs of doing business. Here Metcalf brought in the same detailed arguments he had used so effectively in the McCarran hearings era, which ended with public domain grazing fees still far below those charged by the Forest Service, the Indian Service, and by private landowners who had pasturage to rent.

Matt Triggs, legislative representative of the American Farm Bureau Federation, put his nationwide organization behind the bill,[23] and used all the livestock lobby's usual terminology: The bill would "stabilize and clarify the rights" of permittees; encourage private improvement of range; provide "security of tenure" that was "compatible with the public interest"; and insure "relationships" more nearly like those existing under the Taylor Act.

There was little debate between members of the Senate committee and the livestock witnesses. Questions were asked, but these generally were friendly, to try to complete the record or for some similar purpose. Not so when the House hearings were held a month later. Congressmen Harold A. Cooley of North Carolina and W. R. Poage of Texas put in a number of licks that we of the conservation movement relished.

When Sam Hyatt of Hyattville, Wyoming, speaking for the American National Livestock Association, testified that the existing grazing fees on the national forests were "fair and just," Cooley retorted [24] that they were "ridiculous," that a rancher could "feed a bull a month for the price of a few postage stamps" (at a time when first class mail went for three cents). Further to Hyatt, "You can't tell me you permittees will improve permanently the forest land of this country; you'll get anything out of it that you can, and that is it."

Poage countered [24] the point so often made by the spokesmen for the livestock industry to the effect that they needed all the favoritism they could get because of their heavy base property investments, by saying he had all these costs on his Texas ranch plus the burden of paying a higher fee for rented pasturage. He told Hyatt that having paid all those costs, "from my side of the fence it looks like you have an awfully green pasture."

Congressman Lee Metcalf of Montana called [26] the bill "special interest" legislation and said it and all similar bills should be killed. Grazing "in most cases is the least important" of the multiple uses of natonal forests. The "insecurity" ploy by the stockmen testifying was "largely fanciful," since some permittees had been on the national forest ranges from the start to the present. The "best evidence of the security the stockmen enjoy," he declared, was that when they sold a ranch property the grazing permit often had value "greater than that assigned to the ranch itself." The idea of a top-level appeals board consisting of one man chosen by the Secretary, one by the user, and a third from another state chosen by the first two, was "a clever device" to assure a board "dominated by the representative of the grazing interests," because he would be the only one "who knows local conditions." As for ultimate court adjudication, Congressman Metcalf felt the permittees already had two effective procedures available for user protection: injunction to prevent an illegal or capricious agency act, and mandamus to force an official to do what the law said he should or must do.

Charles H. Callison, conservation director of the National Wildlife Federation (now executive vice-president of the National Audubon Society) and a generally sound, effective advocate of the prevailing natural resources conservation viewpoint, appeared at both hearings [27] and before Senator Aiken's committee expressed the opinion that the bill was an "effort to placate . . . a noisy minority" of permittees, and had been introduced for the very reason that the Service had "performed its duties faithfully and well." At the House committee hearing his statement was similar and, in addition, declared the bill was a "result of the very stability" of national forest grazing, implying, I believe, that without that stability the industry might not be in position to press forward so strongly.

The Izaak Walton League was represented in the record with letter–statements prepared by Penfold,[28] the gist of which was that the only thing we liked about the bills were the sections dealing with multiple-purpose advisory councils. In other respects we considered them "unnecessary and undesirable." It was "imperative," Penfold wrote, that national forest administration should be "predicated on the principle . . . that privileges granted to any one class of users should never transcend the rights of the public as a whole."

The Senate committee did not bother to wait to see what Hope's group on the House side would do. Aiken reported S. 2548 favorably on February 17,[29] and it was passed after brief debate on March 8, 1954. Nothing happened of public note, then, until July 14 and 15, when Congressman Hope held further hearings on both bills, for S. 2548 had long since been signed and sent over to the House for concurring—or differing—action. Hope then put both bills in a pigeonhole. We of the League kept our fingers crossed but were hopeful they were dead.

Sometime between the end of February and mid-July the spokesmen for the National Wildlife Federation had a radical change of opinion. An NWF letter to Hope dated June 25 and put in the record [30] said in part that, as passed by the Senate, S. 2548 was "a fair and just bill giving Congressional approval to all uses of the national forests and providing for the protection of each use against any use becoming dominant to the detriment of other uses." Carl D. Shoemaker, counsel both to the NWF and the International Association of Game, Fish, and Conservation Commissioners, concurred [31] and indicated that he liked the fact that the bill, as passed, would allow the multiple-use councils to advise the Secretary of Agriculture "on their own initiative" as well as at his request.

So now the respected National Wildlife Federation had defected and gone over to approval, alone among all the conservation organizations. We were told later that the change came about after consultations between Callison, Shoemaker, and Hugh B. Woodward, Albuquerque attorney and NWF director.[32] The change was exceedingly distressing to the rest of us in the movement. Up to that point we had moved almost as a drilled team, thanks in part to the coordination of information possible through the Natural Resources Council. We were further disconcerted when Michael Hudoba of Washington, offering a statement [33] to the Hope committee in behalf of the Outdoor Writers Association of America—to which many of us opposed to S. 2548 belonged and about which we had not been consulted—shifted to the NWF point of view.

Then followed an unusual sequence of occurrences. The Senate began debate on what was considered "sacred cow" legislation, the administration's farm program bill, S. 3052 and H. R. 9680. Senator Clinton P. Anderson of New Mexico, former Secretary of Agriculture whom we conservationists had long considered sound as Gibraltar on national forest questions, made the motion by which S. 2548 was added *in toto* as a rider to the farm bill.[34] This was dismaying, to say the least. It was hard to believe that a farm bill would be voted down, and even less believable that one containing what remained of the essence of the 1952 public lands plank of the GOP platform would be vetoed by President Eisenhower. Further, we saw Anderson, a Democrat, by this act pulling Republican chestnuts out of the fire. What had become of his former even-handed approach to range problems? Was his long-time friendship with NWF's Woodward involved?

Congressman Don Magnusson sent out a news release [35] in which he called the attachment of the stockmen's bill as a rider to the farm bill the culmination of "the slyest legislative bootleg play of the 83rd Congress," adding that it was "special interest legislation at its worst" and might "well mark the beginning of the end of the jealous safeguarding of the people's right to our public lands."

Beyond this, the rider ploy put a bitter reverse twist on strategy that had been used by conservationists to good advantage in the nineteenth century. Then the rider had been the tool employed to bring the federal forest system into being in the first place. Now it was being used to try to grant special privilege to a single type of national forest use.

We read that Senator Sam J. Ervin of North Carolina opposed [36] the rider, as did Senator Wayne Morse of Oregon, who declared [37] that if it became law the most that could be said thereafter was that the forests were "quasi-public lands and no longer public."

Morse then put in the Senate record a statement that already had appeared in the House sector on July 28 as an extension of remarks by Congressman Metcalf of Montana, in which Metcalf declared the "big livestock interests who have vigorously fought the whole farm program and condemned it for years, now are hitching onto the price support bill to try to get their foot in the door and control grazing on the national forests."

Then the heaviest gun in the White House arsenal was turned toward Capitol Hill. On August 12, 1954, President Eisenhower sent identical letters [38] to Senator Aiken and Congressman Hope in which he wrote:

"Another item of concern is the bill introduced *at my request* relating to the management of forest land for grazing purposes. The Senate version is fair to all users of the national forests and a forward step in the management of forest lands. Because its approval would complete several conservation measures recommended by this administration to the Congress, I am especially hopeful it can receive the approbation of your colleagues" (italics added).

The existence of the letter was not then known to the conservation groups; if we had heard of it, no doubt our hopes would have plunged lower than they already were.

When the Senate voted favorably on the rider and sent the farm bill to the House, Hudoba suddenly became more concerned than his favorable July statement to Hope's committee indicated. He alerted J. Hammond Brown, outdoor editor of the Baltimore *News-Post* and president of the Outdoor Writers Association, and messages of alarm went from "Brownie's" office to leading outdoor writers across the nation.[39] All of us in the conservation movement were filled in, and many responded. Congressman Hope's name was appropriate, for his would be a decisive voice during deliberations in the conference committee named to iron out differences in the Senate and House versions of the farm bill. Likely just as decisive were the voices of Congressmen Cooley and Poage, who had been critical of the industry in the earlier House hearing, and who also were on the conference committee. At any rate, the rider was stricken before the farm bill was reported out and passed.

It was a near thing. We conservationists rejoiced. We believed that what had taken place could be interpreted as a clear signal to the Forest Service that it had public support for the kind of range program that would accomplish the most in the shortest time. We thought that this time the Eisenhower administration itself must be convinced that its 1952 platform plank was rotten and should be junked. I don't think any of it worked out that way.

It was in July 1972, almost two decades after the events recounted, that I learned of the prescience of Dr. John W. Scott, the modest, self-effacing University of Wyoming professor who, in retrospect, was one of the most underappreciated conservationists of our time. In a letter to Charlie Moore on July 3, 1953, shortly after the old D'Ewart–Butler–Barrett authority grab bills had so abruptly been pigeonholed, Dr. Scott wrote: [40]

"From statements in the press I understand H. B. 4023 would not be reported out by committee. . . . When Bills of this kind appear before Congress it is not hard to kill them, provided they receive adequate publicity. *The chief danger present is that this group may be able to insert an amendment in some other bills on a different subject* that would gain . . . a part of their objectives" (italics added).

Which is exactly the strategy the livestock lobby and the administration adopted.

The hubbub came to a legislative close with the death of the rider, but that did not end all backstage activity in high levels of the administration. A year later, on July 8, 1955, a memo "for current legislative files" signed by Harry McKitrick, chief of the Resources and Civil Works Division of the Bureau of the Budget, quoted from the July 15, 1954, letter from Ike to Aiken and Hope, then said: [41]

"In view of this specific endorsement by the President, we would think that the 83rd Congress Senate-passed version [S. 2548] would, at least, be the starting point for executive branch position now.

The burden of proof would seem to be on anyone . . . wanting to shift from this position. The USDA's letter to BB advances no reasons of this sort" (italics added).

The file did not contain a copy of the "USDA's letter to BB" referred to. There was, however, a BOB "route slip," also dated July 8, 1955, from McKitrick to several other Budget Bureau officials, containing information [42] supplied by one Roger Jones, which said Senator Barrett "does not want a bill put in at this time; he would probably not be willing to sponsor a draft bill at any time." Senator Aiken was critical, Jones was quoted as reporting, because a bill had not been sent to him in 1955 from the executive branch. However, arranging sponsorship in the House would be difficult; Congressman Hope would probably be unwilling to introduce it again.

Secretary Benson remained active. He wrote [43] to Rowland Hughes, Budget Bureau director, on August 3, 1955, proposing that S. 2548 be reintroduced. The Department of Agriculture would have only one objection to it; it would be adamantly opposed to opening the appeals procedure to all users of the national forests. In other words, that should be reserved for the livestock permittees. No others need apply.

S. 2548 was not reintroduced, and the BOB folders on the subject contained nothing else of significance that I saw. The files leave us without hint of the reason why Barrett had grown reluctant to sponsor a bill for the livestock industry that he had so eagerly supported before. I have a theory as to why he took his new position; it is that the livestock lobby, in all its forms, had come to recognize that the Forest Service was by then figuratively on its knees. My hypothesis is that the Service had already suffered severe internal bleeding, and showed symptoms of its weakened condition to which we, its almost blindly loyal conservation friends, should have paid far more attention much earlier than we did.

It is, of course, wishful thinking, but it would be nice to be able to say that henceforth there will be no more riders, on bills or on horseback, galloping for privilege at the expense of public values on our national forests. The most we can say is that none had passed as of mid-1975.

Look at the Range,
Not the Cow

"The public is increasingly unhappy with us," read a 1970 memorandum [1] from the chief of the Forest Service to his staff. "This will continue until we get balance and quality into our program, as well as public involvement in our decisions." Such language might be expected in a showcase trial of dissidents in a dictatorship, but in a message to personnel from our chief forester? Yet it was so.

"Many employes have recently expressed concern on the direction in which the Forest Service seems to be heading," it began. "I share this concern. Our programs are out of balance to meet public needs for the environmental 1970s and we are receiving criticism from all sides." The cure, Chief Edward P. Cliff went on, lay in part in the age old remedy of "more money and people."

At no point did this extraordinary message refer specifically to livestock or grazing. Rather, Cliff seemed concerned about getting more national forest timber cut and on the market to help meet national housing needs. And his wish to initiate "public involvement" appeared to reflect a desire to ward off additional court cases [2] and other doings that challenged Service actions, chiefly with respect to the clear-cutting of trees in conspicuous places and to commercial recreational ventures on national forest land.

I do not conclude that the absence of reference to grazing meant all was as the public should have it in that area of Service activity. In 1970 grazing on national forests no longer engaged the concentrated attention it once received from the nation's conservation community, and both the industry and the Service seemed happy to have it that way. Of course, the report [3] of the Public Land Law

Review Commission had been issued and in some places was critical. It doubtless was a factor. I hold that belligerent actions by both veteran conservation groups and militant new environmental organizations had jabbed a deeply embedded nerve center of the Service and roused it to defensive response.

In grazing matters the previous decade and a half had been relatively calm out on the western range. The livestock associations no longer agitated constantly for additional privilege through legislation. There was little more for them to agitate for. Through what Walter Hickel called [4] the "buddy" system the industry and the Service had grown chummy. The latter was laying on few directives the former could consider adverse, and it was spending money as freely as Congress appropriated it on range improvements and rehabilitative measures; it was furnishing detailed guidance on range use but was not cutting down AUMs of grazing routinely where the land was in bad condition. The slight but regular annual decline in range use that came about did so mostly on the initiative of ranchers who had business reasons for slacking off or who quit entirely. Either would allow the Service to let an allotment lapse or be reduced in numbers or time without affecting a going concern. Such cuts as were initiated by the Service were often a consequence of the development or expansion of a campground or something else related to recreation.

Today Service officials say the trend of its ranges is up—which may be a regional truth or valid in favored smaller areas, but does not change the persistent reductions that show in the statistics. It would be strange if at least some of the ranges had not responded to the yearly infusions of rehabilitation funds since the Anderson–Mansfield Act became law. Yet the Service has not so far stabilized animal unit months of use at a maintainable figure, nor has it managed to bring about and sustain a servicewide increase. Numbers rise slightly in this or that category here or there on occasion, then slide gently downward again.

The places where an upward trend may be found seem to relate to where the foundation forage and weather prospects were better to begin with, and where field officials made better starts toward reductions to grazing capacity levels before the great change in policy took place. To make a point in this regard we return to Region 2, Wyoming and Colorado. At Denver in 1972, Deputy Regional Forester Crane used language [5] indicating that major reduction efforts had been to obtain later spring starts, which he considered the

Spaced water tanks help spread use of skimpy forage, near Desert Range
Experiment Station, Utah, 1957. *USFS photo*

principal element. He conceded that basic range had been superior
in Region 2 to that found in certain other national forest areas, because of the quality of the native grasses, and soil and moisture
conditions. "Once we cut the seasons back, along with reductions in
numbers," said Crane, "it was amazing how the forage came back."

These were precisely the measures Sandvig and his associates
had commenced, insisted upon, and been purged for. And there is
further evidence. A letter [6] from Sandvig quoted one he had received
in the early 1970s from an unnamed Forest Service official stationed
in western Colorado.

"I'm known as a 'Sandvig man' in Region 2," the letter read. "Because of this some of the older stockmen and I get together and
talk about you. . . . Floyd Beach [one of the more intransigent association leaders] . . . once agreed with me over a beer that . . . *you
forced the livestock man to look at his range instead of his cows*"
(italics added).

This should be linked to Sandvig's stated [7] philosophy:

Cattle in good condition on range sprayed in 1962 to kill sagebrush, Salmon National Forest, Idaho, 1964. *USFS photo*

When I saw violations of solid principles of range ecology I felt it deeply, that this can't go on, that it defeats everything we've been taught, and violates natural laws. . . . Why should anyone do such things . . .? Over the long run it does not benefit the stockman dependent on forage for his livelihood. He is in the business of growing grass that he markets through the stock he raises to sell. The more grass he can grow the more stock he will have to market. I was seeing decreases in the forage crop on a wholesale scale, and in every way I could I tried to bring that message to my associates . . ., and to whoever would listen. . . .

The requirement that everyone concerned with livestock must "look at his range instead of his cows" has been implicit in nearly every communication I have had with Forest Service officials in recent years. It was so with Crane, and in exchanges [6] with Frank Smith, director of range management until his retirement in February, 1975. Dutton came close to saying it in his repeated declarations [9] that the Service had always been too optimistic in allotting seasons and numbers. Why, seventy years after the service's beginning, and twenty-six years after the accelerated range betterment program started under Anderson–Mansfield, can't the Service say, and prove, that the national forest ranges everywhere are on the upgrade? Why don't its ranges support at least a stable number of AUMs of grazing annually instead of showing an almost continual decrease?

Laws the conservation community helped get enacted have in my opinion been beneficial, on balance, though they probably have contributed to the conclusion I reach that the Service may be somewhat confused by its multiplicity of orders as to the direction it is supposed to travel. Before the Multiple Use and Sustained Yield Act [10] was made law the Service had a certain built-in discretionary power with respect to the emphasis it might give to this or that phase of its management functions. The department showed little enthusiasm for the Multiple Use Act at hearing time in 1959.

Recreation interests were instrumental in bringing about this law. Recreation had always been enjoyed on the national forests. Vast areas gave elbow room not found in crowded cities. Streams and lakes were numerous, productive, and generally free from the increasing volumes of pollution that threatened where it had not already damaged or destroyed those in urbanized and industrialized parts of the country. Scenic qualities were superb. In earlier years recreational use of the national forests grew at a fairly steady pace that more or less paralleled the rise in population and automobiles, and in miles of improved roads. The increase slowed in World War II for obvious reasons, then leaped skyward immediately afterward. The 1956 report of the chief forester said [11] annual visits rose from fewer than ten million in the war years to 52.2 million a decade later—and the growth has continued apace.

As recreational visits mounted, cries were heard for more campgrounds, roads, foot and horse trails into back country, facilities to serve skiers, and other amenities. The Service responded as funds could be made available, but the demand was for ever more, and the pleas began to bring reaction in Congress. Livestock interests had asked for and got the grazing use of the forests locked into law. Now the recreationists insisted on equal status. They did not want their activities restricted to a permitted privilege any more than stock interests had liked having their grazing so prescribed.

Recreationists took a somewhat different tack, though, from that of the stockmen in earlier years. They did not ask that gratification of their desires be exclusive. They went after equality for all the multiple uses found on national forests. When the Multiple Use and Sustained Yield Act was at hearing stage the departmental attitude —doubtless put in draft form by the Service—was lukewarm. Assistant Secretary E. L. Peterson [12] said "recognition of wilderness, and wildlife habitat as beneficial uses . . . , and a requirement that the national forests be administered under principles of multiple use and sustained yield *may be* found advantageous" (italics added), which does not read like overwhelming enthusiasm.

Then Chief Forester McArdle muddied the hearing waters somewhat by presenting [13] a forty-year long-range program proposal for which he wanted congressional blessing. Priority goals would be "desirable watershed conditions and a sustained high level production of forage." He talked at length, but dwelt throughout on range betterment, after which the chief livestock spokesman present, Edwin Marsh of Salt Lake City, executive secretary of the National Woolgrowers Association, yearned [14] aloud for dominating legislation "like that proposed by stockmen several years ago."

It is tempting here to diverge and comment on the fact that watershed protection was in the original directive given the embryo Forest Service in the organic Forest Reserves Act [15] of 1897, and that sixty-two years later the chief forester was saying that compliance with the Service's initial marching orders would require an additional forty years.

Conservation organizations at the hearing warmly endorsed the multiple-use idea, which may have helped bring the committee's attention back to the legislation before it. When the bill was signed into law it was intended to assure equal consideration by the Forest Service for "outdoor recreation, range, timber, watershed, and wildlife and fish purposes." It must be said that in the annual report for 1960 the Service praised [16] the multiple-use concept more warmly than Peterson did at the hearing. Whether it had misgivings for the future, though, is questionable. I have found no overt criticism of the act, which undoubtedly has resulted in close scrutiny of Service actions since then by each interest—basic or splinter—to make sure it was getting not one whit less than its fully equal share of attention.

Two other laws must be regarded as also tending to lessen Service flexibility. They were the act [17] creating a National Wilderness System and that [18] authorizing a Wild and Scenic Rivers System, both made law in 1964. Most of the statutory wildernesses so far established have been national forest land, corresponding generally to previously established areas administratively labeled "wilderness," "primitive," or "wild." There has been controversy on these, usually concerning boundaries or permitted use. Wilderness advocates have wanted certain acreages, commercial interests have opted for others, and the Service has had its own ideas as to where lines should be drawn. Similar problems have been encountered with respect to the Wild and Scenic Rivers System, with about the same line-up of interested parties.

Anderson–Mansfield solidified and regularized an internal Service policy that practically eliminated imposed livestock grazing reductions. Multiple Use and Sustained Yield made mandatory what had previously been discretionary handling of the multiple resources of the national forests, and the uses to which they were put. Legalizing wilderness and wild and scenic rivers put new and different duties in official laps. All had their individual measures of impact on the livestock use of the forests, and all but Anderson–Mansfield were restrictive to a degree. Each caused more field work and paper work.

I have not looked into other of the multiple uses, but have sensed how cumulative weight has burdened those bearing responsibility for managing national forest ranges. Charles A. (Chic) Joy succeeded Walt Dutton as director of range management in 1953 and retired in 1967. Before he died in 1972, Joy was interviewed [19] on tape by Herb E. Schwan for the Conservation Center of the Denver Public Library. I dubbed the Joy interview, and have listened to it more than once, to capture his earnestness, his tonal inflections, his careful choices of words to express thoughts without openly criticizing a Service he obviously loved. Even in retirement he sounded as though still under Service discipline; he was trying hard not to appear disloyal.

Chic Joy was a happier man in the field than in Washington, and he referred in guarded terms to his dissatisfaction with range policies imposed over his objections. And he longed for a return to times when permittees were "not so politically minded." Washington had been "a trying experience," though he conceded that a tour of duty there would be enlightening to men who had served only in the field. Closed doors in Washington were much on his mind, a lack of communication with superiors and between branches of the Service who should be working closely together to avoid friction where functions impinged.

Speaking of Ed Cliff, who was his superior both as assistant chief for national forest administration and as chief forester, Joy said:

My boss and I got along; he never bothered me or me him.
The chief was in my office perhaps one or two times in my seven years there and the assistant chief only five or six times. . . . One division director seldom knew what the others were doing. . . . We and Research were located next door to each other, and we got along fine. . . . The chief was more or less sealed off from the directors of divisions . . .; he was limited in his sources of information. Nowadays it is hard for a [division] director even to get to his assistant chief. We had to go through assistants to the assistant chief.

The spare words, spoken in a monotone, disclosed how disturbed Joy was because of the impenetrable walls of bureaucracy that had been built and that, he felt, hemmed him in and blocked him from easy access to and consultation with responsible superiors when range problems piled up. A Pennsylvania Deutsch friend used to say of something that had overgrown itself, "It iss too big oudt." So has the Forest Service grown—too big out—too sprawling a bureaucracy, unable to maintain close liaison within itself or with the general public who, collectively, are owners of the National Forest System. The ailment is not limited to Washington. Here is Joy again: [20]

"In my younger days we'd spend three or four weeks on the range, camping. We'd cook our bacon and eggs for breakfast and move on. When we got back we'd make out a Service report and go to town for more groceries. Now it is hard for a ranger to go more than two or three days before he has a crisis of some kind. Questions concerning appropriations, personnel, or something else have to be met."

Personnel numbers have swollen in all segments of the Service. One account [21] notes that a supervisor at a conference at forest headquarters did not recognize the name or face of one of his own rangers. Joy commented: [22]

"Should the pendulum swing back? I'm not sure. We do need more qualified men on the ground."

In context, it appears that Joy meant that there was a need for more knowledgeable people actually on horseback and in pickup trucks and four-wheel-drive vehicles, out talking with and demonstrating range truths to permittees, rather than putting more bodies at desks piled high with papers that might or might not be read or, if read, acted upon. Joy spoke of the proliferation of paper work brought on by the increasing emphasis on rehabilitation and the complex system of allotment management that was evolving.

"My assistant chief [Cliff] was not sympathetic to [prevailing methods of] range management survey; so we got into allotment analysis. I argued against it. So did a couple of men in Research. If you get 3–400 rangers doing allotment analyses they will all be different. Before I left Washington I found a lot of field men were projecting analyses. I know that by 1967 on some national forests analyses had been projected four or five times and likely would be done a sixth."

He was skeptical that rangers could make perhaps one grazing allotment analysis the hard way, on the ground, diligently following all the involved instructions, and thereafter need only to feed old data into a computer to calculate what range conditions and trends would be five or more years later. That, he was convinced, was no substitute for getting out on the ranges to observe vegetative and other changes first hand. Near the close of Schwan's interview with him, Joy mused that one day "there must be a reckoning on some of these things."

Sandvig questions whether the "reckoning" Joy envisioned will come of the Service's own volition; he feels external forces will have to apply sufficient pressure to overcome what he considers today's inertia. In one communication [23] he said he feared both the Forest Service and BLM were "pinning their hopes" for optimum range conditions "on miracles." No miracles have been passed and no such outside pressure has appeared to weigh on the Forest Service up to now. Militant environmental groups concentrate on the precise boundaries of areas to be proclaimed wilderness or to be included in the list of wild or scenic rivers. They raise questions of the propriety of allowing corporate interests to install an elaborate resort in a specific western national forest area. They wrangle over clear-cutting of timber in large blocks, fearful of accelerated erosion as well as unsightliness before soil-building new growth comes along. In recent years almost the only outcry from the conservation community directly related to national forest grazing has been over questions involving fees; whether they were too low, or protesting postponement by the land-managing agencies of next year's increment. The chief exception to this was the unanimity with which Wayne Aspinall's H. R. 7211,[24] which would have granted grazing a dominating place wherever it was the chief use being made of public lands, was opposed. Conservationists feared a dominating use policy would be substituted for the existing multiple use principle.

I find it small wonder that Chief Cliff was constrained to send out his 1970 memorandum, and doubt if corrective action taken as a result of it before his retirement in 1972 has brought results he would consider adequate or Chic Joy would approve. So the Service lumbers along, moving slowly and ponderously. It has many voices to which it must listen. It continues to listen intently when the livestock industry whispers in its ear. It did so at the start of 1975, agreeing apparently without objection—as did the Bureau of Land Management—when the stockmen's leaders requested that the year's normal raise in the planned progression toward fair market value grazing fees be held in abeyance. With all the prerogatives the stock industry enjoys, there does not seem to be much need for it to ask wesern members of Congress to bullyrag the Service, as was so common in prior years. The Service has become preoccupied with its mounting paper work and cryptic computer symbols. And the ranges are given annual injections of rehabilitative money that, no matter where or in what volume spent, seem unable to check the inexorable decrease in forage production that is reflected in annual records of dwindling animal unit months of grazing use.

III

Three Steps Forward, Two Back

19

Closing the Open Range

Little major decision-making in the West has entailed more pain and uncertainty than that of determining what should be the ultimate fate of the remaining public domain after homesteading had run its practical course and the bulk of the national forests had been sundered from it by the end of the first decade of this century.

Mining and other powerful interests were in the thick of the debate and had significant influence, but none more than the western livestock industry's leaders. It is they with whom we are primarily concerned, and with what they wanted or did not want or did not know whether they wanted—all of which would keep the West, and Congress, in ferment for thirty years after the forest reserves had been shifted from Interior to Agriculture. In the end a combination of events and actualities would force the issue. Congress had been obsessed with the idea that one or another kind of homestead would solve western land-use problems, but the lawakers were unrealistic; many voted from ignorance or motives far removed from the hopes and fears of the nesters whose praises they sang for the record. Successful homesteading had to slow down close to the wavering north–south line where long-grass prairie gave way to short-grass plains, except in favorable nooks that became increasingly scarce or unavailable.

For decades—centuries in the Southwest—lands that would be passed up as worthless by settlers had nourished livestock and wildlife. True, in some places a cow or sheep had to ramble across a lot of acreage to fill its belly, but that was no particular problem in earlier times. Heaven knows that at first there was plenty of territory over which they could forage. East of the 100th meridian a landowner might look upon his eighty or 160 acres and usually find them sufficient for subsistence and a little more. The westerner, on a home base where he had perennial water for his needs, often grazed out as far as eye could reach upon vacant land that he could utilize but with a degree of success or efficiency only with domestic animals a link in the chain. Even when the West began filling with people and livestock, here and there to the bursting point, it still was the rancher with large acreage at his disposal who made the most economic use of the public domain. It was a lonesome life that fostered individuality. There were years when the only stranger who might pass the home ranch was a prospector looking for some kind of valuable mineral on which to file a claim, or a hunter from the East or abroad who pursued deer, elk, antelope, or bighorn sheep for sport as much as for table meat. The people the stockman usually encountered near home were visiting ranchers, and the folks he saw in his distant "home" town were generally connected with business enterprises and who bought from or were dependent on purchases made by the cowman or woolgrower.

It was natural that a belief should grow that the remaining public domain was "worthless except for grazing," for that was its dominant use at the time and, in fact, millions of acres of it are still seldom accorded high value for other human purposes. The first white people there could be widely separated by choice as well as the necessities of the region, not subject to the frictions and tensions that attend overcrowding. It was not until the last vacant reaches of the West had become filled with more livestock than they could safely accommodate that the thoughts of the more sagacious of the still relatively small human population turned strongly toward ways and means of controlling excessive grazing use.

And it was logical that stockmen should take the lead, both in advocating control and in the seemingly inevitable trait of splitting several ways over how control should be achieved. Ranching of all kinds in the West had undergone a variety of shaking-out situations, so that a layering or class-creating effect was achieved. It had economic and social implications. At the top were a comparatively small number of very large operators who ran thousands of head over baronial spreads. Below them were a more numerous group, cowmen and sheepmen in middle economic strata who were considered merely well to do. The bottom layer consisted of the little fellows, numerically a majority but politically and economically less impressive; ethnic

Heavily used stock trail and overgrazed slopes on public domain, California. Picture taken for Hoover Commission which wanted states to have the land as a gift, 1930. *USFS photo*

considerations entered at this level more than at the others. Many factors worked to bring this layering about—the boom-and-bust era, the winds of political change, periodic droughts, and others—but perhaps most of all the simple fact that the West was edging toward a degree of stability in its institutions and mores.

But all out there were individualists in one way or another. It took initiative for settlers from the relatively secure East or Middle West to pull up stakes and undertake the arduous journey when the West was untamed. That same independence of action was instilled in many an offspring. It showed in attitudes of ranchers toward the destiny of the open range.

The basic schism was on whether there should be any control at all. The principal contending forces were the cattle interests, who generally favored it, and the sheepmen, who ordinarily did not. It would be misleading to say the woolgrowers were dominated by transients who operated from camp wagons that constituted their homes on the range, but they had a certain influence. Put the public domain under law and regulations and the nomads would be driven out of business or converted to home base ranching. Some tramp stockmen ran cattle, but they were few; cattle could not be handled as sheep were, kept in bounds by herders with well-trained working dogs.

The day of the nomad peaked around the turn of the century and started downward when the Forest Service was shifted into the hands of Pinchot and his associates. They moved swiftly to prevent trespass by transients on national forest range, and that restricted nomad freedom of movement. Settled ranchers who used public domain range found them more and more a nuisance and a threat to their comparatively stable operations. After the Forest Service was created it became merely a matter of when and under what circumstances the transient would have to disappear from the scene. He was a significant and controversial figure as the debate went on over closing the open public domain.

The movement toward regulation at times seemed so slow as to be imperceptible. In the decade before World War I little real progress was made, though thoughts here and there were being sorted out. During the war nearly all were preoccupied with making as much money as they could while dealing with shortages of help, supplies, and equipment. Afterward, when postwar depression struck, the Forest Service began cutting back permitted numbers. This forced still greater competition for public domain forage, and when grazing regions were withered by drought and depression, the far-sighted ones moved more purposefully. Constant wrangling between settled rancher and nomad, between cattlemen and sheepmen in general, between the big and the little, and over every variety of complaint that can arise between neighbors, whoever they be, all served in their separate and sometimes devious ways to further the cause of control and hasten its coming.

Dozens of bills to accomplish the purpose were introduced in the Congress in the first quarter of this century. According to one source,[1] eighteen went into the Senate hopper between 1899 and 1925, while twenty-five were introduced in the House between 1900 and 1921. All failed for one reason or another.

The situation in 1925 was more or less typical. Ferment over what to do about the public domain was great, and the Forest Service had been in existence long enough for a goodly stack of complaints against it to have piled up on the desks of westerners in Congress. Senator Robert N. Stanfield of Oregon took the initiative. He would conduct a double-barreled investigation. He had little love for the Forest Service because of troubles over his ranching operations back home, and more public lands legislation was pending. In addition, the Departments of Agriculture and Interior had collaborated on drafting still another bill, one seemingly intended to be legislation and to end all legislation on the subject of public range management. The hearings began in Washington. What they brought forth there and in the field with respect to the Forest Service was related in Chapter 6.

Edward C. Finney, First Assistant Secretary of the Interior, told [2] the committee of the virtual chaos that existed on the public domain for want of control. He spoke freely of the need for regulation, but drew back cautiously when Stanfield tried to commit Interior to specifics prior to enactment of a law; Interior would gladly administer it after it was on the books, but final decision on its language was the province of Congress. Should ranchers on the public domain have tenure for stability of operations? Certainly, said Finney, but for a term of years, not in perpetuity. Shouldn't a rancher be free from prejudicial actions by Washington bureaucrats? Let Congress put whatever restraints in the law it felt belonged there, but please give the administrator a little wiggle space in the toes of his shoes. Is a "reasonable" fee one that returns full rental value of the land or just the cost of administration? Revenue would be secondary, but Interior had in mind more than the bare cost of keeping range situations under control. If the abused lands were restored, would the United States get a fair return if it sold them so they could be put on state and local tax rolls? The United States would benefit either way. But Finney hedged still more when Stanfield pressed him for a "yes" answer to whether Congress should pass a law so detailed that rules and regulations under it would be unnecessary. He quickly affirmed, though, that Interior could administer public domain grazing at less cost than the Forest Service, an attitude that was to backfire a few years afterward.

After that polite sparring match, the free-swinging oral exchanges between committeemen and witnesses in the less inhibited West made the hearing record more lively reading. Practically all the usual arguments one way and the other came out in forty-nine hearings held in thirty-eight cities and towns. Most of the opinions given had been heard time and again, and were merely variations of the standard patterns of the era: (1) Give the public domain to the states and let them do what they wished with it; (2) DON'T give it to corrupt state politicians; (3) keep it in federal hands but put it under control, leasing it to ranchers; (4) leave it as it is; and (5) give it to present users, or (6) sell it to them cheap.

In Arizona the president of the state organization of cattlemen said "we've petitioned and resoluted and asked in a thousand ways" since 1900 "that the public domain be controlled"; it had suffered "tremendous damage," and might never "completely" recover. Putting it under federal lease, with prior users given prior rights to graze it, would help.[3] Most other cowmen took a similar position.

Generally, the sheepmen opposed sweeping federal control. A nice distinction was made by the head of the Arizona Woolgrowers Association: If control had to come, keep it out of a federal department; instead, establish large districts under local boards or commissions. Nevertheless, the chasm between the two groups had narrowed perceptibly over the last quarter of a century. Now the differences voiced by the leaders were matters of degree, not totality, and the gap would close still more as time passed. In the end, each would win something. The cowmen would achieve federal control and prior rights; the sheepmen could claim that district boards provided home rule on the range. The Stanfield hearings themselves, however, brought nothing definitive.

Calvin Coolidge was President when Stanfield and his investigating teams were holding their hearings. His New England conservatism recoiled from the wholesale give-away attitudes of some of the westerners in Congress, and the grasping by livestock leaders. In a 1927 message to Congress he stated his determined opposition to wholesale disposal of the public domain. His successor, Herbert Hoover, took an entirely different view. Hoover's Secretary of the Interior, Dr. Ray Lyman Wilbur, sounded out one conference of western governors in July 1929 on whether they would take the remaining available public domain as a gift, and Hoover himself repeated the suggestion at another governors' meeting a month later. Don B. Colton, a congressman from Utah, introduced a resolution in 1930 calling for a commission to study the idea and make recommendations.

Colton made a point of noting[4] how badly irrigation reservoirs, many of them by then federally built, were silting up because of grazing-induced erosion of watersheds, nearly all of which were public land. Maybe, if public domain was under state control, authorities close to the ranchers could persuade them to quit the damaging range practices. It was no good to spend large sums of money for irrigation works to make the desert bloom if, shortly thereafter, they would so fill with sediment that their water-holding capacity was diminished or lost.

Its labors completed, the commission proposed that the remaining vacant, unreserved, unappropriated public lands be given to the states, with any minerals present reserved to the federal government —and the governors refused the offering.

Preoccupied by the deepening Depression and its effects on many economic and social fronts, Congress did nothing more about the public domain until after FDR came into office. When his celebrated "first hundred days" were behind him, Roosevelt's bent for social engineering—Calef called it social "experimentation" [5]—helped bring on the Taylor version of a control law.

Congressman Edward T. Taylor, representing a western Colorado district loaded with stockmen who used both national forest and public domain range, would have been considered the last man to permit his name to go on such a bill. He was an ardent states-rights advocate, and back in 1914 had declared [6] his everlasting opposition to federal control of the public lands that now bear his name. In fact, he was not the law's author. Don Colton of Utah wrote the basic bill, but under committee changes it at last bore the name of the chairman, Ed Taylor of Colorado. In 1934, as the Taylor bill was moving through Congress, he recalled,[7] those earlier times, when he and others with similar leanings had fought the Teddy Roosevelt–Gifford Pinchot conservation crusade "to the utmost limit."

> Even with our vigorous western vocabulary [he said on the floor], we couldn't find words vehement enough to express our denunciation of the Roosevelt-Pinchot policy of taking over control of the public domain. We felt that was our . . . unrestricted right, to graze stock upon the free, open public domain. . . . Today there isn't a corporal's guard . . . anywhere in the West that would think of turning that domain back to free, open unrestrained use, exploitation, and loot, to be occupied by force and the law of the jungle.

When a district judge in the late 1880s, Taylor went on, he had presided over eight murder cases in one court term, nearly all a result of conflict between cowmen and woolgrowers. From that the nation had progressed to a point where there was recognition of the need to preserve this vast public estate from such "wanton destruction" as had been visited upon it, "to systematize the use of it, to bring order out of chaos, to stabilize the livestock industry . . . the same as it is in the forest reserves."

"We of the West," he concluded, "have slowly and reluctantly come to see the wisdom" of the national forest range program, and are now "trying to repeat that policy on the fast deteriorating and vanishing" reaches of the public domain.

There might be less point to this narrative if it could be said that the bill Taylor pursued to enactment had allowed the administering agency as much authority as was vested in—and is still retained by—the Forest Service, and the agency had consistently used it. It was not so. The law passed was patchwork, intended to try to please all western factions, to parcel out New Deal goodies, and silence critics of do-nothingism.

The preamble declared that the law was to "stop injury to the public grazing lands by preventing overgrazing and soil deterioration; to provide for their orderly use, improvement, and development; to stabilize the livestock industry dependent upon the public range; and for other purposes." They were noble words. The question is whether they have at all times been followed [8] nobly.

In 1934 FDR was rapidly building a record as a conservationist. He may have seized upon it as expedient or may genuinely have wanted to outdo the Roosevelt–Pinchot achievements, and in Harold L. Ickes he had an equally ambitious Secretary of the Interior who would try to go him one better. What was taking place on the public domain was the antithesis of conservation. Ickes, too, was unhappy over it, and was powerless in the absence of statutory instructions. I suspect neither Ickes nor FDR liked the Taylor bill when it came to the White House, but it nevertheless was signed into law.

Section 1 was controversial from the start. It stated that the law was being enacted for the public domain "in order to promote the highest use"—then implied that it was all temporary, "pending its final disposal." No definition was given for "disposal," a word whose precise meaning, as used, would cause years of argument. Was it intended merely to arrange for "orderly management," or actually to "get rid of?" A desk dictionary gives both definitions, and puts the latter in a subsidiary position. The former reflected the view conservation groups took. Stockmen, on the other hand, came to believe "disposal" could denote nothing but gift or sale.

In the same section the establishment of the local boards desired by the woolgrowers was made a permitted option that shortly would be riveted in positive legal language, thanks in part to the zeal of the first director of the newly created Division of Grazing in the Department of the Interior. The act provided that rules for choosing the lucky ones allowed to use the district grazing lands would be formulated so they would go to "bona fide settlers, residents, and other stock owners." Thereafter the boards would "advise" the division employes stationed out there—and again argument would arise; in this instance over whether the boards merely advised or dominated the federal officials.

Section 3 stipulated that fees charged were to be "reasonable"—that old ambiguous term—"in each case," which seems to mean clearly that they need not be uniform throughout the ten states in which districts were organized. However, a low uniform fee was set when charges first were levied in 1936, and it has remained uniform to the present.

Once a rancher got a permit to graze, all he had to do to guarantee its renewal at term end was to borrow money on which his livestock was put up as collateral. This ingenious clause was inserted at the insistence of the stockmen's perennial friend, Senator McCarran of Nevada.[10] One may be sure few stockmen threatened with reductions in numbers or time on the range, no matter how great the need, or who were merely cautious, would let term end approach without a loan of some amount, with stock as security therefor, from the nearest friendly banker or other money source.

Isolated tracts, said Section 15, were to be leased to adjoining ranchers. These were administered by the General Land Office, and the "reasonable" fees would be on an acreage basis, without reference to numbers of stock or season of use; both would be left entirely up to the judgment, good or not so good, of the lessee.

Of whatever fees were collected, half would immediately be returned to the states from which the money came, to be used as the states decided. Nearly all were politically dominated by livestock interests, and in short order most dutifully enacted laws under which the district advisory boards had exclusive control of spending these funds. Better roads and schools were badly needed, as well as other general public services, but evidence from many sources is to the effect that in earlier years much if not most of the money was spent on the ranges to please individual permittees. The law also provided that 25 percent of the income from fees might be appropriated by Congress for agency-ordered range improvements. These provisions would assume considerable significance in troubled days ahead.

The act left Interior in charge partly because of a reckless promise by Secretary Ickes to administer the lands at the ridiculously low annual cost of $150,000. The record is not completely clear as to whether this was a result of poor advice by the Secretary's counselors, a misunderstanding of the area to be administered, or a belligerent effort to assure that the public domain would not be turned over to the Department of Agriculture's Forest Service. At hearings on the Taylor bill the Forest Service had been more realistic about costs, saying that on the basis of its experience in range management, sound administration would require appropriations of more than a million dollars a year. Ickes's was a Pyrrhic victory; it would bring on years of misunderstandings and of angry recriminations when appropriation requests mounted ever higher each succeeding fiscal period. And the administered lands suffered greatly.

On and after June 28, 1934, though, most speeches and newspaper editorials would lead the public to believe that all grazing problems affecting public domain grazing had at last been successfully resolved. A few had, but others had only been accentuated.

A Controversial Start

Secretary Ickes chose as his first director of grazing, to get the public domain range program on course under the Taylor Act, a man nominated by stockmen who would both please and exasperate. He was Farrington R. Carpenter of Hayden, Colorado, an Ivy League college graduate who mixed lawyering with cattle ranching. It likely was as good a choice as Ickes could have made for the tasks immediately ahead. "Ferry" Carpenter was not experienced in the brand of politics played in Washington, but he was a persuasive speaker, trusted by his livestock-raising brethren. His legal schooling and ranching experience could come in handy as he went about his new business, and he believed heartily in the new law.

Carpenter plunged at once into the basics of the Taylor Act: (1) setting rules under which ranchers would be chosen to enjoy grazing privileges and to guide that enjoyment; (2) fixing "reasonable" fees; and (3) organizing districts. All were done in consultation with industry leaders, and for the most part with solicitude for their desires.

The words of the act [1] governing the allotment of grazing privileges—to "bona fide settlers, residents, and other stock owners"—were not picked at random. Settlers and residents thus given top priority could by definition be stockmen who had home bases and were established at specific locations in or adjacent to public domain. That left the nomad at the end of the line, an "other stock owner," and if he had any hopes of securing a grazing allotment he was not likely to realize them. Too many others had priority positions.

A formula had to be devised for choosing among those who

possessed the prescribed *bona fides*, and here the bigger or more astute operators clearly came out on top. Chosen were ranchers who could show they had run stock on the public domain three of the five years before the law was passed, at least two of them consecutively. Nearly all that time we were in the Great Depression. Numbers of ranchers had been driven to the wall, as had businessmen in all other lines. Many "settlers" and "residents" would not be able to qualify, and the majority who lost out were smaller ranchers who had less in reserve, lacked flexibility, boasted fewer resources for survival, to say nothing of expansion, in those formidable years. They had been forced to sell their stock, sometimes all, sometimes only a portion; often they also had to part with home base acreage. Either left the rancher with a rather bleak outlook under the act, for the expanses of range were awarded in proportion to the size of the operation in those critical priority years. The stock-supporting capabilities of the home base were as vital as the record of past use It would not do to allot a rancher a high AUM permit if he was unable to feed the cattle or sheep adequately in the months they were not grazing Taylor lands. Past use and commensurability combined to favor the sizable rancher. The record of the McCarran hearings [2] is replete with grumblings of small ranchers who felt they got a raw deal, especially during McCarran's first round of hearings, through 1943; after that a projected fee increase monopolized time and preoccupied witnesses from Taylor country.

Fixing "reasonable" fees did not prove difficult for Carpenter. In fact, Carpenter had little to do with it. The livestock associations thrashed out the matter quite thoroughly. The biggest argument appeared to have been whether there should be any charge at all. However, since the act called for something "reasonable," the associations determined that in the absence of no fee at all nothing could be more reasonable than a nickel a month for a cow or horse and a penny a month for a sheep or goat. Carpenter was agreeable and went along.

As these decisions were being arrived at, Carpenter was busily flitting around the western circuit, organizing grazing districts. This, too, had to be approved by the resident stockmen, but was smooth going in most places. After all, it was stockmen who, through their associations and friends in Congress, saw to it that the district provision was written into the law. At first districts were optional but a 1939 amendment incorporated them into the act.[3] In Nevada Carpenter held a statewide meeting at which he called for a vote on whether all the public domain there in unreserved and unappropriated status should be put in districts. The vote then was favorable; this later was to cause displeasure when a sizable number of ranchers decided [4] they did not want district organization in their areas.

It must be said that Carpenter performed minor miracles of district formation. It was no easy task to determine boundaries for areas that ran to several million acres each. In certain respects, this was similar to national forest selections carried out by Pinchot for the Forest Service in its earlier years. Areas of comparable size and complexity were involved. In addition to determination of approximate borders, to be finalized by survey, there was before Carpenter the task of persuading a majority of local ranchers to go along on the considerable organizational detail involved, including selection by votes of the stockmen of advisory boards consisting of up to a dozen members who would themselves have permits on district allotments.

The advisory board system was a key to acceptance of district status in some of the areas through its assurance of home rule to the ranchers based there. Carpenter inaugurated the method of having nominees for board membership chosen by grazing users of affected districts, and this was followed in the amendment to the law. There was a provision that the Secretary could remove a district advisory board member, after notice, "for the good of the Service." In 1972 I asked the Bureau of Land Management whether that right of removal had ever been exercised, and the answer [5] was "no," which I thought remarkable. There have been up to sixty districts at times, and presently are fifty-two, which means approximately six hundred board members in any one year, from the mid-1930s forward.

These district boards form the basic government of grazing on 142 million acres of Taylor lands—raised from eighty million in 1936 by statutory amendment [6] after Carpenter's whirlwind organizing tours—and deal with the operations of from 15,000 to more than 20,000 ranchers. They are called "advisory," but their recommendations seldom over the years have been overruled by district graziers or higher authority. One would suspect that at least once in all that time one of so many humans might have slipped beyond "the good of the Service." The only record I have found that is pertinent here is that of the McCarran hearings.[7] The most accusatory information it contains is that in some instances boards have tended toward what may be called cronyism. Board members are supposed to take no part in deciding issues where their own operations are concerned—

but their fellow members who do make the decisions know they affect one of their own, and surely will want friendly treatment when their own cases come up for decision at other times. The likelihood, as I see it, is that board members who may have gone flagrantly out of line, as their friends and neighbors drew the line, were simply suffered, or ignored until their terms as members ran out, and thereafter were not re-elected. Under such circumstances, ouster cases would not reach the desk of the Secretary for determinations.

While director, Carpenter was also close to if not part of the inner circle of the livestock industry's leadership. Rendering judgment on what could or could not be done over tens of millions of acres of Taylor land must have been an exhilarating experience for the lawyer–rancher from west of Rabbit Ears Pass. The record shows he was rather free-wheeling in his ways and in decision-making. His independence of movement and interpretations of his duties and prerogatives put him in bad more than once with Secretary Ickes, who was himself of imperious nature and known to the press of the era as "the old curmudgeon." Their personalities were bound to clash. In his naïveté concerning national politics, Carpenter often would talk freely, extemporaneously to his western audiences. Perhaps he did not dream it would make news when on one occasion before a rural western audience he referred to Washington as that "big county seat" on the banks of the Potomac,[8] which was not bad phrase-making and must have delighted his hearers, but Ickes was not amused.

The upshot was a lengthy exchange of allegations and responses between Ickes and Carpenter as early as the fall of 1935.[9] Carpenter had been given his original appointment for one year, starting in mid-September 1934. On October 31, 1935, Ickes reminded Carpenter that his provisional Civil Service appointment, plus extensions, would end as of November 11, 1935. Carpenter had assured Ickes, the letter read, that he could get the whole Grazing Division program going in a year and did not want to stay on forever. There was a strongly implied threat in that language. Then Ickes went on to itemize reasons why he was unhappy with Carpenter's doings.

One of the requisites of bureaucratic performance is the establishment of a firmly based staff. Ickes was perturbed because Carpenter had failed to hire competent people to carry on when his provisional appointment should run out. "You have relied upon a skeleton staff, plus the advisory [boards] for such administrative work as has been accomplished," Ickes complained. Carpenter had been authorized to select required personnel from the staffs of three other bureaus in Interior; the Division of Investigation, the Geological Survey, and the General Land Office.

"Notwithstanding these ample provisions for the setting up of an administrative force," Ickes wrote, "the Division of Grazing has but 17 employes in addition to the director, five of whom are clerks and three stenographers, leaving but nine other persons to assist in the administration of 33 grazing districts embracing nearly 80 million acres. . . . In addition there have been 19 employes transferred from the . . . Geological Survey but they are still paid from Geological Survey funds," which implied that they could be returned to their former positions at any time. "The total force selected by you for this enormous undertaking is therefore but 37 and after almost 14 months the Grazing program has not only never been completely organized but you have not developed sufficient personnel even to protect the government's interest let alone develop an adequate range conservation program."

The last clause in the sentence—to establish "an adequate range conservation program"—was one of the chief nubs of the situation. Ickes, partly so he would be remembered in history as a powerful conservationist, embraced the expressed intent of the Taylor Act, especially the clause in the preamble that declared that it was "An act to stop injury to the public grazing lands by preventing overgrazing and soil deterioration," and the precise language on "protection" and "improvement" in Section 2. Carpenter, on the other hand, was of the clique that read more significance in the first section's declaration that whatever was done was to be done to and about the public domain "pending its final disposal." In short, his directorship was that of a custodian, a caretaker who was fixing boundaries of hinterland fiefdoms of advisory boards that would do the actual administering up until the time the government quit this control foolishness and undertook a final massive give-away program.

Through the years, efforts by officials to institute "an adequate range conservation program" have resulted in the resignation, forced or otherwise, of more than one man since Carpenter's day. I am not convinced that the livestock leadership at any time intended that "an adequate range conservation program," realistically established, vigorously pursued, and broad gauge in nature, should ever be a primary objective of the administering agency.

After aiming a rifle at Carpenter's lack of an adequate staff, formed in necessary depth to handle anticipated administrative matters, Ickes fired a scattergun load of accusations at him in the 1935 letter. Carpenter, Ickes alleged, had not laid down firm policies and had made changes in those established, "frequently" without consulting responsible Interior officials, including Ickes. Carpenter made "ill-considered announcements;" he made "untimely decisions from the platform" that he was forced to retract and, in the retracting, had tried to blame others "either directly or by inference." He, Ickes went on relentlessly, had held fourteen months of meetings before grazing groups "to secure their support," but in all that time had "never progressed beyond the promotional stage. His message had "lost its tang by repetition" and his promises "their virtue by nonfulfillment." Continuation of the speaking tours would be "permanently detrimental" to the Taylor Act program. Yet, "on October 1 you embarked on another series of 22 meetings and as of this moment I have no knowledge of your discourses or their purpose." Because of his long absences from the office and unpredictable changes in policy, Carpenter's subordinates had been handicapped, not only by their lack of numbers and depth to handle the tasks before them, but also "the difficulty of knowing where you have stood at the moment on a particular question."

There was more along similar lines. Then Ickes gave details of a promise Carpenter had made to stockmen in Nevada that could not be kept. This appears to have been the incident on which Ickes based his allegation of "nonfulfillment" of pledges and of blaming others for erroneous pronouncements. Ickes wrote that Carpenter, on October 19, 1935, had indicated to a subordinate that the division would proceed with the organization of another district in Nevada even though the eighty-million-acre limitation then in the law would be exceeded. Carpenter, Ickes wrote, had told the subordinate that in going ahead they would rely on securing an increase in the allowed acreage through an amendment to the law that Senator Joseph C. O'Mahoney of Wyoming had "pledged" to see through to "early enactment." Meantime, the subordinate was to "keep this matter confidential and go ahead as outlined before." Carpenter, said Ickes, had not only shown himself "indiscreet" but had demonstrated "a lack of essential frankness." More than that, he had not yet "cleared with your Reno audience your serious mistake in judgment."

Ickes did not at all like the abdication of departmental authority that was inherent in a letter Carpenter had written to an Oregon correspondent on October 21. Carpenter had told this person that in the advisory boards "we hope to build up an hierarchy of local advisers which will be able to act as a policy advising council *and determine all-important matters of fees, cuts, needed legislation, etc., for grazing districts"* (italics added). This, Ickes declared, meant that the federal government would retain "nothing but appellate power, . . . thereby delegating to the [boards] practically the entire administration of the act."

Carpenter replied in a forty-two-page letter dated November 8, 1935. In it he took up Ickes's accusations and allegations one by one and denied wrongdoing or wrongful intent.

"I have been so engrossed in getting the grazing districts organized and under administration that in doing so in an economical manner without building up a large new federal bureau I may have neglected what is considered in governmental activity as almost as important as accomplishing one's mission; that is, keeping the department fully informed at all times as to details. . . ."

Carpenter complained that the work of the Division of Grazing had never been assigned to an assistant secretary for oversight, and the Secretary's own time had been too occupied with other matters to hope to meet with him often. He emphasized that, in his view, the success of the grazing program depended in great measure upon the cooperation of the stockmen affected, which was "why I conditioned my acceptance of the position of Director of Grazing on the right to develop local autonomy as an integral part of the proposed administrative organization." He quoted a page and a half, single-spaced type, from a speech Ickes himself had made about how nearly self-regulating the districts were to be. All in all, Carpenter appeared to me to have shown that his actions were not entirely out of line with what his boss's wishes and policies were—that is, as Carpenter interpreted them.

Be that as it may, Ickes kept Carpenter as director of grazing until the end of 1939. He found a way to get around the Civil Service time limits. But this is not to say there was internal peace and harmony for the rest of Carpenter's tenure. In March 1937, Ickes unbraided [10] Carpenter for proposing to write letters to members of Congress in which he commended western state legislatures for passing laws that would let the district advisory boards have full discretion in the spending of the 50 percent of the grazing fees collected that, under the act as it then read, were to go back to the states.

"Here again," wrote Ickes reprovingly, "is a move on your part which might have the effect of dispossessing the Department of the

Interior and United States Government so far as the public lands are concerned. And just why should we go out of our way to advise members of Congress that we approve certain types of state legislation? . . .

"Questions of such importance as are involved in situations such as this sort must be brought to me personally."

No Carpenter reply was found in the Denver Public Library file.

In March 1938, Ickes ordered [11] "a complete investigation made of the Grazing Administration with a view of determining (1) Whether a fair deal has been given the small stockman; (2) whether there has been any discrimination against the small stockman, and how many small stockmen there are compared with big stockmen." The response by Interior's Division of Investigation, dated July 22, 1938, indicated that "small" stockmen ran two hundred cattle or one thousand sheep or less; that medium-sized operators ran from 201 to six hundred cattle or 1,001 to three thousand sheep; and all who had more stock than that on public land were "big." Some 73 percent of the 17,589 "applicants for grazing privileges" were small under that formula; 20 percent were medium; the remaining 7 percent were large. The investigators could find neither "concerted" effort to discriminate nor "general" unfairness.

"However," the report said, "it appears that in a number of instances the rules and regulations have not been applied correctly and that improper actions have been taken in a number of cases seriously affecting small operators. It also appears that many small operators have been affected adversely by the operation and application of the Federal Range Code of 1938." (The Range Code was the Division of Grazing's book of regulations.)

In a relatively short time Senator McCarran would begin hearing the stories of small operators and complaints that application of the rules and regulations—actually drafted by the district boards and refined by the state boards and National Advisory Board Council before being made operative by the Division of Grazing and its successor Grazing Service—had hurt them. He would hear from many others, for his was the widest ranging and longest lasting of all inquiries made by congressional committees into the workings of our public land agencies. This would be initiated early, in February 1940, but not begin until over a year after Ferry Carpenter had gone back to his livestock and law practice in Colorado.

In his approximately four years as director, Carpenter had put all the approximately 142 million acres in districts, had started the districts on their way, had set up the first Range Code to govern grazing in the districts, and begun the massive task of adjudicating the grazing. The latter task was not completed until some thirty-five years later, for it entailed settlement of questions over grazing nearly all allotments, in fact parceling out the tracts to be grazed under approximately 16,000 [12] permits. And Table 4 lists AUMs only since 1959.

The record is substantial, and was no small accomplishment. Yet the question must be asked whether the results Carpenter accomplished did not virtually assure that the industry leadership would rule the public domain range pretty much as it wished, given the blessing of statutory language contrived by the industry's elected allies in Congress. Lacking substantial staff—partly for the reasons Carpenter gave in his reply to Ickes, partly because of Ickes's own rash forecast of a cheap administration; even the help Carpenter did hire was paid less than those in comparable work in other agencies and this continued to be true until after World War II [13]—it seems unquestionable that industry rule through the advisory board system was not only inaugurated but riveted in place before Carpenter left the directorship.

It was to his credit that Carpenter took full advantage of the presence of the Civilian Conservation Corps, which was in full career by the time the Taylor Act was made effective. For the most part the CCC did well in range improvement work on the public domain, including the usual types of devices beneficial to the ranges and the industry that were being constructed on national forests in the same years. The CCC had been established long enough before the Division of Grazing was activated so that some of its errors of experimentation were behind it and it could thenceforward point generally to sound accomplishment. The very presence of the CCC, however, and the passage of the state laws giving district advisory boards virtually exclusive say-so in spending half the fees collected from permittees, make it inevitable to speculate that the 50-percent funds would and did go in considerable part to such activities as predatory animal control and range undertakings not justified under even the liberal charter granted the CCC.

When McCarran began hearings, Carpenter had been succeeded as director by R. H. Rutledge, a veteran Forest Service official who was regional forester for the intermountain country when he accepted office. Rutledge was convinced he could instill some of the Forest. Service's elitist spirit in the young, newly renamed Grazing Service. He was thoroughly familiar with Taylor land conditions and was determined to bring out the best in range productivity of which those 142 millions of acres were capable. And to do so, there would have to be more money to work with. Some of it, at least, should come from increased grazing fees. The nickel per AUM set up under Carpenter, in Rutledge's opinion, simply was not "reasonable." Rutledge's optimism was no more justified than that of his Forest Service contemporaries and successors in judging the grazing capacity of national forest lands. He was in for rude awakenings.

21

Fending Off Controls

At the end of February 1940, the Senate Committee on Public Lands and Surveys held a hearing [1] in Washington. No bills were pending before it, but a delegation of western stockmen had come to town and Chairman Alva Adams, a Coloradan, heard them formally. Several other members of the committee, including McCarran of Nevada, were on hand. Grazing Service officials were there but no others. All doubtless had been arranged before the stockmen arrived.

The livestock delegates identified were J. Elmer Brock of Kaycee, Wyoming, president of the American National Livestock Association; A. D. Brownfield of Deming, New Mexico, a soon-to-be president of the ANLA who also spoke in behalf of the National Woolgrowers Association; and William B. Wright of Deeth, Nevada, McCarran's home state, who would be the head of the ANLA six years later in the Great Land Grab era. Brock acted as parade marshal for the industry people. R. H. Rutledge, the new Grazing Service director, was the only spokesman for the Department of the Interior.

Wright led off. Here it was, he said, over four years after the department had begun organizing districts under the Taylor Act, and the administrators had not yet adjudicated enough applications for allotments so it could issue the ten-year term permits called for in the law. Instead, it was issuing one-year revocable licenses. Stockmen felt insecure under this temporary arrangement, that their operations had no stability. He implied that banks were hesitant about granting loans because ranchers could not guarantee that they and their herds or flocks would be there long enough to pay out. This would have been reasonable enough, if the task had been simpler;

but the delay was caused in considerable part by Ferry Carpenter's headlong rush to organize the entire public domain into districts.

Nevada stockmen had previously begun to question the legality of uniform fees under the Taylor Act. In 1936 a group of fifty-five filed suit in state court; they reminded that the law called for a "reasonable fee *in each case*" (italics added). The case had gone through various stages and then pended before the Nevada Supreme Court. Meantime the Grazing Service had ordered the protesting stockmen to pay back fees promptly or be cited for trespass. Wright called this harassment. He wanted the parties who were to blame punished. An effort by Interior to have the case transferred to federal court was considered an end run by Wright, one designed to get around an anticipated adverse decision in Nevada. (Later the U.S. Supreme Court did decide in favor of Interior, holding that Congress had approved the uniform fee by appropriating funds for administration of the Taylor Act while the fee was in effect.[2])

The stockmen brought in few other direct complaints, but doubtless there was a general fretfulness over the direction the Grazing Service might be going. The new director might try to curtail some of the privileges the permittees and lessees enjoyed under Carpenter's free and easy rule, or increase the fee. This I consider implied; it was not said at the hearing in so many words.

One of the more complicated situations that was complained about had to do with New Mexico's District 7, which Brownfield described [3] at length. Number 7 had been organized within the outer confines of the state's District 2 under special rules and auspices to try to find range for a mixture of mostly small ranchers. Indians, Mexican–Americans, Anglos, and others were using intermingled ownerships that included private lands and public lands administered by the Indian Service, Grazing Service, Bureau of Reclamation, Soil Conservation Service, the state, and certain counties. A few large operators were involved. The basic problem, with some revision of language and ethnic residencies (which were large factors in District 7), could have applied to either Interior or Agriculture in much of the public land West. Demand had outrun supply of forage many years earlier. There were no new lands to be opened. What existed had to be shared by all. The users had to make do with what the land could produce, and they must use it prudently if it was to serve the needs of their livestock without costly supplemental feeding. Somehow, that lesson has been a hard one for the West to learn.

None of the testimony touched on the question of higher fees. It would be more than a year before that subject would be opened and bring its usual adverse reaction. Instead, the hearing appeared to have been planned by the association people and friendly western senators to lay a base for heading off any managerial or fee steps the new director might hanker to undertake. It would be a good idea to let him know at an early date what they considered his role to be. The hearing closed with a stockman demand for an investigation of alleged misuse of power, coercion, and other wrongs—none of which had been spelled out in specific detail before adjournment.

McCarran introduced S. Res. 241 shortly afterward, but the Senate held off action until May 1941, when a modified form of the resolution was adopted. The delay looks much like McCarran strategy; the resolution was in channels but he would not ask that it be moved along until he determined that Rutledge was indeed starting to behave like an administrator who intended to be more than a temporary caretaker. When the resolution did pass, McCarran rode it for all it was worth until after the close of World War II. This required two congressional extensions of authority.

Under S. Res. 241 McCarran would investigate a wide range of public land matters. The resolution's language was, as usual, imprecise but broad. Forsling has expressed [4] the opinion that McCarran's "paramount" purpose was to "restrain the Grazing Service from becoming an effective administrative agency." The hard core of stockman philosophy in Nevada at the time, Forsling indicated, was to provide permittees with all the prerogatives of ownership without attendant responsibilities. The verbatim report of the investigations would exceed six thousand printed pages and there were partial reports and a final rendering that, strangely, would concentrate almost exclusively on the Grazing Service, ignoring the many other things inquired into, and would not be published until a year and a half after the hearings ended. McCarran would delve into nearly every conceivable aspect of Grazing Service operations, into a variety of Forest Service activities including wildlife management, into the bumbling of the venerable General Land Office, into doings of the Indian Service, and miscellaneous other matters. It would even stumble, probably accidentally, into what appears to have been a fringe of atomic fission's Manhattan Project. Why McCarran at the end chose only to report concerning the Grazing Service was never made generally public by him.

The hearing would close with the consolidation of the Grazing

Service and GLO into today's Bureau of Land Management under conditions that virtually assured that the thoroughly cowed new agency would have the utmost difficulty in rising from custodial into genuine managerial status. In its course the initially hortatorial calls of a few association leaders would develop into the great attempted Land Grab of the immediate postwar years.

I find it hard to believe that, other than preventive action, there was a grand design in all that took place in the course of and following the McCarran investigations. Part of what occurred simply had to be fortuitous. At its beginnings the public land users were restless. They had believed that with passage of the Taylor Act their problems would disappear. Instead, after five years there still was no stable administrative pattern. Long-term permits were not yet being granted. Most applications for grazing had not been winnowed and the typical Taylor land rancher's economic outlook was uncertain. Dissatisfaction was popping up nearly everywhere. Ranchers who were being denied permits because of their public land grazing record during the priority years were definitely unhappy. They criticized the five-year term chosen by their contemporaries for basing lease or permit decisions. Allegations of favoritism were flying in various areas. The Range Code of the Service—counterpart of the Forest Service's Use Book—had been written to try to please everyone, and ended by displeasing ranchers who received adverse rulings as it was interpreted. Big game herds were increasing and often were looked upon as unwanted competitors for forage that cattle and sheep would otherwise eat. Their own man, Carpenter, now back home in Colorado, had been succeeded by a Forest Service veteran schooled, trained, and experienced in rangeland management; Rutledge could be a threat to industry control in Taylor Act country if not promptly put in his place.

The resolution of bothersome matters such as these would take time and what on some occasions appeared to be carefully planned happenings; in other instances events seemed to occur as improvisations. My opinion is that a few in leadership positions were taking a very long view, and others were merely trying to discern what was beyond the nearest horizon, when McCarran took the road westward for his first field hearing in June 1941.

Ely, in eastern Nevada, was a shrewd choice for that hearing. It was a center of one of the touchiest problems the Grazing Service had to deal with. Section 3 of the law specified that preference in the issuance of permits should be given to "those within or near a district" who were "engaged in the livestock business" and owned land or "water or water rights." There was the catch. Dependable moisture was, with some exceptions, more abundant in northerly reaches of the West, scarcer the farther south one traveled toward the Mexican border. Land ownership was the ruling criterion to northward. In Arizona and New Mexico possession of existing or developed watering places, with state-approved water use rights, was precious and justly recognized in allotting leases and permits. There the ownership or use of large tracts of land meant nothing if water was not within easy traveling distance for the herds and flocks. In the wetter and drier extremities of the Taylor lands clear-cut decisions could be made without protest. Troubles rose in middle country, neither mildly moist nor dreadfully arid. Ely was close to the wavering line that divided the regions; there hard choices had to be made. Neither those who had land nor those who had water were happy if others were allotted the ranges they coveted. And the Grazing Service was in the middle. The selections were made by the district advisory boards, but it was a Grazing Service official's signature that was written at the bottom of the permit or lease.

Ely came close to being a microcosm of Grazing Service problems; most that surfaced through the hearing years could be found there. Testimony given involved or was related to such aspects of Grazing Service administration as the Range Code, range management, the priority years, shortcomings of the General Land Office, arguments about district advisory boards and their actions, squabbles between permittees or claimants to range use, and so on.

At Ely, as at other stops on McCarran's earlier itinerary, Rutledge's testimony appeared to follow a predetermined course. He talked of overall policy, and Grazing Service goals. Not that he dodged issues of lesser scale; these were properly delegated to local or regional officials for response, with Rutledge reinjecting himself into a matter only if it appeared that broader policy was affected and required resolution. He gave the Ely audience, mostly ranchers, an overview [5] of the ramifications of range management. How deeply that penetrated may be a good question. In the more remote places McCarran chose to go the ranchers attending usually had driven or ridden to the courthouse in the county seat from rugged hinterlands, far from large cities and the sources of information available through a metropolitan press and other communications media. Those people were often isolated for considerable periods. They tended to hear rumor that might have been distorted in repeated tellings. Small irritations grew large if not attended to promptly and properly. Happenings right around home were usually more important than those in Washington or even the state capital, but the home folks could not escape rulings and decisions made in those far off places. The logic the ranchers used might be based on premises that differed greatly from those of the distant decision makers.

Rutledge acknowledged at Ely that the going had been rough for ranchers in earlier times because of (1) lack of recognition in law of the place of grazing on the public domain; (2) insecurity of tenure; and (3) instability of policy concerning range use matters. Under the Taylor Act something had been done to ease all three. The district advisory boards provided local government, grazing law rulings at home, so to speak. Attaching grazing rights to the headquarters ranch provided inherent tenure; stability lay in the fact that the grazing privilege—whether a ten-year permit or one-year lease pending adjudication of conflicting claims—could not be denied at the whim of an administrator. He seemed to be saying that everything the ranchers could logically desire from the resources available was theirs and would be provided as quickly as the Service could solve its administrative and adjudicative problems.

These extracts from the record outline Rutledge's overall administrative design for the Taylor lands. He had gone to work for the Forest Service when it was young and not yet battered and made weary of countering assaults upon its idealism. He had risen through the ranks to be regional forester at Ogden, and range management had been a long time concern. He knew every clause and nuance of the Taylor Act and to him "disposal" didn't necessarily mean "to get rid of." It could as well mean setting district resources in order, which I believe was his overriding desire. The act contained strong conservation language, and he preferred to believe that this should dictate how the land was applied. He was eager to see the Taylor lands put on the road to complete recovery from the effects of decades of misuse and overuse. He wanted those acres to contribute their natural maximum to the economic and social well-being of the region and the nation. At hearing after hearing over approximately two years he addressed himself dutifully to local problems brought up by witnesses, but unfailingly included a sentence or two of comment that could only be construed as supporting a sound management program for the long pull, not a temporary custodianship.

Events on a large stage thwarted the basics of the Rutledge plan almost at the outset. Timing proved to be a critical factor. He was using the Civilian Conservation Corps for a full range of improvements on the land, but felt it was an insecure base on which to rest long-term plans. Changing conditions, economic or other, could wipe out the CCC source of help in a hurry—and did. And income from grazing should be greater if large-scale appropriations for management and rehabilitation were to be justified before skeptical committees of Congress.

Consequently, soon after taking office Rutledge engaged Mont Saunderson, respected former Forest Service official and university professor, to study the economics and related phases of public land ranching. He wanted to learn whether an increase in fees was defendable. It seems a certainty now that knowledge of the fee study was a prime reason for the livestock leaders to converge upon Washington in February 1940, even though they did not mention fees at that time. The strategy decided upon between McCarran and the leaders could have been to find other reasons for conducting investigations and to let the subject rise more or less naturally when fee facts surfaced as hearings were being held.

McCarran himself brought it up at Ely in an exchange [6] with L. R. Brooks, Grazing Service grazier for Nevada. The United States had been assisting Britain and France in every way short of direct intervention in the early stages of World War II and near-war conditions already prevailed here at home. Prices were rising, yet McCarran did not believe the permittees should be paying higher rates. He wanted them to enjoy increasing prosperity after dreary years of drought and depression. His discussion with Brooks was almost philosophical, and was inconclusive. Rutledge was not asked to comment and volunteered no information. Most of the Ely hearing had to do with lesser problems, local disputes and misunderstandings.

Likewise at Elko, in northeastern Nevada, on June 27, 1941, fees received only marginal attention. Most of the discussions there had to do with the intricacies of ranching operations in checkerboard land, where railroad interests long before had been granted alternative square mile sections of land for distances of up to twenty miles out on each side of the right-of-way as inducement to extend trackage and mass transportation. Saunderson, often accompanied by J. H. Leech, a Rutledge assistant, had traveled across much of the public land West to interview ranchers, bankers, and others, and to study ranch economics on the ground. Thus it came to the attention of Vernon Metcalf of Reno, a staff head of the Nevada Livestock Production Credit Association, a quasi-official lending agency. Metcalf approached the subject obliquely, merely testifying then that a fee increase, or a range management program that included cuts in animal unit months of grazing, would reduce the borrowing power of his clients, and he was opposed.[7] He wanted to be assured that "values that we have loaned on won't be sucked out for a direct revenue for the Federal Treasury." Again, as at Ely, a possible rise in fees was not pursued vigorously by either the livestock industry or the Service, nor was that touchy subject of cuts in permitted grazing.

The scope of the Saunderson study and details of its findings emerged at Casper, Wyoming, in September, 1941, and were elaborated at Salt Lake City early in the following month. At Casper, Rutledge disclosed [8] that the paper work of the Saunderson study had been completed, and its recommendations were before him for determination whether they should be sent to Secretary Ickes for decision.

Leech went into details of the study, which involved going rentals for private pasturage of comparable quality, taxes paid on private range, ranch operating cost and income data, interest paid when livestock were bought with money borrowed from the several available public and private sources, and so on. To these figures were applied a complete formula to judge what part of residual income might go for fees. Rating factors included land grazing capacity, water availability, improvements, topography, distance to shipping point, and distance of range from ranch; all received weighted values. Under the formula, Leech said,[9] the proposed fees ranged from a minimum of seven cents per AUM in New Mexico districts to eighteen cents in Colorado.

As Leech finished a storm let loose. The industry's highly charged objections were presented in chief by J. Elmer Brock, with Senator Joseph C. O'Mahoney of Wyoming, joined by McCarran, asking questions that stirred additional objections. Brock argued that charging no fees at all could be justified. O'Mahoney did not like the idea of higher fees for stockmen who, he said, already were paying excessively high taxes and rental charges for private pasturage. McCarran said in effect that no question that could come before his subcommittee was more important. When Leech reminded that half the added revenue would return to the states of origin for range improvements and another fourth would be subject to appropriation for similar purposes, McCarran paused and grew thoughtful. Rutledge ended the debate at Casper by reminding that an increase was not yet accomplished fact; the entire subject was still open for further consideration.

The chief difference between the fee aspects of the Casper hearing and the one that followed a few days later at Salt Lake City was that Rutledge ˙brought Saunderson there to describe and defend his methods and the results of his study. Rutledge, in preliminary remarks,[10] obviously wanted to forestall an instinctive industry objection; he emphasized that no final decisions had been made, that the Service was merely following the law which said reasonable fees were to be fixed, and he needed to know whether the existing fee was, in fact, reasonable. Saunderson, then, repeated [11] and elaborated upon the study carried out much as Leech had done at Casper.

Vernon Metcalf followed [12] with a carefully prepared negative response, the upshot of which was that the figures were all wrong, that no increase was justified, and if one was imposed it would bring hardship to the entire western livestock industry. The secretary of the National Woolgrowers Association and his chief assistant immediately echoed [13] Metcalf's objections.

Fees were again discussed at Reno on October 8, where McCarran [14] said he had the subject broached deliberately at his hearings in the hope that an increase could be forestalled. In his discussion, Metcalf [15] referred to disposal, saying that "if the states were given the lands, as near as I can see they would be given no new values they don't already have." I interpret that to mean that the lands were being used to the utmost as it was, and if they took title, the states would, in fact, be money out of pocket. In exchange for the small fees paid by the stockmen, the federal government already was returning funds that brought about range improvement. His friends the stockmen would have to dig in their pockets to pay for range improvements or do without. Before the close of the Reno hearing on October 10, Metcalf [16] said that all the industry wanted was enough administration of the Taylor lands to regulate traffic including herd and flock trailing, and to see that the fellow entitled to it got the available range for his grazing use; "that is about all. . . ."

From Reno, McCarran went on to hearings at Las Vegas, Nevada, and Kingman and Phoenix, Arizona, before closing for the year on December 2, just five days before the Japanese struck fleet and shore installations at Pearl Harbor. Fees were discussed at all these, with about the same alignment of forces found earlier. After December 7 virtually all subjects not directly supporting our war effort were set aside. McCarran suspended hearings for nearly a year.

Grazing fees were in limbo; Rutledge and the National Advisory Board Council agreed [17] that further consideration of a change in charges should be held in abeyance for the duration. Rutledge's health caused him to resign in early 1944, and on May 11 of that year he was succeeded by Clarence L. Forsling. The Forsling story comes later and is related to a subsequent round of McCarran hearings.

Testimony in the 1941 McCarran record discloses conclusive evidence, in my view at least, that the Great Land Grab attempt of five years afterward was not a spontaneous outburst of greed, and likewise was not universally supported by public land using ranchers in the West. It tends to support the view of the conservation groups that a small clique led the way and persuaded others to follow.

We have seen that Metcalf, at Reno, expressed doubt that the states would gain new or additional values even if the Taylor lands were handed them as a gift. Nevertheless, he conceded there that the lands might well go into private hands if they were cheap enough. At Salt Lake City a few days previously, F. C. Marshall, chief staff officer of the National Woolgrowers Association, testified [18] that at noon he had tried out on friends the idea of the users acquiring the lands at a low cost, with the invariable answer that "we can't afford to own the lands." Despite this, he was personally in favor of their sale at "fair" or "reasonable" prices—upon which he did not elaborate.

In the two Arizona hearings in 1941, high-level livestock sentiment seemed more in harmony with Brock and his Wyoming clientele than Metcalf and Nevada or Marshall and Utah. The principal Arizona advocate of sale or gift was Frank Boyce, a vice-president of the American National, who introduced into the record [19] the obviously false proposition that the action would be a "return" of real estate to the states or private owners. It was false for the simple reason that those lands had never been in what we know as "private" ownership. Even when the Indians owned it they did so in common, not as individuals. Obviously the federal government could not "return" to the states or to private owners what had never been theirs. At the same hearing a spokesman for the American Farm Bureau affiliate in Arizona echoed [20] Boyce's call for a "return" of the lands. Smaller ranchers tended to concentrate on other problems and spoke little of disposal.

Ten wartime months passed before McCarran again headed west from Washington. The hearings record noted that E. S. Haskell was then the subcommittee's field investigator. A titillating tale of how he happened to succeed George W. Storck in that capacity is told in McCarran's final report.[21] He wrote that the Grazing Service assigned two high officials to travel with his first investigator to get him drunk nightly or as often as practical and extract from him whatever his investigations had discovered.

McCarran's second round of hearings where grazing was a major factor started in November 1942 and ended before Rutledge departed from the Service scene. They were held in Colorado, Utah, Nevada, Arizona, New Mexico, and Washington, D.C., and ranged across a broad spectrum of subjects, with some, in fact, touching more upon problems involving the national forests than upon the administration of the Taylor Act. Earlier chapters relate to the Forest Service phases of these hearings. Yet they were not devoid of interest with respect to the Grazing Service.

At Glenwood Springs, Colorado, in November 1942, Dan H. Hughes of Montrose, who in 1946 as chairman of the Joint National Livestock Committee on Public Lands would take charge of the grab effort, declared[22] that federal officials should have ultimate authority over district advisory boards when decisions were made on range use. However, he leaned toward the user having a "property right" to the use of public lands by reason of his ownership of a base ranch. And he wanted no part of a merger of the Grazing Service and the Forest Service. They should remain separate, so there would be "competition" between them for the stockmen's favor; it provides "a better break for the livestock industry." Hughes had merely advocated his version of the old divide-and-conquer proposition. The agencies would be weaker if not merged, and the industry could play one against the other to gain favors.

Much attention was given in 1942 and 1943 hearings to problems caused by the rapid increase of the big game herds in the West before and during the war years, a subject touched on in Forest Service chapters. Taylor lands were affected as well. The Grazing Service administered some high altitude areas where deer and elk summered, and a majority of the lower elevation public lands where they, and the antelope, wintered. As a rule, privately owned base properties lay in lower reaches of the mountainous West, usually in stream valleys. Deer, elk, and antelope know no boundary distinctions and browse or graze where they find forage to their liking and can get to it.

A brief review of common facts seems desirable. Unbridled killing in earlier years and other factors caused decimation of big game herds, and alarmed state officials went from no or little control to excessive restriction. They did so mainly through absolute protection of females in a polygamous wild world. The herds naturally proliferated beyond the carrying capacities of their ranges. And there was competition with livestock for forage. Elk are fond of grasses and compete with cattle. Deer prefer browse and are more likely to vie with sheep for food.

Arthur Carhart, then an official of the Colorado Game and Fish Commission, told [23] McCarran that where there was an overpopulation of game or an overgrazing situation attributable to livestock, or both, "you cut the food supply to the point where the livestock go to their second or third feed preferences on the one side and the game animals do the same on the other, and when they get down to eating stumps they are head on" toward collision.

It was about this time that McCarran brought forth his bill, S. 1152, to allow federal land managers to slaughter what they considered excessive numbers of game animals in the event an affected state failed to take action to control numbers. McCarran said [24] he wanted to protect public ranges against overuse by the wild creatures "for the higher purpose of the sustenance of mankind." That was an attitude calculated to be highly popular in wartime, when the nation was straining every effort to war's purposes, including food rationing at home. Several months later, during which state and federal authorities, sportsmen's groups, and conservation organizations had fiercely debated with McCarran the merits and demerits of S. 1152, the senator used his strongest argument for effective state control of game numbers in overpopulated areas. He declared [25] at Ely in August 1943, that bitter as the S. 1152 medicine appeared to be, a worse dose of federal game killing could be prescribed under a simple presidential executive order. His view was that a problem existed and unless something constructive was done by the states and their people, so that his bill would not have to pass or an executive order be issued, they would have no one to blame but themselves. The conundrum had to be solved one way or another.

McCarran's and the stockmen's complaints about excessive big game numbers were carried to extremes in some instances, yet in others were fully justified. In my earlier years in Colorado—1938 to 1942—I came face to face with the problem, being what one friend called an "eyeball witness." Even earlier, in Pennsylvania in the mid-1930s, I had seen what good herd management, through legal hunting of antlerless—presumed female—deer could do to help balance population with winter habitat. The states of the West used a variety of techniques for corrective purposes, including open seasons on females and longer hunting seasons; these did result in the shelving of S. 1152 by McCarran, and the White House did not issue any executive orders related to big game slaughter. McCarran explained [26] to a Reno audience late in 1943 that he felt he had put his message across effectively enough that drastic action by federal authority could be averted. However, complaining stockmen were not stilled.

To this point McCarran and the industry, with the timely intervention of World War II, had successfully blocked Rutledge's more significant goals of realistic grazing fees and the widespread institution of sound practices of range management. He had helped prod the states into greater recognition of the need to manage their game herds with an eye to the grazing and browsing capacities of their several ranges. Yet the paradox of advocating sound game range management while avidly pursuing an attitude of *laissez faire* as far as livestock range was concerned, appeared not to have entered the minds of either McCarran or his livestock constituency. To them the two blood brothers seemed not even remotely kin to each other. It was all right for stock to chew out the ranges; it was horrible for game herds to eat their share.

In passing, McCarran had looked critically into the treatment accorded the descendants of our first human inhabitants, the red men, but as he pursued the subject it became clear that the matter of primary concern was to guarantee that Interior, through the Indian Service or any other agency, would not deprive white ranchers of what they considered their rightful portion of available range. This became a bit ticklish in New Mexico, where grazing allocations were complicated by the presence of Spanish-speaking Americans with a long history [27] of range occupancy, and a few large Anglo operators with big intermingled spreads.

At Vernal, Utah, McCarran had heard in February 1943 how the three bands of Ute Indians—the Uintahs, White Rivers, and Uncompahgres—had been concentrated on 360,000 acres of Utah rangelands and mountains, the remnant of a reservation that once encompassed twenty million acres.[28] Pawwinnee, spokesman for the Uncompahgre group, told McCarran through an interpreter that the Indians were losing virtually everything to the white man. He and others had even gone to Washington "seeking some way that the white man, one time at least, will wake up and open his heart, open his eyes, to the needs of the Indians. . . ." There were no questions by McCarran after Pawwinnee finished. Another hearing was held in Washington in June 1943 at which Interior officials presented [30] a plan under which the whites in Utah would surrender a fraction of their grazing to benefit the Indians. However, where white stockmen lost grazing they were to be compensated with range allotments somewhere else close to their home bases. McCarran remarked that this would give someone a headache, and he suspected it would be Rutledge. The outcome left no one satisfied and the problem still alive. McCarran chided both the Indian Service and the Grazing Service for what he felt had been poor handling of a touchy subject.

Considerable testimony adduced at various points had to do with mining claims. There had been a great to-do at Salt Lake City in November 1943 about the withdrawal of approximately three million acres of grazing land where mining interests were primarily benefited; few stockmen participated, for, in fact, the southerly Utah lands involved supported little vegetation. Some of the lands withdrawn were believed to contain vanadium and uranium. The testimony was filled with suspicion and speculation—there were almost 150 pages of it in all—but of course none touched on the possibility that the uranium, in particular, would become publicly recognized soon as critically important; in less than two years the world would learn of the detonation of the first atomic bomb.

At other places mining claim testimony had to do mostly with whether claimants were fraudulently filing in order to gain grazing rights which they could use themselves or lease to nearby ranchers at a profit. The rich shale oil deposits of the Colorado–Utah–Wyoming areas that have since been the subject of extensive experimentation in search of an economically successful method of extracting the oil, were touched upon in passing. It was done mainly in relation to whether shale leases had been obtained from Interior so surface grazing values might be fraudulently exploited.

This chapter has leaned rather heavily upon the McCarran hearings and their influence in searching out meanings and significances regarding the uses of Taylor lands during the first part of our full participation in World War II. It is clear from them, as well as other sources consulted, that even as the nation was preoccupied with war's demand and stringencies, McCarran and his allies in Congress would do what they could to relieve or prevent bureaucratic pressures upon the livestock industry. And after the war? Doubtless there would be another depression, as there had been after the First World War, but deal with that when the time comes. Stress now that the Service must not tamper with grazing fees while there's a war on, and must forget any foolish ideas that the Grazing Service might evolve into a Grazing Management Service instead of just a holding operation for Taylor land, "pending its final disposal."

22

Prelude to Dissolution

Clarence Forsling became the third director of the Grazing Service imbued with high purpose and, though he could not know it then, at what might have been a strategic time.

The purpose was so to manage the Taylor lands that damaged ranges would be rehabilitated and produce forage to the limits of their potentials. His confirmation by the Senate on May 11, 1944, was strategic for the reason that we were approaching a moment when victory in World War II could be forecast. The swift movement of the Allied forces through Hitler's Fortress Europe that came soon afterward could allow forward planning at home. Manpower and other things critically needed would once more be available for nonmilitary uses.

Forsling was assistant chief of the Forest Service, in charge of forest and range research, when he moved from Agriculture to Interior. He accepted nomination for the directorship with his eyes open, knowing he was assuming a charge where odds were heavy against achieving his brand of success. Yet, if he could pull it off, the very difficulties faced would make reaching the goal that much more noteworthy.

"To me," Forsling informed [1] me late in 1974, "the public domain in the western states seemed a great challenge I felt I could meet. I'd grown up in a public domain environment in western Nebraska. I was a pioneer student of range management. I was familiar with the public domain in the West, had done research on range typical of Taylor lands in New Mexico, Utah, Idaho, and western

Montana. I knew the condition of the public domain and saw an opportunity to make a major contribution to conservation and believed I was up to it."

He knew many ranchers and was convinced that most were fine people who would support sound practices they understood, even as they would fight against any they did not or with which they disagreed. He also knew a few things about McCarran, his methods and their potency, and "was not dismayed."

In two years his hopes would be dashed, his dream of a major contribution to conservation crushed, even the agency he was determined to lead to a hitherto unreached plateau of achievement disbanded, its functions merged with those of the tottering old General Land Office in an emasculated new Bureau of Land Management. The livestock leadership would adamantly refuse to accept any part of Forsling's program. Indeed, it would by then be plunging headlong into its massive attempt to grab off not only the Taylor lands, but also national forest and National Park System range. And it would have the advice and leadership talents of some of the shrewdest political operators in the Congress from the West.

Not that Forsling would be tossed brusquely out of government. He remained on the staff of the Secretary of the Interior until the Eisenhower administration chose to consider him politically expendable, after twenty-nine years with the Forest Service and ten in Interior. After that he happily pursued public service activities in New Mexico and, though 81 in November 1974, wrote [2] that he was "looking forward to anyway 15 years more."

The cross currents and obfuscations that would make success in the Grazing Service out of the question began as early as the hearings of the Senate Committee on Public Lands and Surveys where Forsling's nomination was being considered.[3] The first adverse symptoms showed when Senator Joseph C. O'Mahoney of Wyoming, acting chairman, invited [4] a delegation of stockmen to sit with the committee and interrogate Forsling as though they were Senate members. Most were from the Legislative Committee of the American National Livestock Association, including its president, A. D. Brownfield of New Mexico; two vice-presidents, W. B. Wright of Nevada and A. A. Smith of Colorado; and the executive secretary, Ferdinand E. Mollin of Denver. Also present was Moroni A. Smith of Utah, a large cattle and sheep operator, one of the white ranchers who had vehemently opposed the granting of any additional grazing rights to those Ute

Indians who had been squeezed from an original multimillion-acre reservation into a few hundred thousand on the southerly, and drier, slopes of the high Uintah Range.[5]

McCarran made it a practice to allow his livestock industry friends to interrogate federal witnesses as though they were members of his investigating committee—a phenomenon I have not encountered elsewhere over a good many years of attending congressional hearings. On occasion a spectator might send a scribbled note to the rostrum and, if the hearing examiner chose to do so he might ask a question based on the message received, but the McCarran hearings were the first where witnesses such as Vernon Metcalf or Bill Wright or Norman Winder or Elmer Brock could and did freely cross-examine officials of the Grazing Service and Forest Service. And now a delegation of stock association leaders actually was invited to the front table, to sit with the senators and take part as freely as they chose in the questioning of the witness.

Senator McCarran, who had to leave to chair another meeting, almost immediately moved [6] to delay the hearing until a subcommittee—of which he would be a member—could hold an "inquisition" on Forsling's qualifications and philosophy. He was "resolved not to let this matter go by without a very careful and close study" of "theories and policies" of the nominee who, as Grazing Service director, would be dealing with matters "of vital concern to the West." Of course, he had no doubt that Forsling was a fine fellow and all that, but just the same, he must undergo prolonged quizzing that he, McCarran, intended to master-mind. O'Mahoney pacified McCarran by pledging that the record would be complete and that no precipitate action would be taken. In fact, another hearing was held [7] on May 9 at which McCarran grilled Forsling at length.

In his opening statement Forsling quoted [8] conservation language in the Taylor Act, then said, "In accomplishing these objectives, I recognize that action shouldn't be too drastic or too sudden. The program should be worked out by a gradual and orderly process that will safeguard . . . private dependent investment, avoid creating hardships, and maintain the stability of the . . . industry. The important thing . . . is that a policy be applied which in due time will attain the desired objectives" of Taylor land rehabilitation and practical management. He thought the advisory board system was admirable yet would not restrict himself to the boards in seeking suggestions for the administration of the law. "I believe strongly in cooperation with all agencies having a legitimate interest . . . ," he said.

It seems to me remarkable that, after such declarations, Forsling was confirmed at all in his new job, that the livestock leadership failed to seize upon his stated beliefs then and there and angrily demand his head. Perhaps Forsling lulled them somewhat with his repeated assurances that he had "no changes in mind" at the moment, and would at all times operate strictly within the framework of the Taylor Act.

Late in the hearing Senator Edwin S. Johnson of Colorado began asking questions about Forsling's strongly critical passages in the Forest Service's 1936 "Green Book," Senate Document 199 of the 74th Congress. Forsling had been the chief author of two chapters in the Green Book, which Senator Johnson obviously had not previously read. His attention had been called to it by one of his constituents, and after scanning it hurriedly he was perturbed. Forsling was in a tight spot for a moment, but was able to avert disaster through his candor in admitting authorship and expressing [10] belief that many of the things he had criticized had been corrected. Nevertheless, he did not recant, saying he believed the situations then had been as he had described them.

Perhaps, if some of Forsling's more highly critical comments and proposals regarding Taylor lands had been somewhere nearer the front of the book than page 457, reaction would have been stronger. His remarks there were brutally frank. In addition to reductions in numbers, the needs he outlined included (1) grazing systems that would promote revegetation; (2) correction of improper seasonal use; (3) protection of sensitive watershed areas; (4) analysis of needs of and provision for wildlife; (5) rodent control only "where damage is excessive;" and (6) a beginning on needed research. Even though he conceded that these actions must be taken "in a gradual and orderly" fashion, the package must have roiled every leading permittee who read it.

His next suggestion was outright abrasive, given existing conditions and habits of thought. Forsling wrote that the above program "necessitates a well planned, closely knit, aggressive administration," which he obviously did not believe had existed to that point. Then, "forage resources on the public lands have value for which the user should pay a fair fee." Since the grazing act provided for the "blocking up of private lands through exchange . . . , much of the intermingled, submarginal, privately owned lands should eventually be returned to public ownership if management for the perpetuation of the resource is to result." Where water holes were a key to range use and could cause monopoly situations to arise, the areas should be acquired by the United States. Otherwise, the preference language in the act "may become an instrument for giving rights and a monopoly in the use of the public range."

Those declarations in Senate Document 199 were diametrically opposed to the views of the livestock leaders and their allies in Congress and elsewhere. If there had been better organization of files relating to their friends and foes in the offices of the stock associations, I am confident there would have been found a dossier naming Forsling among their chief enemies. Yet reference to Forsling's heresies were few and disjoined at the March hearing. No other Senators present picked up the subject at all vigorously after Johnson had fumbled his way through it; Forsling did offer to have copies of his two chapters sent to members of the committee and the offer was accepted. None of the stockmen in the room mentioned the book. They had asked pointed questions on other topics earlier, and Forsling had replied frankly enough. He obviously had studied Taylor situations closely and appeared to amaze some of his listeners by his command of subjects brought up. Nevertheless, the first hearing ended inconclusively. Between March 29 and May 9, doubts about Forsling grew, probably through additional study of the Green Book. Brownfield was official spokesman for the American National when the committee reconvened on the confirmation, and his long letter [11] to the chairman was blunt.

In it, Brownfield said he was not in favor of letting Secretary Ickes "foresterize" the Grazing Service, which this choice of a director seemed likely to do. He was unhappy that Ickes had not consulted the National Advisory Board Council; it would have put forward candidates of its own. Forsling, he feared, would follow the "case hardened" Forest Service brand of bureaucracy. Yet Brownfield made only one almost casual, backhanded sort of reference to Senate Document 199, and he did not ask rejection of the nominee.

Floyd W. Lee did, however. Lee was a large New Mexico rancher whose brother Lawrance, as president of the Chamber of Commerce of the United States, would support the land grab a few years later. He wrote [12] as spokesman of the woolgrowers of his state, saying they "formally protest" Forsling's confirmation. He was against the appointment of "theorists" to high administration jobs, and this one would be "just one more aggravating straw which will again upset the livestock industry."

At the May 9 "inquisition," McCarran questioned [13] Forsling long and closely on his attitude toward all manner of Grazing Service matters, and tried especially hard to pin him to a pledge that he would not attempt to raise grazing fees. Forsling frankly told [14] the senator that "offhand" the fee looked "fairly low for some areas." He had "a responsibility under the act" to keep abreast of the situation and "determine what is a reasonable fee." Yes, of course he would consult those in the advisory board system, would "take into account every factor that is involved," and the resolution of questions concerning fees would not be "arrived at . . . precipitiously."

Here Forsling may have dug out a shovelful of earth for his Grazing Service grave for before the end of the year he would be accused of acting unduly quickly and undiplomatically in presenting a new fee schedule to the National Advisory Board Council. However, on the same day the second hearing was held, Forsling's name was put before the Senate with a recommendation that he be confirmed. McCarran presented the committee report, but was himself still dubious; his report [15] contained small praise for the nominee. Forsling just hadn't had enough experience in the Grazing Service's "line of work" to satisfy McCarran's and the industry's misgivings. However, the time was not right for further delay in deciding on a director. Two days later Forsling was sworn in.

His first few weeks were the usual ones of a new appointee to high office. He got acquainted with and sized up his staff. Some of it was "not top flight," and he felt [16] the overall level did not rise greatly during his regime. The Service had never had a strong personnel program, with systematic selection and training. The sum was that "too many jobs" were done inadequately or only in part. His men had to be "jacks of too many trades." His predecessor, Rutledge, having no deputy, had leaned heavily on Joe H. Leech, chief of lands, to fill the gap. Leech, said Forsling, while "hard working, earnest, and loyal," lacked "experience in land administration."

"And so, when I became director, with all the other woes of the Grazing Service and much—too much—of my time taken up with Senator McCarran and Company, and the battle of grazing fees on my hands, there was neither time nor funds nor candidates available" to fill the position "on short notice, and I . . . let Leech carry on much as he had before."

The Service's main offices during the war were at Salt Lake

City. "At the other end of the line, in Washington as liaison officer, was Archie Ryan," who had at times acted for Rutledge and carried out field investigations as well. Forsling perforce used Ryan in the same capacities.

These functions and those performing them would assume some importance when the final accounting was made to Congress by McCarran. He chose to single out these two men as special scapegoats. Forsling, as we have seen, defended them. He called [17] McCarran's accusations "exaggerated and mostly invalid," saying Leech and Ryan were "unjustly persecuted."

It was seven months after taking office that Forsling put his foot in the fee trap. At a meeting in Salt Lake City in November 1944, he proposed to the National Advisory Board Council that the rate be raised immediately from five to fifteen cents per animal unit month. This 200 percent increase—McCarran began calling it a 300 percent raise and stockmen by the score believed him and followed suit—would be on an interim basis. It would be subject to change after figures and other supporting data could be studied more thoroughly; then the rate could be refined as need be. The proposal was fuel for an already lively flame, and Forsling thereafter had no chance of making progress with the Service or the lands in his charge. He was marked for humiliating retreat or ejection.

McCarran took the floor [18] of the Senate on December 16, 1944, to assail the proposal. It had "struck consternation in the industry and in the financial institutions which stand behind the industry," he said. As an outcome, he went on, the Senate Committee on Public Lands and Surveys had adopted a resolution demanding that there should be no new fees before the committee had an opportunity to study them. There would be a hearing by the full committee in Washington in January 1945, and field hearings by the subcommittee in May and June, playing out McCarran's string before the end of the fiscal year.

At the January hearing Forsling was given full critical treatment by Senators McCarran, O'Mahoney, and others, and by Representatives Barrett and Rockwell, who sat with the senators. They questioned Forsling's reasoning and judgment from start to finish. Forsling conducted himself in a sober but confident manner as he recounted the work load the Service was carrying under stringent wartime circumstances, with inadequate finances and staff. He completely avoided mentioning demands to increase fees that had been made to the Service by Congressional Appropriations Committees. That would come out later, and would be twisted [19] by McCarran into allegations that the Service rather than the committees had initiated discussions that led to demands.

Here let us see what pertinent records disclose on that subject. Back in February 1940, Rutledge was being questioned [20] by Congressman C. H. Leavy of Washington at a hearing by the House Interior Appropriations Subcommittee; Leavy wanted to know if there was any chance of getting more revenue from grazing on the Taylor lands. Rutledge was dubious.

Leavy: You wouldn't raise fees now?
Rutledge: No, sir, I would not.

Rutledge did want higher fees soon after but was halted by our entrance in World War II, and the subject then lay dormant until after he had departed. In February 1944, Interior appropriations for the next fiscal year were again being discussed, and Representative A. E. Carter of California led the questioning of Leech, Ryan, and DePue Falck, the Service [21] chief of operations. The three took turns answering Carter's questions.

Q. Have you any plans projected . . ., figuring out when [grazing] might be on a paying basis?
A. We know this land is worth much more. You will notice in this statement that the federal range should be worth over $5 million to the stockmen. . . . We collect less than $1 million. . . .
Q. If it is worth $5 million to those people, why did you not get a larger amount than $850,000?
A. Because we have a set fee at the present time. . . .
Q. But you set the fee. I do not want to be antagonistic . . ., but I want this thing explained to me. . . . Why should you not receive a better fee?

The reply was that most people in the Service felt the permittees should pay more, but on the other side the prevalent belief was that any increase should be justified by rendering greater services. Congressman Ben F. Jensen of Iowa did not distinguish between goods and services, and remarked that people usually pay before they get them. He wanted the ranchers to realize what a problem it was for Congress to find means to pay the huge dollar costs of the war and to accept their obligation to pay "just compensation" for their grazing.

These records seem to indicate that in Forsling's time the demands for higher fees did originate with members of the appropriations committees, not the Service. The record seems clear, though, that Forsling felt fees were too low as far back as 1936, when he was writing for the Green Book. I have no doubt he was ready and willing to broach the subject as soon as the time could be considered right, and the progress of the Allied forces in Europe and in the Pacific gave him an inner signal to do so.

Toward the end of the Washington hearing in early 1945, O'Mahoney appeared to soften slightly, saying,[22] he feared the Bureau of the Budget was more to blame than Interior for the proposed increase, through its habit of issuing what amounted to directives to agencies whose activities were revenue-producing. Nevertheless, he felt Forsling should have made a more thorough study of the fee situation before he put his plan for a raise on the NABC conference table. As he presided, the senator had at hand a letter [23] from Secretary Ickes saying in effect that he would not approve an increase in fees without giving the committee prior notice.

For about three months the situation in the Grazing Service remained relatively static, but it is apparent that throughout the West someone was busy stirring up more Grazing Service troubles. In the next sixty days, through May and June, Forsling was put through seven hearings lasting sixteen days, where his principal opportunities to take a breather came only on occasions when Forest Service feet were before the inquisitorial fire. McCarran's charter was running out, and it was arranged that others would conduct hearings he could not attend. Chairman Hatch presided at two in Arizona and New Mexico in the earlier part of May; McCarran ran a lengthy one at Salt Lake City; and Senator Glen Taylor of Idaho chaired three held at Boise in his home state, and at Baker and Burns, Oregon. Later, in September, O'Mahoney would hold two-day hearings at Grand Junction, Colorado, and Casper, Wyoming, with attention divided about equally between stockmen complaints over any Grazing Service fee increase and Forest Service cuts in grazing.

It was an exhilarating period for America and much of the rest of our world. Hatch was presiding in Phoenix on May 11—Victory Day in Europe. It must have been on many tongues, but the record says nothing about it. Nor were there more than casual references to the closing stage of World War II at other of the hearings. The record concentrated on Service–stockman controversy to the exclusion of other subjects. It is perplexing that this was so; nevertheless it was. The livestock associations were fighting their own war and were not to be diverted by the collapse of the Hitler regime or the accelerating advances against the Japanese in the Pacific Theater. They would bear down on Forsling and the rest of the Grazing Service people, and let nothing appear in the record about the men in service coming home or the collective sigh of relief throughout the nation that war was at last behind us. That is precisely how the record makes it look.

And so, in the Southwest, in the Great Basin region, and in the Pacific Northwest, at hearing after hearing it was a case of pound, pound, pound away on the theme that a raise, any raise, would ruin the industry, was not justified by its economic condition, and the permittees simply would not stand for it. At first Forsling remained steadfast in his contention that increased fees were essential, taking ridicule and bombast and pleading as just something to be endured. The hearings were deadly serious, with little to leaven them or provide surcease from the relentless assaults.

One lighter situation did come, though, at Boise. It was provided by A. Abarrate, a rancher and sheep broker, whose English was broken but whose meaning was unmistakable.

"When Taylor law is being created all I see is long faces," he began. "Now, all happy, and fine clothes. . . . I don't want people criticizing that grazing land is too high, because it is cheapest thing we ever got in Idaho. . . ." Then, to the secretary of the state woolgrowers organization, Abarrate asked pointedly, "If sheepmen always lose money since 1924, how they pay your salary, eh? Where they get money?" The response was a burst of laughter from the audience.

Ordinarily, the hearings proceeded at a measured pace, with Forsling presenting and defending the proposed raise, followed by a procession of spokesmen for stockman groups to dispute his every contention. The Forsling stance was positive to the point of brusqueness at earlier 1945 hearings, doubtless due in part to the effects of long and repetitive questioning. For example, at Salt Lake City G. Norman Winder of Craig, Colorado, top ranking official of the National Woolgrowers Association, tried to pin Forsling down on the method used to arrive at fifteen cents as a "reasonable" grazing fee. The tart reply was that he, Forsling, had fully explained the process at the Washington hearing in January, and "I have no further comment to make on that."

In print, the remark looked somewhat imperious, but even the shadow of a high-handed approach faded as the hearings proceeded. Forsling's opening statements and his responses to inquiries became more subdued, until, as at Boise, he would begin to say [24] that all he wanted was to get information that would help the Grazing Service judge what a reasonable fee amounted to, and "to decide whether . . . any fee that may be proposed by the Secretary is reasonable." He conceded that perhaps he had erred in a "good many ways in the method or manner the whole thing was handled." At one point he was quoted [25] as saying the fee thing "should be decided on its merits, feebly as I can present them." There doubtless was a degree of sarcasm in some of Forsling's comments. He had been on the grill almost constantly, and the pressure seemed to be wearing him down. At Salt Lake City on May 28, 1945, near the end of a long oral sparring match in which McCarran and Vernon Metcalf alternated at taking pokes at the fee proposal, Forsling began to flag and his answer to a question appeared to McCarran not to be fully responsive. This prompted the senator to exclaim, "Please, please . . . face the subject and answer it categorically."

By the middle of June Secretary Ickes was ready to capitulate. The signal was in a letter [26] dated the 14th, to Senator Hatch, in which he said he no longer proposed an increase; he had instructed Forsling to continue his range appraisal study and to work with the users through the advisory board system, with the thought that from it all would come the "basis of a reasonable fee" as specified by the Taylor Act.

With the end of the 1945 fiscal year came also the end of Mc-Carran's authorizations for hearings, and money to pay staff and travel costs. Yet those two additional hearings in Wyoming and Colorado appear in the McCarran record,[27] though he was not present at either. O'Mahoney presided, and most of the testimony concerned national forest matters. The fact that Ickes had surrendered seemed not to matter when the Grazing Service was grilled; Forsling still was assailed for having had the temerity to propose a fee increase. At Grand Junction on September 6, Norman Winder felt he must repeat, doubtless for emphasis, the points originally made by the NABC at Salt Lake City in November, 1944: (1) no increase without an "independent" study made by the industry; (2) no increase without specific approval by the NABC; and (3) Congress must enact a law declaring fees should not exceed the actual costs of administration of the grazing lands.

Here matters rested, as far as surface indications show, but tumult was growing within the councils of the industry's leadership, and marked changes were in the making in Washington. Nineteen-forty-six would be a disastrous year for the Grazing Service, even though the Great Land Grab, whose immediate target was the take-over of the Taylor lands, would fail in its first objective. Ickes would leave after twelve years in office, a long time for any department head, to be succeeded by Julius A. Krug, who was not inclined to stand as firmly against the overloads of grazing. Forsling would find the Grazing Service "Executive Ordered" out of existence, its spirit and morale demolished and his own position abolished.

More Turmoil

Nothing in its young history equaled the disruption and disquiet visited upon the administration of the Taylor Act in the months that followed the close of the McCarran inquisitions and the resignation of Secretary Ickes.

Appropriations for fiscal 1947, passed in the spring, were slashed right and left. At midyear the Grazing Service and General Land Office both were abolished as such and combined in a new agency called the Bureau of Land Management, which was so weakened and disordered that the all-embracive name given it was rather farcical. In August the stock associations formed their Joint National Committee for the express purpose of tearing out of federal ownership the choicest remaining public grazing lands in the West. The industry was riding furiously toward what looked like total demolition of the concept of government management of the ranges. The staff was demoralized and fearful.

In the late summer the new Interior Secretary, Julius Krug, asked Rex L. Nicholson, a Californian acceptable to McCarran and the stock associations, for recommendations as to how the reorganization should be implemented, and the outcome served further to dishearten the remaining staffers committed to principles of grazing moderation and range recuperation. Nicholson's advisers in his study were district and association leaders, and his report was accompanied by a confidential letter to Krug in which he advocated that both the director of BLM and its range chief be men chosen by the industry to be supervised.

To one reading the *Congressional Record*, it might have appeared in the early months of 1946 that a power struggle was going on between the Committees on Appropriations and those on Public Lands and Surveys. The appropriators wanted the Grazing Service to produce more revenue, and higher fees were its only source of additional money. The public land groups, on the other hand, were bitterly against any increase in fees to be paid for grazing. This aspect of the clash shows clearly in debate on the floor of the House over appropriations for fiscal [1] 1947. Three pages of small type were required to print the debate. Congressman Jed Johnson of Oklahoma presented the House Appropriations Committee position, and the upshot was that the $1.7 million asked for range by Interior was hacked to $425,000. Frank Barrett of Wyoming, though fighting against any fee increase, recognized that the reduction would curtail services his livestock constituency wanted, and argued for a larger appropriation. He lost then, but a few months later became author of a $300,000 supplemental appropriation to keep essential programs going. He boasted [2] of this accomplishment often during his Wild West Show hearings in 1947. With the reorganization and reductions in funding, any lingering hopes any personnel may have held for a meaningful postwar reinvigoration of the ranges went glimmering.

While the money actions were ongoing, McCarran's influence and that of those with whom he was aligned led inexorably toward the reorganization that became public knowledge in July. This was when the differences in attitude of Ickes and Krug became apparent.

"Ickes," Forsling [3] told me, "was the only man I knew who could handle McCarran. He demonstrated it when he turned down McCarran's demand that he fire three Grazing Service officials in Nevada. Ickes backed me when I told him these were honest, reliable men trying to perform their duties. Ickes said, 'Thank you; that is all I need to know.' "

Krug, to Forsling,[4] was "an entirely different breed" who thought "the way to get along was through acquiescence" that would gain favor; he apparently did not realize that McCarran was the kind who would "try to gain two yards for every one he conceded."

McCarran was chairman of the Senate Judiciary Committee at the time President Harry S. Truman's Reorganization Plan No. 3 [5] was sent to Congress. When Krug was called as a witness, McCarran demanded that neither Forsling nor Joel D. Wolfsohn, assistant commissioner of the General Land Office, be appointed to head the new agency to come out of the merger. Krug went along. Thereafter,

BLM operated under the caretaker administration of Fred W. Johnson, former GLO commissioner, until Marion Clawson became director eighteen months later.

Nicholson was touted as an objective outsider when Krug asked him to suggest how best to get BLM started. For several months Nicholson traveled over the public land West, interviewing leaders and meeting with district and state advisory boards as well as the National Advisory Board Council. I have not found where he consulted any others. In his report he referred [6] to a "confidential" letter to Krug on the subject of personnel. I have not seen that letter, but the fact that Nicholson recommended hiring top officials chosen by the livestock leadership came out in testimony [7] at one of two BLM hearings conducted in Washington in the spring of 1947 by Congressman Barrett.

There Elmer Brock said candidly for the record that the stock associations and the NABC never would have agreed to any increase whatever in Taylor Act grazing fees unless everything in their "understanding" with Interior had been carried out. Part of that understanding had to do with top BLM appointments.

"We were given a definite commitment," said Brock, "that should we present the name of a man [to head the new agency] whose endorsement or approval would be made by four senators, we could depend on his appointment. *All of these have been disregarded*" (italics added). Barrett interrupted Brock at that point and shunted him to another subject.

The subject came up again in even more specific language on May 10, 1947, when Barrett held his second hearing on whether the new BLM was operating obediently under the new scheme of things. Gordon Griswold of Elko, Nevada, chairman of the NABC and holder of numerous other titles including president of the Nevada Livestock Production Credit Association, whose staff executive, Vernon Metcalf, had figured so prominently in the McCarran investigatory years, was put on the stand to review the whole situation. Nicholson,[8] he said, had met with the NABC and with the Joint Public Lands Committee of the cattlemen and woolgrowers in Salt Lake City in October 1946, "prior to the submission of his final report to Secretary Krug." He went on that Nicholson "gave us to understand that if the Council and the Joint Committee agreed on and would recommend those who would head up the Bureau of Land Management and its Branch of Range Management, and secure their endorsement by a representative group of public land . . .

senators, he felt sure of their appointment. . . ." Griswold said Dan Hughes, chairman of the Joint Committee, and Ed Kavanaugh, a former assistant director of the Grazing Service, were their choices and that they did get the needed senatorial approval.

Griswold declared the NABC's concurrence in Nicholson's report and the change in fees it proposed was based on acceptance by Interior of their whole package, including the appointees, not just whatever parts Secretary Krug liked. All Krug did was to raise the fees without following through on the rest, so now Griswold and his associates were in Washington to declare that they had been misled and they didn't like it.

The NABC chairman showed clearly in his statement how easy it was for the livestock leadership to get whatever it wanted through the Public Lands Committees of the Congress. He asserted that the stockmen would demand that until Interior complied with what they had requested, there would be no increase in BLM appropriations above the limited sum allowed for fiscal year 1947. This appeared in a communication to Krug from the NABC and the Joint Committee in February, 1947. In March the two groups wrote Krug asking him to meet with them and Nicholson somewhere in the West. By this time Krug apparently had grown wary, for Griswold said he replied that he knew of no broken promises and if the stockmen wanted to meet with him, they should come to Washington. So, declared Griswold, the stockmen's position hardened; if Krug would not come to them, the best way to handle him would be through a formal congressional hearing. He said that had been decided on April 23, when the stockmen's group sent a final letter to Krug stating their intentions.

The hearing on May 10 was Barrett's swift compliance with their wishes. This one was unusual in another sense: It was held on a Saturday, a rare occurrence, doubtless for the convenience of visiting stockmen.

Later in the hearing,[9] Krug testified that "at no time did Nicholson or I tell anybody that they could select the director of the Bureau of Land Management, or any of its officers. That is one principle that I, as a servant of Congress, would have to defend to the last breath. A gentleman was suggested from the West, by that group. We found he was legally unqualified to hold the job, because he himself was holding permits to use the public domain."

The fact that Krug testified after Griswold was also unusual. Ordinarily an official of cabinet rank would be heard first. Barrett no doubt wanted Griswold's allegations recorded first so as to put Krug in the position of respondent.

Forsling had little doubt that things would have turned out rather differently if Ickes had still been Secretary of Interior when the merger was brought about. "I had received verbal assurances that I would head the new agency," he told [10] me.

The reorganization and all that accompanied it traveled on tracks parallel to those being used by the stock associations, under McCarran's counseling, to seek a favorable outcome of their Land Grab ambitions. Chapter 1 and chapters in the Forest Service segment of this book have told of the initial organization, of the production of a draft of a grab bill, and Chairman Hughes's unhappiness when the conservation organizations refused to support the grab at the meeting in Denver in December, 1946.

Forsling's comments [11] on the Nicholson operation were that the latter had had "little experience" in public domain matters, having spent much of his life as "a tractor salesman" in California. His report, Forsling went on, followed McCarran's idea that fees should be only large enough to cover the actual costs of grazing administration.

Nicholson's report generally followed the stockmen's association line. He set forth stockman versions of existing situations. He recommended what stockmen wanted him to recommend. Fees were the "major" issue, yet a small increase [12] would be approved. The advisory board system was very good, despite the fact that some boards had a habit of moving in and taking control away from Service officials; [13] he suggested no change intended to curb them. Trespass was referred to as trespass *against* Service permittees on Taylor land,[14] never *by* Taylor land permittees.

Nicholson was on solid ground when he deplored the poor management of the ranges carried out by the Service and advocated a clearly defined long-range national land [15] policy. In another place he called for a long term "policy and plan of operation" for the Taylor lands, and appeared to admit that the lack of such a plan was at the root of much of the prevailing unhappiness in the industry.

Forsling's 1975 comment on the Nicholson report was predictable.[16] He thought it followed McCarran's ideas, especially with respect to fees which, as McCarran had made abundantly clear in his hearings and elsewhere, Nicholson wanted only large enough to cover the costs of administration of grazing. Though McCarran and the livestock spokesmen at his hearings opposed *any* increase while Rutledge and Forsling were in office, they went along without protest with Nicholson's suggestion of a raise to eight cents per animal unit month.

I found no specific reference to the manner in which the eight-cent fee was reached. At Phoenix on May 10, 1945, when Senator Hatch was substituting for McCarran in the chair, a legislator named Ed Jamison who identified himself as one of the architects of the five-cent fee in the early Taylor Act era and as a rather large livestock operator, testified [17] that perhaps a fee of seven or eight cents would not be too far out of line. In the next breath Jamison wondered aloud why the users of the Taylor lands should have to pay any fee at all, since 50 percent automatically came back to the point of origin under the law and another 25 percent was eligible to do so for range improvement. It is little more than a guess, but I suspect that Nicholson and his advisors discussed the fact that an increase of some sort was inevitable, or else the Congressional Committees on Appropriations would continue to clamor, and perhaps it would be better to accede to a small raise in the hope it would silence criticism from that source. At some point someone must have mentioned a specific figure, and from then on it was a matter of choosing from alternatives.

In the end the prevailing system of distributing fee revenues was changed to a formula that gave the districts considerably less than most of them had enjoyed before. The base fee was raised only one cent, to six cents per AUM, which went into the federal treasury. Then, on top of that, an additional two cents was assessed, with all of it to go back to the districts for range improvements. This eight-cent fee remained in effect until 1951, when it rose to twelve cents. Table 5 [18] gives GS-BLM fees from the beginning through 1975.

Nicholson's denunciation of the Grazing Service for its lack of forward management of the range lands in its charge obviously stung Forsling. He told me [19] that if the kind of administration of the lands that he envisioned had been put into effect, recovery of deteriorated ranges would be twenty to twenty-five years further along than it is today. Doubtless Forsling's words must be discounted to some extent, despite the fact that he headed the Service amid the distractions and disruptions of the long series of hearings, pressures from all sides, low agency morale, and in a time that had to be

Table 5*
Grazing Fees on Taylor Act Lands

Years	Fee (AUM)	Years	Fee (AUM)
1936–1946	.05	1963–1965	.30
1947–1950	.08	1966–1968	.33
1951–1954	.12	1969–1970	.44
1955–1957	.15	1971	.64
1958	.19	1972	.66
1959–1960	.22	1973	.78
1961–1962	.09	1974–1975	1.00

* Personal communication from BLM Division of Range, Washington.

difficult at best because of the stresses attendant upon the winding down of history's most demanding war. Nevertheless, it must be said that he never had a chance to demonstrate whether he could transform the weak Grazing Service he inherited into an effective and forward-looking public range managing agency.

Nicholson suggested [20] that another agency, the Bureau of Agricultural Economics in the Department of Agriculture, be asked to study the whole situation affecting the varied uses made of Taylor land and the "public benefits" found there, which he listed as wildlife protection, forest fire protection, erosion control, and watershed protection. He would have BAE separate the costs of administering these benefits from those relating to livestock grazing. The study was carried out [21] and resulted in the proposal that 30 percent of the administrative costs be charged to range and the remaining 70 percent to the other functions. The Nicholson formula, which prevailed, called for a 25/75-percent distribution of costs. Presumably the six-cent grazing fee would cover the 25 percent attributable to administration of grazing functions.

Under Johnson as acting director, the Bureau of Land Management moved with utmost circumspection until after the threat of the Great Land Grab ended. Its officials assumed a very low profile, and spoke softly—with one exception. In April 1947, at Barrett's first hearing in Washington on BLM matters, the Joel Wolfsohn who was not acceptable to McCarran as director but who nevertheless was allowed to serve as associate director, spoke up defensively under stiff courtroom style questioning. With Barrett the chief examiner, exchanges went like this:

Q. Why has it taken you so long to get reorganized?

A. It is harder to merge two agencies than to set up one.

Q. How have you responded to Nicholson's advice to prevent rising administrative costs, to correct your imbalance of manpower as between headquarters and field offices, excessive paper work, and other extracurricular matters?

A. Congress took care of personnel reductions with its cut in appropriations; it left BLM without opportunity for "extracurricular" activities, "whatever that means."

Q. Are you going to reduce your excessive statistical data collection?

A. Figures are necessary if we are to carry out orders from Congress for a range and fee study and if we are to report intelligently when Congress demands such information.

Q. Do you plan range improvement studies as suggested by Nicholson?

A. This is counter to complaints by stockmen and members of Congress that too many statistical and related studies have been made.

Q. Is it your position that a federal agency should seek to make a profit on grazing of public lands, such as private owners do?

A. I stand by a statement I made last year that the federal government should get a return of the full value of the forage consumed. The House Appropriations Committee, in reporting the Interior bill today, critically noted that the Forest Service was charging an average of 31 cents per AUM while the BLM was only charging 8 cents.

[At that point,[22] Barrett went "off the record" for an unspecified length of time.]

Q. What is your interpretation of "reasonable" fees?

A. "Reasonableness" has plagued the agency *ever since Congress put the word in the act* [italics added]; fees should not be so high as to wreck the industry, but permittees should pay for value received.

With the close of the May 10 hearing the stockmen gave up on the proposition that they should dictate who should carry the title of director of BLM. By this time the policy of the livestock bloc both in and out of Congress was swinging deliberately away from that which had prevailed only a few months earlier, with respect to both Interior and Agriculture. It no longer appeared important that the Taylor lands or the forest ranges should be owned outright by the permittees whose cattle and sheep grazed them. The maneuvers that would bring the Forest Service to heel had not yet run their course, but there was no question as to the strangle hold the stock leadership had on BLM. Let Interior appoint whomever it wished as director and as chief grazing administrator; so long as the advisory system functioned effectively to curb actions the boards and council did not approve, it mattered little who warmed the big swivel chairs. Barrett and his cohorts at hearings later in 1947 could ask whether anyone in the meeting rooms was in favor of a land grab in full confidence that there would be an almost unanimously negative reply from the ranchers present. The issue was settled. Barrett & Co. could get on with the attack on the Forest Service—and did.

Bared Teeth

Marion Clawson moved into the office of director of the Bureau of Land Management in 1948 as industry leaders and Senator McCarran looked on benignly, well satisfied with Secretary Krug's choice.

Three years later Clawson's "a good man" image was changed to that most horrendous of creatures, one who wouldn't hesitate to hold that Taylor Act permittees must reduce the grazing use of their allotments and undertake other solidly based range management practices that they indicated unmistakably they were not ready to embrace.

Clawson inherited a Bureau of Land Management that was short of funds and low in manpower. Its people were wary, often on the defensive. Congressional appropriations were above the abysmal low of fiscal 1947, but still under amounts needed to bring about better conditions at headquarters and in field offices, to say nothing of out on the allotments on which their efforts were focused. The livestock leadership had apparently abandoned its Great Land Grab attempt, but outspoken influential individuals kept the subject warm. Field officials of BLM who attended meetings of conservation groups in western states generally stayed in back rows and responded cautiously to questions on "controversial" subjects. At the same time, some with whom I was in touch obviously were eager to have their story—heavily watered and circuitously written so as not to disturb their livestock clientele too much—brought to the attention of the conservation community. However, conservationists had become wary of many BLM officials. Rightly or wrongly—and I now suspect it was a mixture of both—we took it more or less for granted that the stockmen had the agency so under its thumb that we could do little to rescue it. What energies and other resources we had, we thought, would be better employed strengthening the hand of the Forest Service, trying to keep its more versatile and valuable properties from going the way of the public domain. It was a hellish time for a man to step into the directorship of the Bureau of Land Management.

But Clawson, like Forsling before him, was an optimist. When BLM was formed in 1946, he was a regional official of the Bureau of Agricultural Economics in Berkeley, California.[1] His office there was abolished in a shake-up and, at the start of 1947, Clawson became the first regional administrator of BLM for California and Nevada. He had been "assured that Interior had plans to make BLM an outstanding resource management agency and . . . could get the money to do it," he wrote me in 1975.

It shortly became apparent to me that BLM was badly floundering [Clawson wrote]. I was quietly looking for a way out, and at the same time was working with [Assistant Interior Secretary Davidson] to help him find an adequate director. . . .

By December, 1947, Secretary Krug and other top interior people were fairly desperate about leadership for BLM. With the Truman administration under heavy criticism and the likelihood of a change in the election of 1948, it was difficult to attract a first rate, top flight man to the job. BLM was drifting. So, somewhat in desperation, Krug offered me the job.

Clawson believed his was a merit promotion and approached the task before him confident it could be accomplished over time. He thought the eight-cent fee might have proved adequate for the sort of agency structure Rex Nicholson had recommended, but "it never was implemented." By the time Clawson became director, the eight-cent fee was totally inadequate, and in two years he was able to persuade the NABC that the fee should be raised to twelve cents per AUM.

"That group not only accepted the need," Clawson wrote, "but actually helped sell it to stockmen all over the West."

That sort of camaraderie had little longer to live. Clawson was transformed from friend to enemy in the eyes of former supporters by the publication of a slim volume titled *Rebuilding the Federal Range*.[2] It was replete with language that was anathema to leaders of the industry. Those people were accustomed to think of their grazing use of the Taylor lands as "rights;" Clawson wrote as early as page 3 of the booklet, and again on page 11, that instead they were "privileges." That was Forest Service terminology, and must have rankled. What is more, Clawson had the temerity to put "these grazing privileges" in italics, to underscore the importance he accorded the concept.

On page 4 he wrote that although forage production per acre on the public domain was far lower than on average hay lands elsewhere, "income per operator in terms of meat, wool, and leather obtained from the use of these lands . . . is among the highest of any type of agriculture." Long time livestock lobbyists, for years in the habit of putting on a poor mouth in behalf of their clientele, must have shuddered when they saw that.

Further on came a procession of terms that had a bad range country connotation. Clawson wrote that the management he advocated included "use not to exceed grazing capacity"; [3] policing—Clawson called it "supervision"—to prevent trespass and improper distribution of livestock on allotments; and he even hinted that *all* stock might have to be removed from some badly abused ranges.

Though the Taylor Act had been passed seventeen years earlier, under the prevailing federal management and permittee operations less than 10 percent of the total rehabilitation required had been accomplished; [4] large areas were still deteriorating under "present . . . programs;" [5] and in general Clawson wrote like a managerial taskmaster with regard to numbers of livestock, seasons of use, and federal control of range improvement activities.

As though these were not enough, Clawson published [6] pictorial material that could be construed as a direct slap. The left half of a two-panel drawing showed a horde of sheep rushing with bared teeth upon a lone clump of grass in a denuded area; the right half pictured well distributed stock munching contently on lush vegetation, with cattle on one side of a fence, sheep on the other. Clawson commented to me: [7]

"That pamphlet of *Rebuilding the Federal Range* was only one of several things we published during those years. It did have one unfortunate sketch—unfortunate, in large part, because wrong—sheep have no upper teeth. Those of us who wrote and reviewed the manuscript simply missed the artist's error. But, on the whole, that pamphlet was well received by stockmen, as well as by others."

Clawson's recollection may well be right as to the reception others gave the booklet, especially those in the conservation movement. It was strong medicine, needed and overdue. James Lee, long time information specialist on the BLM staff, had a different recollection [8] of how stockmen reacted. His was that the lefthand sketch threw the stockmen into a frenzy of anger and vituperation. I gathered that it upset them so badly even an amended version of the picture would have been unacceptable.

Rebuilding the Federal Range presented a summary [9] of range improvement and restoration work that Clawson calculated still remained to be done on the 142 million acres in districts and the fifteen million outside (Section 15) acres. From it comes the following;

1. Improved range management, including range surveys and inventories on 90 million acres.
2. Improved fire protection on 170 million acres (which likely included private holdings).
3. Watershed treatment of 90 million acres, including:
    a. Revegetation of 22 million acres.
    b. Construction of 40,000 water conservation and erosion control dams.
    c. Water spreading structures on 2.4 million acres.
4. Range management improvements, including:
    a. 38,500 stockwater developments.
    b. 68,280 miles of fencing.
    c. 25,500 miles of livestock and truck trails.
    d. 1,650 corrals, loading chutes, etc.
5. Pest and rodent control on 62 million acres.

Clawson estimated that these things would cost from $400 to $500 million and require twenty years to complete. This was comparable to the 1946 postwar program proposed by the Forest Service. Congress, without strong constituency support for either, did not see fit to approve them.

Despite his setback in the *Rebuilding* incident, Clawson continued in office until the Eisenhower administration came along in 1953, and built an overall record that caused a long-time BLM employe to comment [10] in 1972 that Clawson and Charles H. Stoddard, who served later, had been the best directors in Taylor Act history. Clawson agreed with a Nicholson suggestion that in BLM there should be heavier attention to field-level staffing, with fewer swivel-chair operators in regional and national offices. The men on the ground could then become well acquainted with range conditions as well as with the permittees and their elected leaders on the advisory boards. The combination should lead to better communication and better patterns of land use. Clawson felt strongly that the advisory board system was basically good.

I argue [he wrote [11]] "that advisory boards are often misused, but I think their absence is even worse. In the 1948–1953 period, as well as earlier, it could be argued, and often was, that the BLM boards were too narrowly based, since they consisted almost wholly of livestockmen. But in those days it was only the livestockmen who had any real interest in western public land management. . . . Later, . . . BLM moved to establish much more broadly based advisory boards and I think that was a very good thing but one not really possible while I was there.

Clawson's office had been listed by the Eisenhower administration for Schedule C treatment, but Clawson felt such action really was not necessary, as few officials, even though under Civil Service, could serve effectively once their departmental secretary had asked for resignations.

With Clawson's departure, BLM went into the custodial management that the livestock leaders had wanted all along, and it remained that way until Stoddard was named director in June 1963. Stoddard initiated many changes in BLM's range management program, setting it on the basic course it has followed to the present. Stoddard had a forestry background of schooling and early experience. Early in 1950 Robert O. Beatty, assistant director of the Izaak Walton League, brought Stoddard to my attention and we employed him as program specialist. From our staff Stoddard went to the Interior Department in Washington, then for a time to Resources For the Future, Inc., and from there to the BLM directorship. When he left in 1966 he distributed a summary of the actions he instituted. Highlights must be drawn upon.

He turned around the policy of having strong field organization and a weak headquarters office. In earlier years, he wrote,[12] strong BLM directors had usually been "rewarded by transfers elsewhere or firing. A showing of strength meant controversy and in the Department . . . controversy has always been shunned when powerful interest groups brought on political pressure."

Previously, field programs "were usually in response to demands by interest groups . . . , and "no system existed to give close on-the-ground supervision to all activities. . . ."

In the Stoddard regime, BLM was reorganized into the staff and line system that remains in large part. He strongly supported enactment by Congress of the Classification and Multiple Use Act [13] and a companion Public Sale Act,[14] both passed in 1964.

He instituted range improvement techniques intended to reverse the severe soil erosion that had been taking place for so long; they also would benefit wildlife. When Dr. Glen D. Fulcher, professor of agricultural economics at the University of Nevada, criticized BLM's lack of a sound range program, Stoddard promptly hired him and put him in charge of the BLM standards and technology staff. Fulcher, in turn, recruited A. L. (Gus) Hormay from the Forest Service, where he had fashioned a rest–rotation system of grazing that, he believed, would speed up the rehabilitation of damaged ranges without AUM reductions. The Hormay formulas are the basis of the BLM's range management program of modern times. It is my present view that detailed allotment management plans predicted upon rest and rotation will remain the linchpin of BLM range policy even if Congress enacts the organic act it and the nation's conservationists have wanted for so long.

Stoddard might have remained longer as BLM director if he had not held "so tenaciously to principle." [15] He noted in his parting account that he made many industry leaders furious when he brought in Fulcher and gave him such a free hand in the range aspects of BLM's mission.

The Public Land Law Review Act [16] passed in 1966 had been part of the packet of legislation that included the Multiple Use and Public Sale laws referred to earlier. At that time the Multiple Use Act had been written on a temporary basis, since it was believed that the entire mass of public land laws that had accumulated since the birth of the republic would be revised and regularized by the newly created Public Land Law Review Commission. Stoddard had been one of its staunch advocates. After the PLLRC reported in 1970 several versions of a BLM organic act were introduced, but as this was written in the spring of 1975, Congress had not seen fit to pass one. Consequently the Taylor lands were still being administered under an archaic law that made range allotments the equivalent of private property without the problems that attend ownership. Low fees were still range battle trophies; "stagflation" was the reason given when both Interior and Agriculture acceded to stockman demands that they not impose a 1975 increment intended to lead toward "fair market value" rates. And out on the range, far from headquarters offices, where top level supervision was scant and livestock influence was great, wildlife habitat, recreational values, soil erosion control measures, and the like, were given more promise of future attention than present action. [17]

The outlook is not hopeless. Determined officials in Washington, at the regional center near Denver, and at field offices are more numerous than ever and are patiently awaiting the day when the Taylor Act will be just a memory and they can function under a broader, less one-sided law. Whether they will move into AUMs reduction then remains a question. Under present circumstances they are banking all on rest–rotation and rehabilitative spending. Reductions, if any, are up to the judgment exercised by the permittee.

In a late 1975 news summary, the Washington-based Wildlife Management Institute reported that the bill for an organic BLM act to replace the Taylor Act had been "so polluted with concessions to livestock interests and other user groups that public interest has diminished. . . . The House Subcommittee [considering the bill], dominated by western congressmen, appears determined to let private rather than public interest dictate the measure's content."

Application to Interior's range lands of the National Environmental Policy Act [18] seems likely to be the tool that will in the end bring about stability for the permittee and restoration of forage and other values where needed. Under the NEPA an environmental impact statement (EIS) was put in final form by BLM late in 1974. It is possible that strict adherence to the promises in the EIS may complete the job that Rutledge, Forsling, Clawson, Stoddard, and unnamed others and their subordinates found impossible under the vigilant eyes of the livestock lobby and their elected friends on Capitol Hill.

Evaluation and Challenge

Too Early, Too Heavy,
Too Long

At Prineville, Oregon, in October 1974, a BLM official told [1] a group representing environmental organizations that "basically the problems we are faced with today result from historical situations: too early use, too heavy use, and too long use."

The assertion applies equally to both our major grazing land managing agencies—BLM in Interior and the Forest Service in Agriculture. I question, though, whether the three named symptoms belong entirely in a strictly historical context. These "toos"—early, heavy, and long—are not memories called up from a distant past but are presently widespread in the public land West. Here grazing begins before ground and forage are ready. There grasses, forbs, and shrubs are cropped by too many head of livestock. Yonder the animals are allowed to linger too long in the fall. Elsewhere all three occur. There is ample documentation; [2] the facts should be conclusive to anyone observing the situation realistically.

In significant ways the grazing prospects for our western public lands are not pleasing. The Forest Service has been in existence seventy years, since 1905. The Bureau of Land Management is younger, its predecessor agency having been created in 1934, but in all Interior has had forty years on the job. Isn't it reasonable to expect that by this time each would have the public properties it supervises in good order, with its various activities in smooth operation? Why, after all these years, cannot the administrators say that the ranges—renewable resources all—are being conserved in the best traditions of stewardship? Why is not forage, the primary marketable product of the western ranges, being produced at maximum potential, considering natural variations in character and growing conditions inherent in the numerous terrains and climates that prevail? Some clues may be found in a quick glance backward toward agency leadership and some of the factors that influenced their actions.

In the second part of this account the range record of the Forest Service was presented, along with burdens put upon it and the manner in which its leaders reacted to situations and circumstances. It was duly noted that its chief range public was also its principal adversary, protesting even temporary curtailment all the way. The leadership of its livestock-raising clientele was shortsighted; it had difficulty looking beyond the next annual sale of domestic animals fed in part on public forage. Now a feeling of misgiving lingers, of questioning whether the Forest Service has grown overly cumbersome through the years, so logy it has difficulty moving with dispatch to meet changing conditions and attitudes in what is really a dynamic area of administration. Beyond sluggishness, is there sufficient remaining will to move quickly and act firmly to correct demonstrated unsatisfactory range conditions and trends?

The third segment dealt in somewhat less detailed manner with the administration of the public domain under the Taylor Act, with all that law's built-in bias toward the livestock industry. It told of sporadic efforts by some administrators to upgrade range management despite obvious statutory handicaps.

As we look backward and seek to evaluate performance, by agency and administrators, it is important to remember that the leadership in each has had many areas of responsibility other than grazing—the Forest Service from its beginning, the Bureau of Land Management since it was created out of a merger between the former Grazing Service and the General Land Office in 1946. A 1975 reference [3] listed forty operating programs in six resource categories of Forest Service functions. Nevertheless, grazing still is important, particularly so with respect to BLM; even there it is diminishing to some extent, though not as much as appears true of the western national forests. It need not *continue* to do so, except for a comparatively short term, on either agency's millions of acres of range.

The driving urge in Pinchot's time was to get the new Forest Service staffed and functioning. His choice of a range manager was an official of the Arizona Woolgrowers Association. In an early chapter I suggested this was about as wise a selection as could have been made at the time, and I have not changed that opinion. Yet the question does rise of whether that manager, Albert Potter, might not have tilted toward his former business associates when close decisions had to be made. The record shows that, despite clear evidence of deteriorated ranges resulting from many years of unrestricted grazing in the nineteenth century—before that in the Southwest and California—the Service found it agreeable to increase the AUMs of allowed livestock use annually until after World War I ended.

Some of this came in the years under Pinchot's successor. Graves, like Pinchot, was mainly interested in forestry. It is to his credit that he initiated cutbacks in grazing after the disaster of the war years. All the liberties the livestock industry took in the boom-and-bust years of the 1870s and 1880s could not equal the havoc wrought on the ranges in that world war. It was devastating, and government was fully as responsible as industry. It insisted that ever more stock be crowded upon the allotments. The entire nation was swept up in patriotic fervor. We were Making the World Safe for Democracy. Never mind that the environment being depleted was all we had and must serve our needs for all time; that was subordinated to the short-term production of red meat, wool, hides, and tallow for which hungry allies and the defense establishment clamored.

"I well remember," Walt Dutton wrote [4] me, "when the long arm of the Washington office reached out to me in the hinterland and patted me on the back for having made a good showing in reporting room for more livestock on the Whitman forest."

Graves likely spent much time in the war years close to his Washington desk, and only became concerned enough to act when, after they ended, his field men sent in persuasive reports of damage wrought. The full extent was not recognized even then, it seems. Dutton said it was "much later" before many officials "realized the appalling damage" that wartime overstocking had brought about. The reduction program Graves initiated was just getting started when he retired in 1920.

Colonel Greeley, also primarily a timberman, maintained the pace of grazing cuts begun by Graves. Dutton called him "a gifted administrator" who "had a logical mind and doubtless was the most articulate chief of all." When Greeley, then, had the effrontery to believe that fees should be comparable to those permittees had to pay to rent private pasturage, he felt the heel of the cowboy's boot on his neck and the sheepherder's dog nipped at his heels. As Dutton put it, "he never got the support he needed from the White House and the Secretary's office." Administration superiors didn't interfere with reductions made in Greeley's regime, to try to bring use within grazing capacity, but deserted or overrode him on fees. That question had not been resolved when he left the Service and it fell to his successor, Stuart, to recede from the fair market value formula set forth in the Rachford study of the early 1920s and approve the market price formula preferred by the livestock leaders. Then drought and depression slowed down, and in some instances reversed, the reduction program. Stuart slacked off in other ways, too. He more or less let the several regions run their own show,[5] and discipline got so lax that when Stuart died in office FDR brought in Silcox from the outside—a previously undreamed of step—to tighten the organization.

Silcox could move to straighten out internal affairs, and did so, but had no influence on dry weather and economic doldrums. These led to continued pressure to allow excessive grazing, and Silcox was no match for the livestock lobby. As recounted earlier, he leaned so far toward industry wishes as to give orders at the start of the 1936 permit term that reductions in AUMs for any cause could not exceed 20 percent over the ten-year period, regardless of range condition or trend.

Clapp refused to step up national forest grazing as the economic tempo quickened in early World War II years. His firm order to his people in 1942 not to make the World War I mistake of excessive stocking was a fine demonstration of long-term regard for the future. He held his position against what must have been extreme pressure for permission to graze more and more domestic stock to help supply fighting troops and needy allies. Dutton believed his policies were too liberal, and cited a "secret, confidential letter to Regional Foresters and [experiment station] Directors instructing them personally to make sure the social outlook of new recruits was satisfactory before allowing them permanent appointment," as backing for his view. Could Dutton have misconstrued what was then a common effort by employers to assure that new employees had the correct patriotic attitude? Dutton's and Sandvig's views differed sharply on Clapp. When chief, Clapp did not reprimand Major Kelley and his helpers in Region 1 for reducing livestock use to a point within grazing capacity, war or no war and in spite of the Silcox promise at the start of the permit term. Sandvig, one of Kelley's helpers then, wrote [6] me that he believed Clapp had been the Service's "best leader . . . since Pinchot." Whichever of the two may be right, it is unfortunate for the ranges that aggressive action to reduce overuse during those critical years was spotty to nonexistent in other western regions; Region 1 stood out sharply then and, overall, is probably still in better shape than most others involved in this account.

The Watts regime began bravely in 1943, with high hopes, and ended nine years later in turmoil and unhappiness for service officials dedicated to principles of moderation in grazing use of national forest ranges. He did not abandon Clapp's position on conservative stocking in wartime, and as the 1946 permit term neared he issued directives to cut deeper, to the bone if necessary, in order to repair the lingering damage from earlier times and undo the harm the Silcox go-easy policy had brought about. He probably encouraged decisively the thinking that was translated later into the Anderson–Mansfield rehabilitative law, motivated in part by the promise of experimental work carried out in CCC days. He likely was spurred also by hope that, after passage of the law, actions under its authority would stop the complaining and pressuring being carried on by livestock spokesmen and others supporting them. The circumstances of his closing years, related in Part II, need no elaboration here.

I am convinced McArdle basically wanted to do what was best for the ranges but was handicapped politically. When he tried to speak out against the stockmen's authority grab bill, H. R. 4023, he was muzzled and handcuffed by Ezra Benson and Sherman Adams at the behest of Barrett and Company. Later, under the threat of head-hunting patronage devices, or perhaps because advisers convinced him later modifications of the legislation could be lived with, he came out in approval. Either way, he remained under administrative and congressional and industry pressure until the last of the bills of the sequence was killed in conference by adamant House members.

McArdle was by bent and experience a research specialist. He had less range background than Cliff, who then was assistant chief for Service functions that included grazing, and in general let Cliff handle such matters. In his regime range began to get increasing competition for front office attention. Recreation was ballooning in relative importance and in numbers of people to be accommodated. Timber management trended toward marketing ever more stumpage to help meet a rising demand for housing and other wood products.

These and many other forest activities were locked in place with passage of the Multiple Use and Sustained Yield Act of 1960, and McArdle probably was glad when he reached retirement age in 1962.

The Cliff concepts of range management—detailed, intricate, involving much paper work and avoiding cuts wherever possible—evolved in the Watts and McArdle years and reached today's complex level [7] in his own decade as chief. He had been a range man much of his career, and had a strong desire to see his own management ideas made official practice. By the time he became assistant chief he was in a strategic position for that purpose, for he could then give orders rather than merely make suggestions. Cliff had what Dutton called a "homey personality that stood him in good stead in dealing with committees of Congress or his own organization"—and with the lobbies of the various industries which, by the nature of the resources in his charge, he encountered in day-to-day activities and operations. My view is that no previous chief had the opportunity Ed Cliff enjoyed to exercise prolonged influence over national forest range use—ten years as assistant chief and another decade as chief forester.

A fundamental tenet of the Cliff formula was that through almost exclusive dependence on rehabilitative devices and techniques, soil erosion could in time be halted and forage production be increased to its natural peak. Best of all, it could be done that way without reducing the rate of grazing through mandatory downward adjustments. Cuts angered permittees and roused the industry lobby. Cliff wanted to get along with both. If permittees saw fit to quit their preferences, and their ranges or parts of them could then be put to other uses without industry protest, well and good; that would help speed the processes of recuperation. The records I have seen disclose no strong or widespread actions in the Cliff years to bring range use by livestock within grazing capacity, in which he differs little from most of his predecessors. Dutton commented that Cliff "had little to do with grazing policy except to maintain the status quo" while he was chief. True enough; the policies had been set in the late Watts years and in the McArdle era, when Cliff sat at their right hands. Dutton also notes that in Cliff's regime "there was a period of relative calm in relations between stockmen and the Forest Service." On the other side, forest officers who opposed Cliff policies feel—or felt, as this refers also to men now dead—quite differently about him. Nevertheless, Ed Cliff retired in 1972 proud of his range record, and took with him the Agriculture Department's highest citation for meritorious service.

My basic conclusion, after a good many years of observation and study, is that when the Service did try to impose a firm will upon the industry its successes were few and short lived; most often it was outsmarted, adroitly countered, bulldozed—or cajoled—into positions and policies more to the livestock leadership's liking. In time it tired and sought methods of administration that would not bring recrimination, or was led by officials who agreed with industry points of view.

The Service's reluctance to act promptly and straightforwardly has been especially noteworthy in the twin matters of raising fees to fair market value of the forage consumed, and of reducing AUMs of use to safe grazing levels. On fees the agencies are sometimes loitering on the way but slowly approaching something that resembles fair market value. On grazing levels, side effects more than imposed official will have brought many of the reductions that have been made in the last twenty years or so. Of late, Forest Service reasons for such mandatory reductions as have taken place have included the rise of recreation and conversion to its uses of what once was grazing land, the need for more forage to feed standing big game herds, and the reversion to solid timber stands of what used to be lightly wooded range.

Over on the other side of Washington, in Interior's BLM, the story differs substantially but parallels that of the Forest Service in two important respects. The livestock industry rides herd on the agency more than vice versa, and the three basic elements of too early, too heavy, and too long persist. Though Congress had before it the latest of the several bills [8] for an organic law that have been introduced in recent years, BLM in the spring of 1976 was still saddled with the one-sided Taylor Act, little changed from its 1934 form. The new legislation, if not weakened prior to passage, should give the agency ample power to act in the public interest, and there have been symptoms in recent times that indicate BLM could emerge as a strong bureau. A principal weakness, as I see it, is that it is committed, much like the Forest Service, to courses that seek to avoid cuts in livestock numbers or time at all costs and put virtually the entire burden of correcting bad range situations on the taxpayer-at-large.

In retrospect, Carpenter shows up as a stockman's administrator, with few qualifications for firm direction of a major range managing agency. Rutledge might have put Taylor land under more positive control if his health had held up. He possessed administrative ability, though he was hampered by personnel problems and departmental policies, and in time likely could have brought about substantial increases in fees as well as practical range management methods. It didn't happen. World War II intervened, and he went out for health reasons before it ended.

Forsling's ideas were sound, as I read them. His speed on the imposition of higher fees was bad, though excusable in view of the swift advance of allied forces across Europe and in the Pacific Theater. When he made his approach there was a growing belief the war would soon be over. Even so, he might have survived to be remembered for significant achievement if congressional pressures had lessened and if Ickes had not resigned as Secretary of the Interior at a critical time. He was hampered throughout his brief tenure by the heavy-handed inquisitions of Pat McCarran, his Nevada nemesis.

Clawson's regime was marked by progress despite the failure of the management effort typified by *Rebuilding the Federal Range.* He contrived to get a small fee increase and made some policy changes. He was not ousted by recalcitrant livestock leaders, but was a victim of the political patronage system, and has had a secure place in later years on the staff of Resources For the Future, Inc. There his writings related to public lands and their management have given him standing as a senior economic specialist in that field.

Stoddard leaned strongly toward the Forest Service brand of agency structure and operations, and in his three years as director brought about a number of policy innovations. Key positions held by officials he brought into the bureau or elevated to decision framing rank are evidence of the lasting nature of his influence. His successors have retained a number of policies he initiated. Such improvements as were achieved in BLM attempts to secure a firmer control over what happened to its ranges in the Stoddard regime were more signicant by reason of the statutory handicaps under which they were brought about than by the magnitude of their scope.

The Classification and Multiple Use law that Stoddard supported to enactment in 1964 has given BLM some management leverage, and I gained the impression after talking with BLM officials in Washington and at its chief regional headquarters at Denver that they were pleased with progress made. Some of this was in

Public domain in California before off-road vehicle use became popular, year not given. *BLM photo*

Same public domain area, showing scars of heavy use by motorbikes and other off-road vehicles, 1974. *BLM photo*

the wildlife, recreation, and watershed improvement aspects of multiple-use administration. Agency claims of progress there were then downgraded by the 1974 report of a Nevada study team, which disclosed—to official embarrassment—that the livestock interest, abetted by friendly or complacent officialdom, was still dominant. The outcome may prove beneficial, despite some waffling in Washington. Through chance the Nevada report came to the personal attention of Interior Secretary Rogers C. B. Morton, who peremptorily demanded corrective action. Directives ordered by Morton were issued in a revised version of the report, in which comments that could be considered critical of either the livestock industry or BLM officials were carefully omitted.

The issuance of an environmental impact statement on grazing BLM ranges was recounted in the previous chapter. Taking similar action by the Forest Service was delayed and complicated by the enactment of the Forest and Rangeland Renewable Resources Planning Law of 1974, but something was produced in the late summer of 1975. The 1974 law instructed the Service to apprise Congress of inventory, program planning, and resulting action at stated intervals. The first report was due at the end of 1975. The Service decided to give Congress and the public a double order of information. It would meet the stipulations in the 1974 law and combine with its initial report environmental impact statements on all the six major divisions of service activity—outdoor recreation and wilderness, wildlife and fish habitat, range, timber, land and water, and human and community development—which had evolved from the programs that prevailed under the Multiple Use and Sustained Yield Act of 1964.

As the service acknowledged in its executive *Summary,* its report documents titled *Assessment* and *Program* [9] were both "voluminous" and "quite technical and complex." When the three documents were received I could take time to review only the range aspects, which I found lacking in major respects. They contained little or nothing to indicate that the Service could or was inclined to tighten its belt and seek to operate with greater public benefits on its present sizable resources of men and money. Oh, no! If there was to be improvement, it could come only at huge dollar expense and with vastly increased personnel numbers. The alternative was range disaster, according to the Service.

In later years health of range has become somewhat remote from the size of the fee charged for grazing. I consider this related closely to the practice of putting more of the financial burden of

rehabilitative work on the general taxpayers, less on the range permittee. Knowledgeable former officials have told [10] me more than
once that fees have been of minor importance in dealings and relationships between the Forest Service and the users of its ranges.
The record seems to differ from these views, though at least one of
my informants emphasized somewhat that he referred to the importance of fee changes to the activities of the ranger force rather
than any headquarters group. Where Taylor land grazing is concerned, fees unquestionably have been major items of dispute. The
record indicates that in time both agencies became sensitive on the
subject, reluctant to take corrective steps.

In 1951 Congress directed [11] all federal agencies to prescribe
fair and equitable fees for goods or services furnished. Neither agency
took action then, presumably arguing that their fees met those cri-
teria. In 1958 the Comptroller General recommended [12] that fair
compensation be obtained for use of federal lands, and that there
be more consistency in grazing fees charged by the administering
agencies. His report asked for a joint study by the agencies to arrive
at a uniform fee system. A preliminary outline for a study was developed [13] in July 1960, but no further steps were taken as the Bureau
of the Budget began a *Natural Resources User Charges Study*, which
was issued in 1964 as a directive that included guidelines to be followed. Thereafter an interdepartmental grazing fee group began a
definitive investigation that, three years later, suggested a fair market value for federal forage was $1.23 per AUM. The full amount
should not be charged at once, though, but on a step-by-step basis
over a period of years. The first annual increment was to have been
imposed for 1968, but the livestock industry protested. The Public
Land Law Review Commission was well along with its work and
should report not later than June 30, 1970. That would only be a
couple more years, so why not wait to see what PLLRC might have
to say on the subject? The conservation community protested routinely, and the agencies routinely acceded to the livestock industry's
demand for more delay.

The first increase under the new formula actually was applied
for the 1971 grazing season, and step rises were imposed in each of
the next three years. In 1975, though, the industry used the combination of inflation and recession as leverage and, apparently
without much difficulty, secured the acquiescence of both the Forest
Service and the Bureau of Land Management to at least a one-year
moratorium. I have been informed [14] that this does not mean fair

market value, as described, and will not be achieved by the target year of 1980—only that the 1975 increment was delayed, to be applied at an unspecified later date.

Two questions have been left dangling. One is whether the price agreed upon, after exhaustive discussions with industry spokesmen, actually amounts to the fair market value of the forage being consumed on federal land. A definition is called for, and the Forest Service supplied one: [15] It is "the amount the prospective user of a product is willing to pay for that product—in this case the value of the use of the public grazing resource to the livestock owner." That seems clear enough, though it smacks somewhat of the "all the traffic will bear" thought that was berated in congressional inquiries of the 1940s; so the Service went further. It said adjustment should be made "for differences in the cost of services provided on private lands by the landowners, but not provided on public lands." Then the method used to reach a correct fee, after adjustment, was "to determine the total cost of operation to the user on private leased grazing land . . . and to subtract from this . . . the total non-fee cost of operation to the user on public rangelands."

Was the $1.23 arrived at under this formula truly fair market value of national forest and Taylor Act grazing land? In 1974 the cost of private range rental in Colorado averaged [16] $5.51 per month per cow. The permittee in 1975 would have paid $1.60 for grazing national forest land, which would have been the annual increment plus a figure added to compensate for inflation—if there had been no moratorium. Up to now the leading conservation organizations have not complained that the fees are unduly low.

The second question: Why did it take so long for the two agencies to bring corrective change to the grazing fee system? If it is considered that the recommendation of the Comptroller General had validity and should have been followed forthwith, bringing about the change consumed about twelve years. However, 1964 seems a more realistic year to choose for calculations, and that means a seven-year time lapse before application of the new fees. My conclusion is that the agencies continued to be reluctant to tackle the industry they were supposed to supervise, and procrastinated somewhat. It is ruefully recognized that it was no easy thing for them to counter all the objections that can be produced by the livestock lobby. The industry went so far as to challenge the new system in court, where it was beaten.[17]

Whether the issue be fees paid for goods and services, or reductions in use consistent with range condition and trend, the leaders of that part of the livestock industry that operates on western public lands have repeatedly contested affirmative action by the agencies. Truly fair market value for forage is still a good many years ahead. So is the achievement of range quality that approaches natural potential.

The Forest Service is entangled in a complicated system of range management that entails large expenditures of appropriated funds for rehabilitative measures, with few grazing concessions by permittees. AUM cuts for protection are rare. BLM is wedded to the similarly complex allotment management plan technique in which rest–rotation, usually over a five-year cycle (which the Forest Service also uses), is a prime factor. AUM reductions are minimal, regardless of range condition and trend. In a sample plan studied by the Prineville visitors referred to at the start of this chapter,[18] it was found that a permittee who had an allowable of 11,000 AUMs of grazing would use 46 percent of the total between April 1 and May 31 when, the report said,[19] "grasslands are most vulnerable to damage." The report expressed opinion that the heaviest grazing should not occur during "the most critical period of the grazing season" without reference to range readiness.

As far back as 1949 a treatise[20] on vegetation management contained the following statement:

"From the very nature of [vegetative] climax and succession, development is immediately resumed *when the disturbing cause ceases*, and in this fact lies the basic principle of all restoration or rehabilitation" (italics added).

Perhaps it is indicative of the dilemma of the two agencies as well as the public owners of the lands that authorities on both sides of the question of how best to manage ranges quote the above passage to support their views. Hormay[21] repeats it in his prescription of rest–rotation as a cure for western ranges. Sandvig[22] does so in discussion of the Prineville findings. He emphasizes that the cow is the "disturbing cause" of poor range and, if climax vegetation is a logical goal, the cow should be removed or allowed to graze only in moderate numbers that do not inhibit desired succession, until full vigor returns.

In fairness to BLM, it must be reminded once more that for at least the last forty years a powerful reason for being less than a firm general manager has been the prefabricated shortcomings of the Taylor Act. The Forest Service has no such reason; its statutory base is ample for whatever degree of firmness it chooses to employ. Until the one is given new power and exercises it, and until the other changes its practices, it appears that western public ranges will continue to suffer the ills of "too early use, too heavy use, and too long use."

Less Growl
Than Whimper

Many chapters ago this narrative began with a description of a meeting in Salt Lake City where a bold, aggressive movement to try to wrest the choicest remaining public lands from the public and put them in selected private hands was formalized and set on its course. Disparate forces in the conservation movement rose in outrage and the Great Land Grab came to a swift end.

It was followed by the authority grab against the Forest Service, which succeeded. The Service acceded to livestock industry wishes on nearly all major issues. And despite increasing expenditures that pacify and placate, ranges in many areas remain underproductive in relation to potential.

The Bureau of Land Management, as Clawson was quoted previously as saying, has in some ways been more innovative than the Forest Service, but it has at no point truly been out from under the western livestock industry's thumb. One would think the industry would be content with its gains in influence, with its demonstrated power to move the agencies in whatever direction it seems to want to go, but that has not been so. That old yearnings seldom die completely but still have some life was demonstrated in the late 1960s when the Public Land Law Review Commission held public meetings in the West and in Washington.

Transcripts of what took place at those meetings were read at its offices while the PLLRC was still conducting later stages of its study, and the following are excerpts from and condensations of testimony presented at Salt Lake City on June 7 and 8, 1966, at

Albuquerque on November 10 and 11, 1966, at Billings on July 13 and 14, 1967, and at Washington on January 11 and 12, 1968: [1]

National Wool Growers Association [whose spokesman said at the outset that the National Association of Manufacturers had surrendered some of its time to him]: We believe the majority of the public lands of the United States would be much more productive and beneficial to the nation if they were put in private ownership or under private management.

American National Cattlemen's Association: Fundamental to the recommendations in this summary is that much more federal land ultimately should be placed on the tax rolls under a new set of land laws and policies. [The spokesman went on to say that people and governments at state and local levels should have the power to decide when, how, and under what conditions the public lands should be retained or disposed of.]

American Farm Bureau Federation: We believe there is at this time federal land which should move into private ownership. [The spokesman said he wanted Congress to declare private ownership of land to be the basic policy of the United States, and then make lands "suitable" for private ownership available for "disposal".]

Chamber of Commerce of the United States of America: The National Chamber does encourage the orderly disposal of those public lands not reserved and not needed for a particular government purpose.

Wyoming Stock Growers Association: We concur in the statement of the American National Cattlemen's Association.

New Mexico Cattle Growers Association: Generally speaking, nations have never successfully managed and worked their resources as nations. Only has this been done by individuals within nations. Private ownership or security of expectation in the form of certain tenure is the incentive and spur for development. . . . Disposal . . . should take the form of whatever the individual wants, needs, and is willing to pay for. [The spokesman suggested the long obsolete Homestead Law as a guide for fixing terms of disposal, including price.]

Arizona Cattle Growers Association [The spokesman said his group wanted greater "security of tenure" and advisory boards with "real" power to govern land management policies of federal agencies.]

Montana Stock Growers Association [The spokesman favored disposition of public lands to private owners, but did not favor open competitive bidding for the lands to be disposed of.]

Former President, American National Livestock (Cattlemen's) Association: I agree heartily [with previous statements presented at the same meeting favoring "disposal" and complaining of "lack of security of tenure"].

Former Chairman, 1946–47 Joint Livestock Committee on Public Lands: I agree in the main with the previous speakers.

Former Member, Joint Livestock Committee of 1946–47 [He favored disposal, with the price to be paid by rancher-permittees for the land to be based only on its productivity of forage for grazing.]

New Mexico Farm Bureau Federation: Federal lands suitable for private ownership should be made available for disposal.

Southeast New Mexico Grazing Association [The spokesman said he wanted "equitable disposition of all classes of public lands", with grazing permittees to have a preferential right to buy, paying 10 per cent of the cost down and the remainder over 20 years with carrying charges of 3½ per cent.]

Nevada Taxpayers Association . . . cession of all public lands and their resources, except national parks and Indian Reservations, by the federal government to the states in which they are situated.

Some of my colleagues [2] in the conservation movement were alarmed by such statements. Clawson was less impressed. He told [3] me he believed that except for minor adjustments in ownership patterns that really should be made, the federal estate would remain intact. He said there are and always will be special interest groups, including recreationists and wildlife enthusiasts, who will want many kinds of favors, and they will keep on trying to get them. Much of his optimism, however, appeared to me to rest on the extent to which the guardians of the public estate, in and out of government, keep alert and stand ready to take needed defensive steps.

The PLLRC did exercise restraint in the matter of "disposal" of federal lands when it released its report in 1970. It suggested [4] that where a use of an area was "dominant," that use should be favored above others, but it refrained from any semblance of advocating a give-away or another land grab.

Now, close to thirty years after the Salt Lake City meeting at which the "Joint National Livestock Committee to Grab Public Lands" was formed, the yearning for a giant give-away appears to linger in a few places, but what once sounded like an overpowering growl now seems little more than a whimper. The nation's western public lands seem safely national. It remains to be seen, however, when or whether the full productivity of which they are capable will be achieved.

Notes

CHAPTER 1

1. *Denver Post*, February 2, 1947, guest article by J. Elmer Brock.
2. *Salt Lake City Tribune*, August 16–18, 1947.
3. Under S. Res. 241, 76th Congress, extended by S. Res. 139, 79th.
4. Act of June 28, 1934, 48 Stat. 1269, as amended (Taylor Grazing Act).
5. Reorganization Order No. 3, Truman Administration, 1946.
6. Testimony and other documentation appear at various places in later chapters.
7. Excerpts from the *Congressional Directory* furnished by the late Congressman John P. Saylor of Pennsylvania, show public land committee members of the Senate and House from east of the 100th meridian outnumbered those from west of that line until 1890, after which the numbers were reversed. By 1970 the figures were: one from the East and seventeen from the West in the Senate and twelve from the East and twenty-three from the West on the House side.
8. 30 Stat. 34.
9. See Arthur H. Carhart files, Conservation Center, Denver Public Library, and Charles C. Moore Papers, Western History Department, Denver Public Library, hereafter referred to as AHC/DPL and CCM/DPL respectively.
10. Taylor Grazing Act, Section 1.
11. Consult, for example, *Outdoor America,* Journal of the Izaak Walton League of America, in the decade of the 1930s, and note the paucity of references to the public land West other than as to fishing and hunting resources.
12. Brock in *Denver Post,* February 2, 1947.
13. This is a personal conclusion, bolstered by confirming comment

from Marion Clawson, *Resources for the Future* (Washington, D. C.), as used by me in an article titled "The Plot to Steal the West," in *Field & Stream*, Vol. LXXIV, No. 7, October 1968, p. 14.

14. See, for example, Gifford Pinchot, *Breaking New Ground* (New York: Harcourt, Brace & Co., 1947); Arthur H. Carhart, *Timber in Your Life* (Philadelphia: J. B. Lippincott Co., 1955); and official records of the General Land Office, Department of the Interior, from about 1870 forward, as well as most historical works dealing with the subject.

15. Testimony of opponents of H. R. 1330 in Hearings report on that bill titled *To Abolish the Jackson Hole National Monument, Wyo.*, Subcommittee on Public Lands of the House, Committee Hearing No. 20, Washington, D. C., April 14–18, 1947, and AHC/DPL and CCM/DPL.

16. CCM/DPL and AHC/DPL; also William Voigt, Jr., "An Authority Grab?" in *Outdoor America* (hereafter referred to as *OA*), Vol. 15, No. 2, February 1950.

CHAPTER 2

1. Many historians and other authors have written of the American era of acquisition and dispersal of public domain. An excellent account is found in Marion Clawson, *Uncle Sam's Acres* (New York: Dodd, Mead & Co., 1951), Chapters 2 and 3.

2. Bernard DeVoto, *Beyond the Wide Missouri* (Boston: Houghton Mifflin Co., 1947), p. 5 and elsewhere.

3. Ibid, p. 2. I have drawn freely on DeVoto's excellent account, as well as sporadically from other sources, for basic information in this chapter.

4. Ibid., p. 51.

5. Ibid., p. 44ff.

6. Ernest Staples Osgood, *Day of the Cattleman* (Minneapolis: University of Minnesota Press, 1929, 1954).

7. Charles Wayland Towne and Edward Norris Wentworth, *Shepherd's Empire* (Norman, Okla.: University of Oklahoma Press, 1945); see also their *Cattle Men* (Norman, Okla.: University of Oklahoma Press, 1955).

8. DeVoto, *Wide Missouri*, p. 351.

9. 12 Stat. 392.

CHAPTER 3

1. Daniel J. Boorstin, *The Americans: The National Experience* (New York: Vintage Books, 1965), p. 252.

2. Osgood, *Cattleman*.

3. John Clay, *My Life on the Range* (Norman, Okla.: University of Oklahoma Press, 1962 ed.), p. 7ff.

4. A. W. Sampson, *Range Management: Principles and Practices* (New York: John Wiley & Sons, Inc., 1952), p. 116.

5. Joseph Nimmo, Jr., *The Internal Commerce of the United States.* House Executive Document 7, Part 2, 48th Congress, 2nd Session, Treasury Department Report, p. 122.

6. John Wesley Powell, *Report on the Lands of the Arid Region of the United States* (Washington, 1878; Cambridge, Mass.: Harvard University Press, 1962), p. 30.

7. Nimmo, in *Internal Commerce,* tells of a government trader of 1869 who, caught by a blizzard on the plains, camped for the winter, loosing his stock in the belief that they would starve, only to find them fat and healthy the next spring.

8. Barbed wire was invented by J. P. Glidden in DeKalb, Illinois. Osgood, *Cattleman,* says that 40,000 tons were manufactured annually by 1880, three times as much in 1890.

9. Pinchot, *Breaking New Ground,* p. 23; also Chapter 12, p. 79ff.

10. Commission to Codify the Land Laws, of which Major Powell was a member, p. 297.

11. Among the more important of the several enacted were the 160-acre Homestead Act of 1862; the 320-acre Homestead Act, 34 Stat. 531; the Forest Homestead Act, 37 Stat. Pt. 1, 123; and the Stock Raising Homestead Act, 39 Stat. 862.

12. Osgood, *Cattleman,* p. 89.

13. Ibid.

14. Nimmo, *Internal Commerce,* p. 114.

15. Clay, *Life on the Range,* p. 200ff.

16. Osgood, *Cattleman,* p. 104ff.

17. Ibid., Chapter V, p. 114ff; Louis Pelzer, *The Cattleman's Frontier* (Glendale, Calif.: Arthur H. Clark Co., 1936), p. 73ff.

18. Towne and Wentworth, *Shepherd's Empire,* p. 64ff. See also *The Western Range,* Senate Document 199, 74th Congress, 2nd Session, p. 125ff.

19. S. Doc. 199, ibid., p. 122.

20. Clay, *Life on the Range* p. 208ff.

21. S. Doc. 199, p. 124ff.

22. Hearings, Subcommittee of the Senate Committee on Public Lands and Surveys pursuant to S. Res. 241, Ely, Nevada, June 25, 1941 (hereafter referred to as McCarran), pp. 146–148.

CHAPTER 4

1. Pinchot, *Breaking New Ground,* pp. 26 and 84.

2. Aldo Leopold, *A Sand County Almanac* (New York: Oxford University Press, 1966), p. 217ff.

3. Powell, *Report on Arid Region,* p. 37ff.

4. Personal communication. (Hereafter cited as WV/DPL, lodged in the Conservation Center, Denver Public Library.)

5. Powell, *Report on Arid Region,* p. 121.

6. 26 Stat. 1103; also see Benjamin Horace Hibbard, *A History of Public Land Policies* (New York: The Macmillan Co., 1924; Madison, Wisc.: 1965), p. 530.

7. Richard G. Lillard, *The Great Forest* (New York: Alfred A. Knopf, 1947), p. 266.

8. Pinchot, *Breaking New Ground*, Part III, "Public Awakening," and Part IV, "The President Makes the Issue," have been drawn on freely for factual material in this and succeeding passages.

9. Ibid., p. 111.

10. Ibid., p. 117.

11. Ibid., p. 123.

12. Ibid., pp. 235–236.

13. 33 Stat. 628.

CHAPTER 5

1. Pinchot, *Breaking New Ground*, pp. 181–182.

2. Ibid., pp. 161–162.

3. Operable from 1966 through 1970 under P. L. 88-606.

4. Lillard, *Great Forest*, pp. 265–266.

5. Act of June 28, 1934, 48 Stat. 1269.

6. Pinchot, *Breaking New Ground*, p. 264.

7. McCarran, and Barrett hearings pursuant to H. Res. 93, 1947–1948.

8. Under Memorandum G426, issued by Chief Forester Richard A. McArdle.

9. Pinchot, *Breaking New Ground*, p. 270.

10. Ibid., pp. 270–272.

11. S. T. Dana, *Forest and Range Policy* (New York: McGraw-Hill, Inc., 1956), p. 145ff.

12. Pinchot, *Breaking New Ground*, p. 300.

13. Dana, *Forest and Range*, p. 144; also Jenks Cameron, *Development of Governmental Forest Control* (Baltimore: The Johns Hopkins University Press, 1928), p. 242ff.

14. Cameron, *Forest Control*, p. 332ff.

15. U.S. *v.* Grimaud *et al.*, 220 U.S. 506, and U.S. *v.* Light, 220 U.S. 523. Grimaud was a California case, Light occurred in Colorado.

16. Pinchot, *Breaking New Ground*, p. 264ff.

17. WV/DPL.

18. For an exhaustive study of the ranger, his problems and attitudes, see Herbert Kaufman, *The Forest Ranger* (Baltimore: The Johns Hopkins University Press, for Resources for the Future, Inc., Washington, 1960); also WV/DPL, especially a tape recording from E. D. Sandvig to WV, transcribed September 18, 1972.

19. Pinchot, *Breaking New Ground*, contains a detailed account, p. 395ff.

20. E. D. Sandvig and Walt L. Dutton, in WV/DPL.

21. An animal unit month is defined as the forage required to sustain one animal unit for one month; an animal unit means a cow plus unweaned calf, or five ewes with their suckling lambs.

22. Clawson, *Uncle Sam's Acres*, p. 108.

23. 36 Stat. 961–963.

24. 50 Stat. 525.

25. WV/DPL, especially correspondence with Frank J. Smith, 1971–1972.

26. See Rachford Report in Senate Calendar No. 519, Report 517, 69th Congress, 2nd Session, March 27, 1926, *Grazing on Public Lands and National Forests*, p. 17ff; also see report of joint study of fees by the Forest Service and the Bureau of Land Management pursuant to an instruction from the Bureau of the Budget in 1964.

CHAPTER 6

1. *Hearings, on National Forests and Public Domain*, by a subcommittee of the Senate Committee on Public Lands and Surveys, 69th, 1st, pursuant to S. Res. 347.

2. W. L. Dutton, "History of Forest Service Grazing Fees," *Journal of Range Management*, Vol. 6, No. 6, November 1953, pp. 393–398 (reprint). Additional information was given me orally by Dutton in 1972–1973, and in taped and written communications now part of WV/DPL.

3. "Range Appraisal Report" by the Rachford study team was put in the Stanfield Subcommittee hearings record, p. 17ff, and has been drawn on freely for narrative purposes.

4. Dana, *Forest and Range*, p. 230.

5. Stanfield *hearings, National Forests*, p. 9ff.

6. Ibid., p. 853ff.

7. Ibid., p. 898ff.

8. Ibid., p. 907ff.

9. Ibid., p. 1201ff.

10. Ibid., p. 1223ff.

11. Ibid., p. 1315ff.

12. Report No. 517, 69th, 2nd, March 27, 1926, *Grazing on Public Lands and National Forests*.

13. Dutton, "Grazing Fees," p. 395.

14. Letter report, Dan D. Casement to Agriculture Secretary William Jardine, June 30, 1926; also Dutton, "Grazing Fees," p. 395.

15. Memorandum G436, April, 1953.

16. Dutton, "Grazing Fees," p. 396.

17. Ibid.

18. Act of June 28, 1934, 48 Stat. 1269.

19. Quotations are from letter of transmittal of what became S. D.

199, from Henry A. Wallace, Secretary of Agriculture, to the chairman of
the Senate Committee on Agriculture and Forestry, April 29, 1936.
   20. S. D. 199, p. 467ff.
   21. S. D. 199, Preface, pp. vii–viii.
   22. Ibid., p. vii.
   23. Ibid., p. 48
   24. Annual Report of the Chief, U. S. Forest Service, 1947, p. 10.
   25. S. D. 199, p. 28ff.

CHAPTER 7

   1. A. W. McMahon and J. D. Millet, *Federal Administrators* (New
York: Columbia University Press, 1939), 346–347.
   2. Annual Report of the Chief, U. S. Forest Service, 1936, pp. 27–28.
   3. Ibid., 1927, p. 12.
   4. S. 1152 of 1943, by McCarran.
   5. Circular letter G82, April 2, 1942, Clapp to regional foresters and
directors, western regions and stations.
   6. McCarran, supra.
   7. USFS Annual Report, 1943, p. 25.
   8. Ibid., 1944, p. 14ff.
   9. Ibid., 1945, p. 2ff.
   10. Ibid., p. 21.
   11. Ibid., p. 23.
   12. McCarran, p. 3458 and 3661ff.
   13. Ibid., p. 3997ff.
   14. Ibid., p. 4603.
   15. Ibid., p. 5677ff.
   16. Ibid. p. 5692ff.
   17. USFS Annual Report, 1946, p. 25ff.
   18. Ibid., p. 26.

CHAPTER 8

   1. *Denver Post*, September 11, 1947.
   2. Reorganization Plan No. 3, 1946.
   3. Presidential Proclamation 2578, March 15, 1943.
   4. These were among facts adduced at hearings on Barrett's bill April
14–18, 1947, at Washington.
   5. *Cf.* AHC/DPL and WV/DPL, from which this outline was derived.
   6. USFS Annual Report, 1945, p. 21.
   7. This and following passages in this chapter based on personal participation and communications with principals; see WV/DPL, E. D. Sandvig
Papers (EDS/DPL), AHC/DPL, and Charles C. Moore Papers (CCM/DPL).

8. WV/DPL.

9. Ibid.

10. The first annual meeting of the NRCA was held in Mansfield, Ohio, on September 15–16, 1947. It was viable and growing in 1975.

11. From Sandvig's report to Regional Forester, R2, EDS/DPL.

12. *Cf*. Barrett, at Salt Lake City September 8, 1947, pp. 75, 79, 111, 115, 157, 176, and others.

13. Ibid., Rawlins, p. 208ff; see CCM/DPL for text of statement.

14. Passages of narrative relating to specific hearings are from the official record; see note 12 above.

15. See also Chapter 1.

16. EDS/DPL, AHC/DPL, and WV/DPL.

17. AHC/DPL and WV/DPL, ibid.

18. Transactions, North American Wildlife Conference, San Antonio, 1947.

19. The reference was to an article and an "Easy Chair" column by Bernard A. DeVoto in *Harper's Magazine* for January, 1947.

20. *Cf*. Pinchot, *Breaking New Ground*.

CHAPTER 9

1. Leopold, *Sand County Almanac*, p. 217ff.

2. *OA*, Vol. 13, No. 5, May–June 1948, p. 22.

3. McCarran, p. 305.

4. Ibid., p. 339ff.

5. Ibid., p. 5679ff.

6. *OA*, Vol. 10, No. 4, July–August 1945, p. 16.

7. Ibid., Vol. 10, No. 5, September and October, 1945, p. 3.

8. Ibid., Vol. 11, No. 3, March–April 1946, p. 51.

9. WV/DPL.

10. Some of DeVoto's activities were familiar to me from firsthand knowledge; their scope is admirably recounted in Wallace Stegner, *The Uneasy Chair* (Garden City, N. Y.: Doubleday & Company, Inc., 1974), especially p. 287ff.

11. WV/DPL and AHC/DPL.

12. Issues of July 26 and August 9, 1947.

13. AHC/DPL.

14. *OA*, Vol. 12, No. 5, April, 1947, p. 7.

15. Stegner, *Uneasy Chair*, p. 330.

16. WV/DPL and AHC/DPL.

17. National Archives, Bureau of the Budget files, 1953, re H. R. 4023.

18. Philip O. Voss, *Politics and Grass* (Seattle: University of Washington Press, 1960), p. 138; Louise Peffer, in *The Closing of the Public Domain* (Stanford, Calif.: Stanford University Press, 1951), p. 284, was more

generous, but she attributed most of the Izaak Walton League's opposition
to the land grab to fear of loss of big-game hunting lands, which was but a
fraction of the whole.

CHAPTER 10

    1. Taped conversation, now in WV/DPL.
    2. WV/DPL.
    3. Barrett, H. Res. 93.
    4. Ibid., p. 1ff.
    5. Ibid., p. 6ff.
    6. Ibid., p. 13.
    7. Ibid., p. 14ff.
    8. Ibid., p. 22.
    9. Ibid., p. 40ff.
    10. Ibid., p. 34ff.
    11. Ibid., p. 38.
    12. Ibid., p. 40ff.
    13. Ibid., p. 53.
    14. April, 1947, issue.
    15. AHC/DPL and WV/DPL.
    16. Barrett, Grand Junction, p. 41ff.
    17. AHC/DPL.
    18. Barrett, Billings, p. 172ff.
    19. Barrett, Glasgow, p. 5ff.
    20. S. 1945.
    21. Barrett, Billings, p. 144ff.
    22. AHC/DPL and CCM/DPL.
    23. Barrett, Billings, p. 69.
    24. Ibid., p. 72.
    25. Barrett, Grand Junction, p. 100ff, among others.
    26. Ibid., p. 115.
    27. See taped interview, WV with Lloyd Swift, retired chief of wildlife
management, USFS, 1972, in WV/DPL.
    28. Barrett, San Francisco, p. 65ff.
    29. Barrett, Ely, p. 3ff.
    30. AHC/DPL and EDS/DPL.

CHAPTER 11

    1. Barrett, Rawlins, p. 5.
    2. Ibid., p. 7ff.
    3. Ibid., p. 20.
    4. Ibid., p. 22.
    5. WV/DPL and AHC/DPL.

6. Its title was *Who Owns Our Public Lands?*
7. Barrett, Rawlins, pp. 23 and 25.
8. Ibid., p. 66ff.
9. Ibid., p. 26ff.
10. Ibid., p. 46ff.
11. Ibid., pp. 58–62.
12. Ibid., p. 140ff.
13. Ibid., p. 247ff.
14. WV/DPL.
15. Barrett, Rawlins, p. 105ff.
16. Ibid., p. 135ff.
17. Ibid., p. 208ff.
18. CCM/DPL.
19. Barrett, Grand Junction, p. 78.
20. Ibid., p. 96ff.
21. Ibid., p. 166ff.
22. Ibid., p. 115ff.

Chapter 12

1. January, 1947, issue.
2. Barrett, Salt Lake City, p. 19ff.
3. Ibid., p. 93ff.
4. See *OA*, especially issues reporting on convention resolutions, from about 1945 through 1950.
5. USFS Annual Report, 1945, p. 23.
6. Anderson–Mansfield Act, 63 Stat. 762.
7. Telephone discussion with Dutton May 1, 1974; notes in WV/DPL.
8. USFS Annual Report, 1945.
9. Ibid., 1946, p. 25.
10. Ibid., 1947, p. 47.
11. WV/DPL.
12. USFS Annual Report, 1948, p. 7ff.
13. Ibid., 1949, p. 37.
14. S. J. Res. 53, 81st, 1st.
15. The difference between the four million acres mentioned in the bill and 26 million acres referred to in the 1946 Chief's Report may not be as great a discrepancy as appears on the surface, due to in-service definitions of such terms as "damaged," "harmed," "deteriorated," and "depleted." Range was considered "depleted" only when it was damaged almost to the point of no return. Too, probably neither Anderson nor the Service cared to publicize an excessively large acreage in the bill. Other factors included the raw truth that some forest ranges never had been productive and others were in terrain that made rehabilitation impractical.

16. *OA*, Vol. 15, No. 2, February, 1950, p. 6.
17. 64 Stat. 82–88.
18. House Report 733, 81st, 1st, Committee on Agriculture, on S. J. Res. 53.
19. See taped interview with Charles F. Brannan in July 1972, in WV/DPL; also Dutton file in WV/DPL, concerning letter preparation.
20. *Congressional Record*, April 11, 1949, pp. 4238–4239.
21. William Voigt, Jr., *The Susquehanna Compact: Guardian of the River's Future* (New Brunswick, N. J.: Rutgers University Press, 1972), Chapter 2, p. 11ff.

CHAPTER 13

1. McCarran, p. 5116ff.
2. EDS/DPL, with copy in WV/DPL.
3. Charles C. Niehuis, "Lee Kirby, Lone Ranger," Arizona *Sportsman*, August, 1951, p. 15.
4. Barrett, Grand Junction, p. 100ff.
5. EDS/DPL andWV/DPL.
6. Barrett, Grand Junction, p. 157ff.
7. EDS/DPL.
8. *Ibid.*
9. WV/DPL.
10. Barrett, Grand Junction, p. 46ff and p. 58ff.
11. EDS/DPL, especially correspondence, Williams to Sandvig.
12. EDS/DPL.
13. Ibid.
14. Williams to Sandvig, EDS/DPL.
15. AHC/DPL, WV/DPL, and EDS/DPL.
16. EDS/DPL.
17. Ibid.
18. WV/DPL.
19. *Outdoors Unlimited*, publication of the Outdoor Writers Association of America, carried the full story of the Everett case in spring, 1952, issues. Penfold's calculations showed Everett's claim for antelope damage, translated into AUMS, would have made the equivalent grazing rental for one cow amount to $61.50 a month. *Cf.* AHC/DPL and WV/DPL.
20. EDS/DPL.
21. Ibid.

CHAPTER 14

1. Much of the material in this chapter is from files of exchanges between Sandvig and me accumulated over a number of years. Many were

written; some were taped. All have been sent to the Conservation Center, Denver Public Library; identified herein as WV/DPL and EDS/DPL.

2. Ibid.
3. Forest Service Memorandum G426.
4. EDS/DPL.
5. WV/DPL.
6. EDS/DPL.
7. Ibid.
8. WV/DPL.
9. Ibid.
10. Taped and transcribed interview, WV/DPL.
11. EDS/DPL.
12. Ibid.
13. Ibid.
14. Personal communication, JWP to WV.
15. EDS/DPL.
16. Ibid.
17. Ibid., and WV/DPL.
18. Taped and transcribed interview, WV/DPL.

CHAPTER 15

1. Most of the historical information cited here is from "The Uncompahgre Case" (Summary of History and Points of Contention), undated mimeo prepared by Region 2, Forest Service, prior to 1951 hearings by Appeals Board on grazing controversy, p. 1ff; EDS, in pencilled marginal note, wrote "This is an unexpurgated version."
2. Ibid., p. 2.
3. Ibid., p. 3. See also February 2, 1973, tape recording, EDS to WV, transcribed, in DPL.
4. Ibid., p. 3.
5. EDS tape, supra.
6. Tape recording, transcribed, CKC to WV, in DPL.
7. Taped interview, transcribed; WV/DPL.
8. Letter from W. B. Gallaher, regional range director, March 19, 1975, in WV/DPL.
9. CKC/WV/DPL, February 2, 1973.
10. Barrett, Grand Junction, p. 2ff.
11. About February 1947; EDS/DPL.
12. Summary, "The Uncompahgre Case."
13. EDS/DPL.
14. Ibid.
15. Ibid.
16. Tape and transcript are in WV/DPL.

17. EDS-WV/DPL.

18. Modoc information is from several sources, including EDS in WV/DPL, records of Barrett hearings at Redding and San Francisco in 1947, *Outdoor America*, and personal recollections; see also EDS/DPL.

19. May 4, 1972, in EDS/DPL; copy in WV/DPL.

20. Ibid.

21. Ibid.

22. Ibid.

CHAPTER 16

1. *OA*, Vol. 15, No. 2, February, 1950, pp. 6–7.

2. AHC/DPL.

3. Kirby/DPL.

4. AHC/DPL.

5. 64 Stat. 82–88.

6. Steamboat *Pilot*, March 15 and 29, 1951; also AHC/DPL.

7. AHC/DPL.

8. Letter put in record of Hearings, Grazing Policy and Range Improvements on National Forests, before Senate Committee on Agriculture and Forestry, 83rd, 1st, pursuant to S. Res. 127, September, 1953, pp. 229–230.

9. As cited in *OA*, Vol. 17, No. 5, September–October, 1952, p. 12.

10. Ibid., p. 13.

11. Issue of July 13, 1952; also AHC/DPL.

12. *OA*, Vol. 17, No. 5, September–October, 1952, p. 12.

13. The strong "anti" sentiments at the Barrett hearings in Montana in 1947 caused D'Ewart to have second thoughts about all-out support for the industry.

14. The overt act was a full page advertisement in *The New York Times* urging defeat of the bill that would have authorized the dam.

15. A copy was found in CCM/DPL.

16. National Archives, Bureau of the Budget files on H. R. 4023.

17. *OA*, Vol. 18, No. 3, May–June 1953, p. 10.

18. Memorandum G426, April 6, 1953.

19. Mimeo, dated March 17, 1972. Copy in Dutton folder, WV/DPL.

20. Memorandum G438, April 14, 1953.

21. Dutton folder, WV/DPL.

22. Archives, BOB.

23. Ibid.

24. Dutton folder, WV/DPL.

25. WV/DPL.

26. Ibid.

27. *Congressional Record*, p. 5718ff.

28. As quoted in Ogden, Utah, *Standard-Examiner,* May 30, 1953; clip in AHC/DPL.

29. CCM/DPL.

30. Denver *Post,* May 25, 1953; AHC/DPL.

31. Much of this and several following paragraphs are from a mimeographed memo I sent to IWLA leaders shortly after the hearings; copies in WV/DPL and EDS/DPL. I also found a copy in Archives files of the Office of the Solicitor, Department of the Interior, on H. R. 4023.

CHAPTER 17

1. Folders of Bureau of the Budget, Department of Agriculture, and Forest Service files in National Archives, Washington, relative to H. R. 4023 and S. 1491.

2. BOB, Archives, June 4, 1953.

3. *OA,* Vol. 18, No. 4, p. 29ff.

4. Hearings, "Grazing Policies and Range Improvements in National Forests," Senate Committee on Agriculture and Forestry pursuant to S. Res. 127, 83rd, 1st, September 11–17, 1953.

5. Hearing, "Administration of the National Forests," on S. 2548 before Senate Committee on Agriculture and Forestry, 83rd, 2nd, January 21–22, 1954, pp. 6–8.

6. Senate hearings, "Grazing Policies," p. 2.

7. Ibid., p. 11ff.

8. Ibid., p. 17ff.

9. Ibid., p. 86.

10. Ibid., p. 104ff.

11. Ibid., p. 113.

12. Stegner, *The Uneasy Chair.*

13. Senate hearings, p. 131ff.

14. Ibid., p. 160ff.

15. Ibid., p. 35ff.

16. Ibid., p. 140ff.

17. Section 13.

18. Section 6.

19. Senate hearings, p. 48ff; House hearing, p. 5ff.

20. Senate hearings, ibid.

21. Ibid., p. 60ff.

22. Ibid., p. 72ff.

23. Ibid., p. 81ff.

24. House hearing, p. 62.

25. Ibid., p. 64ff.

26. Senate hearings, p. 85ff and House hearing, p. 87ff.

27. Senate, ibid., p. 98ff, and House, ibid., p. 71ff.

28. Senate, ibid., p. 123ff; House, ibid., p. 40ff.
29. House, ibid., p. 5.
30. Ibid., Serial X, Part II, p. 137.
31. Ibid., p. 153ff.
32. AHC/DPL.
33. House, Serial X, ca. p. 155.
34. August 4, 1954, as Title VIII of H. R. 9680.
35. AHC/DPL.
36. *Congressional Record,* August 10, 1954, p. 13896.
37. Ibid.
38. Archives, BOB File p. 1-3/53.1.
39. AHC/DPL.
40. CCM/DPL.
41. Archives, BOB.
42. Ibid.
43. Ibid.

CHAPTER 18

1. Memorandum sent to supervisory personnel and circulated by them to other employes as of October, 1970.
2. Several were filed by such groups as Friends of the Earth, Sierra Club, and others.
3. *One Third of a Nation's Land,* U. S. Government Printing Office, Washington, 1970.
4. Walter J. Hickel, *Who Owns America?* (New York: Paperback Library, 1972), p. 126.
5. Tape recording and transcript, July 1972, in WV/DPL.
6. WV/EDS/DPL.
7. Ibid.
8. WV/DPL.
9. Ibid.
10. 74 Stat. 215, *supra.*
11. USAF Annual Report, 1956, p. 4.
12. *Long Range Program for the National Forests,* hearings before Subcommittee on Forests, House Committee on Agriculture and Forests, 86th, 1st, May 14–15, 1959, Serial Y, p. 1ff.
13. Ibid., p. 8ff.
14. Ibid., p. 194ff.
15. 30 Stat. 34.
16. USFS Annual Report, 1960, p. 18.
17. 16 U. S. C. 1131.
18. 16 U. S. C. 1271.
19. Tape recording, DPL.
20. Ibid.

21. EDS/DPL.
22. Joy tape, DPL.
23. EDS/DPL.
24. Ninety-second Congress.

CHAPTER 19

1. Stanfield hearings, *National Forests*, pp. 3–4.
2. Ibid., p. 127ff.
3. Ibid., p. 431ff.
4. *Congressional Record*, Seventy-first, Second, p. 408.
5. Wesley Calef, *Private Grazing and Public Lands* (Chicago: University of Chicago Press, 1960), p. 52.
6. *Congressional Record*, Sixty-third, Second, p. 13680.
7. Ibid., Seventy-third, Second, pp. 11814–11819.
8. Calef dedicated his book to graziers "badgered by politicians, ignored by those they are supposed to regulate, unsupported by their department, and neglected by the electorate."
9. 48 Stat. 1269.
10. Clarence L. Forsling file and tape recording in Conservation Center, Denver Public Library; hereafter referred to as CLF/WV/DPL.

CHAPTER 20

1. Taylor Grazing Act, Section 3.
2. McCarran hearings (Ch. 3, n 22).
3. 53 Stat. 1002.
4. Ickes-Carpenter Correspondence, Western History Department, Denver Public Library; hereafter referred to as I-C/DPL. *Cf.* also McCarran, Senate Report 10, 80th, 1st.
5. WV/DPL, BLM folders.
6. 49 Stat. 1976.
7. McCarran, at various places in his 1941–43 hearings.
8. CLF/WV/DPL.
9. I-C/DPL.
10. Ibid.
11. Ibid.
12. BLM has not kept as meticulous records as the Forest Service. In April, 1975, its Denver office furnished figures from 1959 forward, as shown in Table 4.
13. CLF/WV/DPL.

CHAPTER 21

1. Report, "Amending the Taylor Grazing Act," before Senate Committee on Public Lands and Surveys, 76th, 3rd, February 28, 1940.

2. CLF/WV/DPL.
3. Also investigated extensively by McCarran in field hearings later on.
4. CLF/WV/DPL.
5. McCarran, p. 3ff.
6. Ibid., p. 32ff.
7. Ibid., p. 204ff.
8. Ibid., p, 47855.
9. Ibid., p. 491ff.
10. Ibid., pp. 1071–1072.
11. Ibid., p. 1073ff.
12. Ibid., p. 1094ff.
13. Ibid., p. 1107ff.
14. Ibid., p. 1137ff.
15. Ibid., p. 1139ff.
16. Ibid., p. 1273.
17. Ibid., p. 2869ff.
18. Ibid., p. 1107ff.
19. Ibid., p. 1544ff.
20. Ibid., p. 1597ff.
21. Senate Report No. 10, 80th, 1st, January 31, 1947, p. 69.
22. McCarran, p. 1848ff.
23. Ibid., p. 1874ff.
24. Ibid., p. 1879.
25. Ibid., p. 2473ff.
26. Ibid., p. 3742ff.
27. Ibid., pp. 3021–3441.
28. Ibid., p. 2138ff.
29. Ibid., p. 2265ff.
30. Ibid., p. 2405ff.

CHAPTER 22

1. Much of the material in this chapter relating to Forsling came from a lengthy tape recording of his recollections, received late in 1974, and from letters and memoranda from him, all sent to the Conservation Center, Denver Public Library; CLF/WV/DPL.
2. Letter, January 9, 1975, CLF/WV/DPL.
3. Report of hearings, March 29 and May 9, 1944, on Forsling nomination as Grazing Service director; copy in CLF/WV/DPL.
4. Ibid., p. 1.
5. See McCarran, p. 213ff and p. 2405ff.
6. Forsling nomination hearings, p. 3.
7. Ibid., p. 70ff.
8. Ibid., p. 7ff.

9. Ibid., pp. 58–59.
10. Ibid., p. 59ff.
11. Ibid., p. 71ff.
12. Ibid., p. 74ff.
13. Ibid., pp. 78–112.
14. Ibid., p. 98.
15. *Congressional Record*, May 9, 1944, p. 4170.
16. CLF/WV/DPL, January 9, 1975.
17. Ibid.
18. *Congressional Record*, 78th, 2nd, pp. 9558–9559.
19. McCarran's Senate Report 10, p. 9, *supra.*
20. Report of hearings, 76th, 3rd, part 1, pp. 91–92.
21. Hearing, Senate Committee on Public Lands, Washington, January 22–23, 1945, found with McCarran hearing reports, p. 36ff.
22. Ibid., p. 25.
23. McCarran, p. 5393ff., *supra.*
24. Ibid., p. 5298ff.
25. Ibid., p. 5308.
26. Ibid., p. 5855.
27. Ibid., Part 19.

CHAPTER 23

1. *Congressional Record,* 79th, 2nd, pp. 4634–4636.
2. Barrett, Montana hearings, p. 5; Rawlins, p. 1; Salt Lake City, p. 18.
3. CLF/WV/DPL.
4. Ibid.
5. 60 Stat. 1100.
6. Nicholson Report to Krug, p. 34.
7. First Barrett hearing under H. Res. 93, 80th, 1st, April 21, 1947, at Washington, p. 35ff.
8. Ibid., p. 71ff.
9. Ibid., p. 108.
10. CLF/WV/DPL.
11. Ibid.
12. Nicholson report, p. 2 and p. 27.
13. Ibid., p. 7.
14. Ibid., pp. 19–20.
15. Ibid., p. 5 and p. 26.
16. CLF/WV/DPL.
17. McCarran, p. 5088ff.
18. Phoned from BLM, notes in WV/DPL.
19. CLF/WV/DPL.
20. Nicholson report, p. 17.

21. The text of the BAE report is in the report of Barrett's Washington hearing on April 21, 1947, p. 16ff.

22. Ibid., p. 14.

CHAPTER 24

1. Much of the material concerning Clawson in this chapter is from personal correspondence, especially letters from him dated February 20 and March 3, 1975, referred to hereafter as MC/WV/DPL.

2. U. S. Government Printing Office, 1951; long out of print and hard to find, even in Interior Department libraries.

3. Ibid., p. 10.

4. Ibid., p. 20.

5. Ibid., p. 22.

6. Ibid., p. 11.

7. MC/WV/DPL, February 20 and March 3, 1975.

8. Personal communication.

9. *Rebuilding*, p. 20.

10. Tape recording, in WV/BLM/DPL.

11. MC/WV/DPL, February 20 and March 3, 1975.

12. *Report and Summary of Actions*, etc., under his directorship, June, 1963–June, 1966, dated August, 1966; copy in WV/CHS/DPL.

13. P. L. 88-607.

14. P. L. 88-608.

15. WV/BLM/DPL, February 20 and March 3, 1975.

16. P. L. 88-606.

17. The extent to which these values had been neglected or ignored was brought sharply to the attention of the public when an interdisciplinary intramural team wrote a report, *Effects of Livestock Grazing on Wildlife, Watershed, Recreation and Other Resource Values in Nevada*, April, 1974.

18. U. S. C. 4327.

CHAPTER 25

1. As reported for the Oregon Environmental Council and Friends of the Earth by Sandvig and circulated to interested persons including this writer, who received it March 8, 1975. See WV/DPL and EDS/DPL.

2. See papers and tape recordings on subject in WV/DPL and EDS/DPL.

3. *Alternative Goals* under the Forest and Rangeland Renewable Resources Planning Act, P. L. 93-378, published by the Forest Service in March, 1975, p. 2.

4. This and other direct quotations of Dutton in this chapter are from a letter, April 19, 1975, to the writer, in WV/DPL.

5. EDS to WV, April 3, 1975, in WV/DPL.

6. Ibid.

7. For one exposition, see unpublished manuscript on subject by Ralph R. Hill, in Conservation Library Center, Denver Public Library.

8. S. 507.

9. The 1974 act is P. L. 93-378. The documents named, dated August, 1975, were prudently labeled "drafts," to be put in final form after receipt of comment from interested individuals and groups.

10. Sandvig and Dutton were principal informants; WV/DPL.

11. Independent Offices Appropriations Act of 1952.

12. Annual report, 1958, transmitted to Congress in September, 1959.

13. By both agencies pursuant to Bureau of the Budget Circular A-25, September, 1959.

14. BLM issued a news release on the subject, and doubtless the Forest Service did likewise; a letter of March 26, 1975, from R. T. Younger, acting chief, BLM Division of Range, Washington, supplemented the moratorium information.

15. *Grazing Fees on National Forest Range: Past History and Present Policy,* by the Forest Service, June, 1969, pp. 11, 17.

16. *Farm Real Estate Market Developments,* USDA-ERS, July, 1974, p. 43.

17. *Grazing Fees,* p. 18.

18. That of Lister Cattle Company, near Prineville.

19. Prineville report, p. 5.

20. Frederic E. Clements, *Dynamics of Vegetation* (New York: H. W. Wilson Co., 1949), page number not cited by either source referred to.

21. August L. Hormay, *Principles of Rest-Rotation Grazing and Multiple-Use Land Management* (Washington: Bureau of Land Management, 1970), p. 25.

22. Prineville report, p. 11.

CHAPTER 26

1. Previously published in *Field & Stream* magazine, October, 1968, to accompany my article, "The Plot to Steal the West."

2. Joseph W. Penfold, conservation director of the Izaak Walton League of America, and C. R. Gutermuth, vice president of the Wildlife Management Institute, among others.

3. Telephone conversation, 1968, later quoted in *Field & Stream,* October, 1968.

4. *One Third of the Nation's Land,* report of the PLLRC, June, 1970, Recommendation 42, p. 115.

Index